Improvisation *at the* Piano

A Systematic Approach for the Classically Trained Pianist

Brian Chung & Dennis Thurmond

Alfred Publishing Co., Inc.
Los Angeles

Brian Chung serves as Senior Vice President of Kawai America Corporation. He is a past president of the Piano Manufacturers Association International, a former Chair of the Board of Trustees for MTNA Foundation, a past member of the Board of Directors for NAMM and a 2004 MTNA Foundation Fellow.

After receiving an undergraduate degree from the University of Michigan, he studied piano and conducting at the Guildhall School of Music and Drama (London) as a Rotary Foundation Scholar. Returning to the States, he pursued jazz studies as the recipient of a grant from the National Endowment of the Arts. After several years as a professional musician, private teacher and composer, he completed an MBA at the Kellogg School of Management at Northwestern University.

With a diverse career that includes experience as a performer, educator, conference speaker and music industry executive, Mr. Chung is devoted to the cause of advancing music participation across America and around the world.

Dennis Thurmond is currently director of Keyboard Pedagogy at the Thornton School of Music, University of Southern California, was formerly the chairman of the music synthesis department and class piano program at the Berklee College of Music and Teaching Fellow at the MIT Center for Advanced Visual Studies. Summer improvisational faculty at the following: Utrecht/HKU Conservatory, Netherlands; Hochschule für Musik, Freiburg, Germany; Cultural University & Municipal Teachers College, Taipei, Taiwan; Mahidol University, Thailand; Sangmyung University & Catholic University, Seoul, Korea; Shanghai Conservatory & Dalian Conservatories, China; The World Pedagogy Conference, Slovenia & Las Vegas. He is a classical and jazz pianist and keyboard synthesist. His keyboard performances and technical background has included playing synthesizer for the Boston Pops, keyboards for the New York Vocal Jazz Ensemble, being production arranger for the Gospel Review for Symphony Orchestra with Della Reese and Billy Preston, studio pianist for the television series "Party of Five" and ROM card designer for Kawai Japan. He is a composer and technical consultant for the Music Thru MIDI series and co-composer of the Jazz SophistiCat series for Alfred Publishing Co. He continues to perform throughout Asia, Europe and the United States.

ISBN-10: 0-7390-4378-1
ISBN-13: 978-0-7390-4378-3

Editor: Nicholas Janssen
Cover and interior designer: Tom Gerou
Music engraver: Bruce Nelson
Book production: Greg Plumblee

Cover art: Improvisation 26, *1912*
by Wassily Kandinsky (1866–1944)
Courtesy of Planet Art

Acknowledgments

The authors wish to extend our deepest appreciation to many who helped this book become a reality. We offer sincere thanks to Dr. Stewart Gordon, for providing the spark that ignited the initial concept for the book; to the many private and master class students who became a living laboratory for the testing of this methodology; to Jo Anne Chung, for her infinite patience through hundreds of hours of writing and editing; to Carla Dean Day, for her wisdom and insight that helped this text communicate with clarity and accuracy; to E.L. Lancaster, for his steadfast support of this project from its inception; to Nick Janssen, for his intelligent guidance and good-natured collaboration throughout the editing process; and to Bach, Mozart, Beethoven and the pantheon of great composers whose collective works have provided a vast musical foundation upon which improvisation can be built.

Contents

Foreword

Making music began with improvisation. The earliest civilizations' musical expressions consisted of spontaneously creating music and constantly elaborating on music already known. The history of Western music provides ample evidence that the great composers were not only expert improvisers, but that improvisation was the genesis of the music they refined into written compositions. It is thus reported that Mozart improvised his first six piano sonatas on tour before writing them down; that improvisation was a staple in the documented piano competitions between Mozart and Clementi, or Beethoven and Steibelt; that Liszt improvised regularly for his students in his classes at Weimar—only three examples among dozens pointing to the fact that improvisation was as basic to professional pianism as reading music or developing technique.

What happened? How is it, then, that by the late twentieth century many pianists who pursue professional goals did not improvise and, indeed, experienced a sense of panic if forced into a situation where they were asked to create music they had not already studied and perfected? The answer is that by the twentieth century, pianists had so much first-rate literature to choose from that they lost interest in improvising, quite possibly deeming what they made up inferior to the masterworks at their disposal. What they overlooked, however, was that improvisation stimulates creativity, imagination, and expressive exploration, qualities that nourish all performance, including those of masterpieces.

Fortunately, within the past ten years there has been a renaissance of improvisation. Many musicians, who formerly eschewed it, now study it. Teachers include it as an important skill to be developed along with studying and performing written music. Workshops and formal courses in improvisation are now offered regularly. Indeed, increasing numbers of pianists are now reveling in the pleasure of their own spontaneous keyboard creations.

A few astute musicians never abandoned improvisation as a primary skill. These musicians now emerge as grand masters of the art, having practiced and perfected it for decades, even through its period of neglect. It is to these masters the neophytes must now turn for guidance. The authors of this volume are expert practitioners of improvisation, as well as great teachers who have detailed knowledge of the road aspiring improvisers must travel. They are, moreover, celebrants who joyfully lead the way. You are in the best of hands. Enjoy!

Stewart Gordon
Professor of Keyboard Studies
Thornton School of Music
University of Southern California

Introduction

If you can talk, you can improvise.

You may not believe that now, but it's true. Often, very achievable skills appear to be much harder than they really are. You should know at the outset of this book that improvisation is not quantum physics. It is simply the process of saying similar things in different ways.

For example, you could look up toward the sky and remark, "The sky is blue." But would that be the only way to describe what you are seeing? Certainly not. With a little prompting and imagination, you might be inclined to say any of the following:

- "The sky is certainly a beautiful blue today!"
- "Have you ever seen such a gorgeous blue sky?"
- "Look! Not a cloud in the sky! Just blue everywhere you look."
- "That's got to be the loveliest blue sky I've ever seen!"
- "Blue, blue, blue. That's all I can see."

With these statements, you're improvising. By spontaneously expressing the same thought in different ways, you're using words to form improvised phrases. The reason it seems so simple is that you've already developed some basic verbal communication tools and have learned to link them together in meaningful ways that express what you're thinking or feeling.

Learning to Talk

Keep in mind that you didn't learn to talk overnight. It was a process that took time and patience. If you can't remember how you learned to talk as a young child, the process went like this:

1. You had a *desire* to say something.
2. You *"lived" in the language* and *listened* to the sounds made by others.
3. You *experimented* with simple sounds and words.
4. Gradually, you added more words (*vocabulary*).
5. You acquired a framework for using those words (*grammar*).
6. Over time, you learned to *link* the words into phrases and sentences that let you *communicate* in a coherent way to others.

Learning to Improvise

This text will help you learn to improvise by taking you through many of these same steps. But since it is designed for people who already have musical training, this process can go much faster. If you're an experienced player, the challenge will be to remain patient in the areas that require you to slow down and exercise different "creative muscles." So get ready for a journey that will turn the sky into all different colors—not just blue.

Section 1 *Foundations*

What Is Improvisation?

The Desire to Say Something

Whether talking or improvising, the process of learning begins with the desire to say something personal and meaningful. This is the "heart" of improvisation. Learning to improvise is much deeper than just the acquisition of formulas that help add more notes to a melody or add a flourish here and there. It is the process of acquiring tools that help facilitate the creation of personal musical statements.

Rewriting the Script

Think about traditional music study for a moment. What is the primary vehicle for personal expression and communication? It's interpretation. A musician doesn't have much control over the notes since they are provided by the composer. Instead, something meaningful must be created with the notes that are given. This goal is similar to that of an actor who is offered lines by the writer and is asked to bring a character to life through the delivery of those lines.

For many students of the traditional school, however, there is something missing. While interpretation is a noble pursuit that offers a world of creative opportunity, it offers no authority over the actual content—the notes themselves. In other words, traditional performance demands that the musician follows the script. No matter how well it is interpreted, the notes still belong to someone else.

Improvisation flows from a desire to say something truly personal—something that expresses one's own mind and soul. Returning to the drama comparison, improvisation gives the actor permission to rewrite the script and become a co-author of the story. The overall plot may remain the same, but improvisers are allowed to express the "details" in their own way and in their own voice. Those who are willing to pursue this adventure will find it to be an exhilarating and liberating experience.

Training the Mental Muscles

Keep in mind that everyone improvises to some degree. Whistling a new melody while doing a chore or humming a slightly different rendition of a familiar tune are examples of improvisation. It is often forgotten that the composers of most traditional music—Bach, Mozart, Beethoven, Chopin, Liszt, etc.—were all famous improvisers who were expected to include improvisations in many of their performances.

Still, the concept of improvisation may seem quite foreign, even to many expert musicians. If improvisation has been tried in the past with only modest success, it may be frustrating to be highly skilled as an interpreter of music, but limited as an improviser. Why does it seem so difficult? It's because only a particular set of mental muscles have been exercised in the traditional school. Improvising requires the development of different mental muscles. Once these are exercised sufficiently (some will require slow, gradual conditioning rather than heavy powerlifting), they will begin to dovetail with already existing skills. In the end, an expanded array of creative muscles will all be able to exercise together in exciting and fulfilling ways.

CHAPTER 1 Living in the Language

Infants spend a great deal of time listening before they learn to talk. The brain must grasp the way words sound before it can devise ways to physically produce them. Therefore, an infant must "live in the language" and gradually comprehend the basic rudiments before the act of speaking.

Improvisation works the same way. Before it can become natural, the rudiments of the musical language—melody, harmony, rhythm, tone, and dynamics—must first be re-explored in ways quite different from those employed by the traditional school. The following series of exercises will assist in this process.

At first, the exercises may seem deceptively simplistic, especially to the skilled player. But as they are practiced, different muscles in the brain will be exercised and prepared for future steps. Above all, be patient—crawling comes before walking.

Exercise Series One: Ode to Mr. Morse

Exercise 1-1: One-Note Rhythms

1. Set a metronome to ♩ = 110–112.

   With the right hand (RH), use one finger on C to form musical statements. Start simply, and then gradually get more creative. In the example below, note that each rhythmic pattern could be repeated several times before moving on to a new idea.

2. Continue to experiment for several minutes or until all possible rhythmic ideas have been expressed. It may take awhile for spontaneous creativity to occur, so be persistent.

Exercise 1-2: Rhythms in Octaves

The first exercise should have created the feeling of being a Morse code operator (thus, the title of this series of exercises) communicating with rhythmic patterns. For the next exercise, imagine creating a new "language" and trying to convey a message to another person through rhythmic patterns.

1. Repeat the steps of exercise 1-1 using any of the C's located above and including middle C. While there are five C's from which to choose, the example below uses only three.

2. Continue this exercise for at least five minutes or until all possible rhythmic ideas have been expressed.

Again, be persistent. If boredom creeps in, don't give up! There will come a point when every player suddenly breaks through and feels momentum. Some of the most creative ideas will come after doing this exercise for several minutes.

Exercise 1-3: Adding the Left Hand

Having experimented with various rhythms, it's time to involve the left hand (LH).

1. Play the following LH quarter notes in time with the pulse of the metronome:

2. While playing these LH quarter notes, repeat exercises 1-1 and 1-2 with the RH. Be sure to begin with simple rhythms. Start with the example below:

3. When ready, turn off the metronome and let the LH control the tempo. This offers complete control of the exercise and increases creative freedom.

The addition of the LH may feel uncomfortable at first, especially as more complicated rhythms are played with the RH. If adding the LH seems too difficult at this point, skip it for now and try again tomorrow or the next day. With practice, the LH notes will become automatic, allowing greater focus on the creation of ideas with the RH.

Exercise 1-4: Adding Other Musical Elements

The previous exercises have focused primarily on the use of rhythm. But there are other elements of "musical language" that have not yet been utilized. Repeat the elements of exercise 1-3; but this time add dynamics, duration and tone to the palette of expressive tools.

- **Dynamics:** Play the example below and then spend several minutes creating new, more colorful phrases by adding dynamics to the rhythmic ideas developed earlier.

- **Duration:** The length of time notes are held can strongly affect the character of a phrase. The example below uses staccato, legato and marcato markings to express different durations. Play through the following example, and then spend several minutes experimenting.

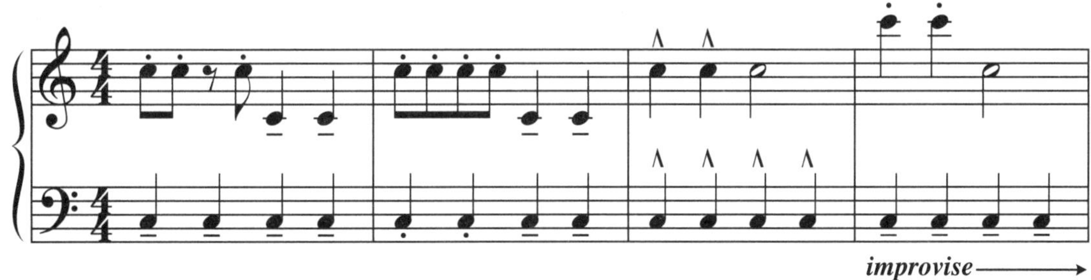

- **Tone:** Since it is difficult to describe the element of tone with traditional notation, spend several minutes experimenting with the example above using different variations of tone (e.g., mellow, strident, round, thin, etc.).

When focusing on the creation of rhythmic and melodic ideas, it's easy to forget dynamics, duration and tone—essential musical elements that add interest and musicality to one's playing. Throughout the early chapters of this text, remember to utilize these tools to add character and depth to improvisations.

Exercise 1-5: Silence

There is one more element that should be introduced in this chapter—silence. Silence is not always viewed as an expressive tool. But in verbal communication, people often express as much by what they don't say as what they do say.

One who has experienced the drudgery of conversing with a person who talks incessantly can fully appreciate the value of silence. Improvisers should remember that, in many cases, less is more. Pauses and extended moments of silence can bring great power to improvisation.

Repeat exercise 1-3. But this time, introduce silence in strategic places to communicate in a more balanced, conversational way. Play the example below and then experiment further with silence.

While playing through this example, notice that silence in the RH gives the mind some time to regroup. This relieves the pressure of having to create something new every moment. By using silence intentionally and creatively, one's mind and future listeners will both benefit.

Exercise 1-6: Be Adventurous

Turn this entire series of exercises upside down by placing the steady quarter notes in the right hand while "speaking" with the left. This may seem uncomfortable at first, since it will flex some new mental muscles. Spend some time doing this each day and watch how the mind gradually adjusts.

How Long Should This Series of Exercises Be Practiced?

- Practice the entire series daily until the concepts feel comfortable.
- With each exercise, continue as long as creativity flows.
- During each practice session, start with simple statements. Then, gradually stretch creative boundaries with new ideas.
- Feel free to change to a different thematic note at any time (use only D's for one session and G's for another).
- Try playing the repeating LH quarter notes in different octaves.

Something to Think About

While practicing the *Ode to Mr. Morse* series, remember to imagine speaking to someone through the notes played. Try to express a range of emotions—happiness, anger, tiredness, uncertainty, sadness, etc. By using rhythm, dynamics, duration, tone, and silence, it may be surprising how much can be said with just a few notes.

Try experimenting with short verbal expressions that match a rhythmic pattern. Early opera singers were given great license to improvise with vocal passages. In that same spirit, try taking some of the phrases from *The Sky Is Blue* example (in the introduction) and sing or say them with the played notes like the example below:

Try inserting words to help articulate the emotions that are conveyed through the notes. During this experimentation, the key is to have fun!

Congratulations! The first important steps toward becoming an improviser have now been taken. It should seem clear that this deceptively simple set of exercises is much more valuable than it first appeared. If the brain feels stretched and engaged, that's a good sign. It means the new mental muscles described earlier have been exercised. When ready, move on to chapter 2.

Key Points from This Chapter

- Improvisation is similar to talking.
- Improvisation requires the development of new mental muscles.
- Improvisation involves more than notes—it includes rhythm, dynamics, duration, tone, and silence.

CHAPTER 2 Upper & Lower Neighbors

The first chapter was limited to just one note in various octaves. That's because "living in the language" requires the player to understand all of the various tools that are vital to effective musical communication—notes can sometimes get in the way. As the element of melody is added to the artistic palette, don't forget to use all of the other expressive "colors" explored in chapter 1.

This chapter introduces two important notes that are the backbone of all improvisation—upper and lower neighbors. These names refer to the notes immediately above and below any "defining" note.

But first, what is a defining note? In verbal and written communication, certain essential words define the meaning of a statement. For example, the traffic sign below has a way of communicating a concept with very few words—each one vital to the meaning of the phrase.

If the sign was expanded to a full sentence, the message would read as follows:

Your LANE *is* ENDING.
You *should* MERGE *into* the lane on *your* LEFT.

The original four words (shown in capital letters) are the defining words. If all other words are omitted, the defining words still convey the intended meaning. But the longer version helps illustrate the function of upper/lower neighbors (shown in italics).

The upper/lower neighbors help to "frame" the defining words. In some cases, they are descriptive (as in the word "your" to describe which lane). In other cases, they are verbs and prepositions that bring continuity to a phrase (such as "is" and "into"). These adjacent neighbors are not absolutely necessary, but they do help to express a fuller, more eloquent statement of communication.

In music, upper/lower neighbors perform the same function. They "frame" the defining notes. For instance, assuming a defining note of C, the upper neighbor would be D (a whole-step higher) and the lower neighbor would be B (a half-step lower).

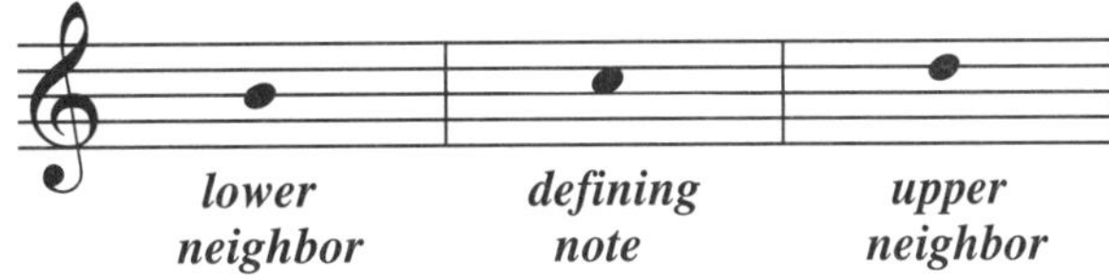

It's important to note that sometimes upper neighbors will only be a half-step higher, and lower neighbors will be a whole-step lower than the defining note. These adjustments can be made at any time to suit a particular harmony.*

* This concept will be discussed further in later chapters.

Assume that the example below is made up of the defining notes of a musical phrase, similar to the defining words in a traffic sign.

Now examine the following expanded phrase with upper/lower neighbors (the arrows identify the defining notes).

The addition of upper/lower neighbors adds beauty and fullness to the phrase and creates a sense of melodic tension. They are constantly trying to resolve to their corresponding defining notes. The continual push-and-pull of tension and resolution makes the phrase interesting to one's ears. This is why upper/lower neighbors are so valuable to the improviser.

The next series of exercises will experiment with defining notes and their upper/lower neighbors.

Exercise Series Two: The Three-Note Waltz

Exercise 2-1: Experimenting with Upper & Lower Neighbors

Begin with a defining note of C. This makes the upper neighbor D (a whole-step higher) and the lower neighbor B (a half-step lower).

1. As with *Ode to Mr. Morse*, play steady quarter notes with the LH using only the C below middle C. This time, the quarter notes should be played in $\frac{3}{4}$ time. If playing LH quarter notes still feels uncomfortable, use a metronome set at ♩ = 100.

2. With the RH, use the defining note and its upper/lower neighbors to form simple musical statements like the example below:

3. Continue to create phrases with the three notes for several minutes or until creativity wanes.

Exercise 2-2: Using Multiple Octaves

- Repeat exercise 2-1 utilizing the same three notes in any octave. Play the following example and then explore new possibilities.

- Experiment with dynamics, tone, duration and silence to express various emotions as done with *Ode to Mr. Morse* (see pages 7–8).
- Repeat this exercise for several minutes or until all current ideas have been expressed.

Exercise 2-3: Exploring Different Keys

It is time to begin practicing improvisation in all 12 keys. This is an important step in understanding how notes relate to one another for improvisation.

1. Each day, practice exercise 2-2 in a few different keys using the same intervals for selecting the upper/lower neighbors. For example, in the key of F, the upper neighbor will be G (a whole-step higher) and the lower neighbor will be E (a half-step lower).

2. When the major keys have been fully explored, try the previous example in D minor (with a defining note of F). Notice how the character and feel are different in a minor key. Experiment with new phrases in different octaves and minor keys.

3. Repeat steps 1 and 2 of this exercise for several days (practicing in a few keys each day) until the creation of phrases across a range of octaves in all 12 keys (major and minor) feels comfortable.

Exercise 2-4: Be Adventurous

Turn *The Three-Note Waltz* upside down (with steady notes in the RH while improvising in the LH) as shown below. Practice this exercise periodically until it feels comfortable.

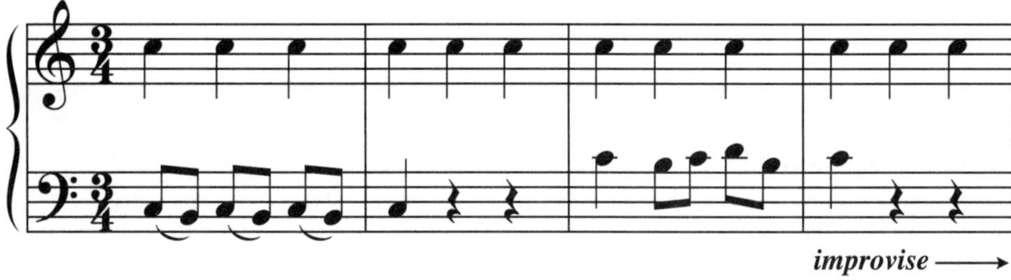

Key Points from This Chapter

- Just as word statements are made up of defining words and adjacent neighbors, musical phrases are composed of defining notes and corresponding upper/lower neighbors that add richness and continuity to the phrase.
- Learning to play in all 12 keys (major and minor) is an important skill for improvisation.

CHAPTER 3 Elaboration

Remember the traffic sign in the last chapter?

LANE ENDING. MERGE LEFT.

A slightly expanded version was used to illustrate defining words (in capital letters) and upper/lower neighbors (in italics).

Your LANE *is* ENDING.
You *should* MERGE *into* the lane on *your* LEFT.

In addition to defining words and upper/lower neighbors, there is another concept that adds further detail called "elaborating" words. By using these words (underlined below), the following statement communicates even more information than the previous two:

The LANE *in* which you are now traveling will soon *be* ENDING.
If you don't want to run off the road, you *should* MERGE
into the lane on *your* LEFT *side* as soon as possible.

This augmented sign clarifies which lane is ending (the lane the driver is occupying). It explains why the sign should be obeyed (to stay on the road). It also tells the driver when the action should take place (as soon as possible). These additional words elaborate upon the original meaning.

In a similar way, the next series of exercises will expand upon the previous exercises by encouraging elaboration. While *The Three-Note Waltz* provided hundreds of melodic combinations to explore, the exercises in this chapter will offer thousands of ways to improvise through different combinations of notes.

Speaking In Longer Phrases

In previous chapters, one might have felt restricted to the random creation of short musical statements one after another. From this point on, begin to think in longer musical sentences. Start with short simple statements, and then elaborate in longer phrases that may extend across several measures.

Strive to maintain cohesiveness in these longer phrases. In the road sign example, the elaborating words didn't branch off in random directions. They "flowed from" or "led to" the defining words to create more complete thoughts. While practicing the next exercise series, make sure the elaborating notes relate closely to the defining notes as in measure 2 the following example:

Defining-Note Melody from Haydn's Symphony No. 94, "Surprise Symphony"

Sample improvisation

In the sample improvisation, mostly upper/lower neighbors are used. Although the elaborating notes in measure 2 move in wider intervals, they still correspond closely to the natural movement of the melodic line.

Exercise Series Three: The Six-Note Sojourn

Start in the key of C. The six available notes will consist of the root C, the upper/lower neighbors (D and B), and the three notes above the upper neighbor (E, F and G).

Exercise 3-1: Thinking in Longer Phrases

1. Play steady quarter notes in the LH using only the C below middle C in $\frac{4}{4}$ time. (If a metronome has been used instead of the LH quarter notes so far, now is the time to begin playing with the LH.)
2. As with exercise 1-1 of *Ode to Mr. Morse* (page 5), start by using only one note in the RH to improvise in shorter phrases.

   Example of One-Bar Phrases

3. Gradually expand the improvisation to include the upper/lower neighbors as done with *The Three-Note Waltz*. Think in longer phrases. Try to convey ideas that stretch across the measure lines.

   Example of Two-Bar Phrases

4. Improvise using all six notes. Try to think in longer musical sentences. If possible, connect themes to form "musical paragraphs."

   Examples of Four-Bar Phrases

Example with Faster Harmonic Rhythm

5. Practice this exercise for several minutes or until all current ideas have been exhausted.

Exercise 3-2: Expressing Emotions

Repeat exercise 3-1 using dynamics, tone, duration and silence to express a range of emotions (e.g., happy, sad, angry, listless, etc.). Feel free to alter the tempo or switch to the relative minor in the bass (in this case, A) to expresss these emotions.

Exercise 3-3: Different Keys

Each day, practice *The Six-Note Sojourn* in a different key using the same relationships for selecting notes (the first five notes of the major scale, plus the lower neighbor of the defining note). Continue this exercise until longer phrases can be created using the six prescribed notes in all 12 keys.

Exercise 3-4: Octave Switching

For this exercise, utilize the same six notes in all octaves. In addition to moving complete phrases into different octaves, try another technique called "octave switching." This technique focuses on the transposition of selected notes of a phrase to a different octave, while leaving other notes of the phrase unchanged. The results of octave switching can be quite interesting as in the following example:

Original Melody

Octave Switching

By comparing the two versions, one can see that switching the octave of selected notes can create an entirely different (and interesting) passage. For this reason, octave switching can be a valuable tool for improvisation.

1. Spend several minutes creating phrases using different octaves and the octave switching technique.
2. When creativity diminishes in a given key, change to a different key.

Exercise 3-5: Be Adventurous

As in earlier chapters, turn this exercise upside down. This may feel more difficult, but it will be well worth the effort. Plus, it will be great preparation for the next series of exercises that utilize a more active LH. Start with the sample measures below and then experiment.

Key Points from This Chapter

- In verbal communication, "elaborating" words allow the creation of more complete thoughts. In music, "elaborating" notes help to create fuller musical sentences.
- Just as in speaking, musical sentences can be combined to create paragraphs of ideas.

CHAPTER 4 Speaking to One Another

When learning a new language, a point is reached where live conversation becomes important. Interacting with another learner can help to strengthen one's skills and make the experience much more enjoyable. This exercise is a fun way to flex new creative muscles with another musician.

Exercise Series Four: The Musical Conversation

Exercise 4-1: Initiating Communication

1. **Getting a Partner:** Find someone who is also interested in learning how to improvise (or someone who just wants to have some fun). Sit together on the piano bench in "duet" style.
2. **Conversing with *Ode to Mr. Morse*:** Have the person on the left side of the keyboard play steady quarter notes on C. The person on the right should begin creating musical statements using only C's as described in exercise 1-1 of *Ode to Mr. Morse* (see page 5). Continue for eight measures in $\frac{4}{4}$ time, and then switch roles (i.e., the person on the right will play steady quarter notes, while the person on the left creates musical statements).

3. **Exchanging Ideas:** After exchanging roles every eight measures for awhile, begin to trade roles more often. Try switching every four measures and then every two measures.

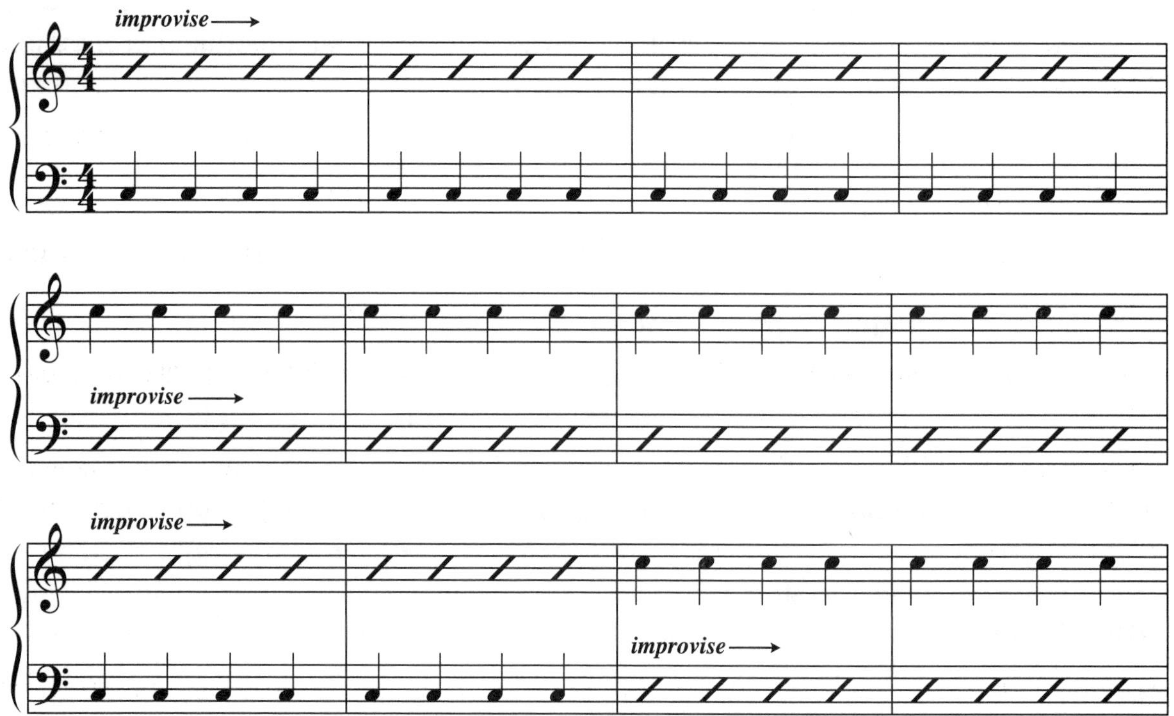

When the trading becomes more frequent, try to continue the other player's ideas as the roles are switched. Complete each other's musical statements and start new ones as appropriate. Think of this as a conversation—talking to one another using musical notes.

Exercise 4-2: Conversing with *The Three-Note Waltz*

Repeat step 3 of exercise 4-1 using upper/lower neighbors (in any octave) as done with exercise 2-2 of *The Three-Note Waltz* (see page 13).

- Play in either $\frac{3}{4}$ time or $\frac{4}{4}$ time, whichever feels more comfortable.
- Start exchanging eight-bar phrases, then four bars, then two bars.
- Converse in various keys. If time permits, travel through all 12 keys.

Exercise 4-3: Conversing with *The Six-Note Sojourn*

Repeat step 3 of exercise 4-1 using the notes prescribed for *The Six-Note Sojourn* (see page 16). Again, if time permits, explore all 12 keys. Remember to think of this exercise as a conversation.

Exercise 4-4: Using All the Tools

Repeat exercise 4-3 utilizing the complete array of expressive tools described in chapter 1—dynamics, duration, tone and silence. Have fun communicating with the other person!

Key Points from This Chapter

- Improvisation is a skill that encourages interaction with other players.
- Interactive musical improvisation uses the same skills as verbal conversation.
- True musical conversation involves careful listening to others.

CHAPTER 5 Spreading Your Wings

This final chapter of the *Foundations* section combines all the material explained in the previous four chapters:

- *Ode to Mr. Morse* explored rhythms, dynamics, duration, tone, and silence.
- *The Three-Note Waltz* experimented with upper/lower neighbors.
- *The Six-Note Sojourn* connected phrases into musical sentences and paragraphs.
- *The Musical Conversation* explored musical communication and collaboration.

The capstone exercise will provide the opportunity to apply all these skills while using any notes of the keyboard.

To help integrate the elements above, there are two new concepts to introduce—charting paths and meandering. Rather than adding new information, these two concepts offer a wider framework for improvising.

Charting Paths

Suppose Mrs. Smith wanted to walk from one location in her home to another—perhaps from the kitchen to the bedroom. To make the trek in a two-story home, she might have to walk around the corner, down the hall, up the stairs, down another hall and make a right turn into her bedroom. It probably wouldn't take her more than a split second to determine this route. She would simply chart the path and go!

In improvisation, the same thought process occurs. In a split second, the path of a musical phrase can be decided. For example, a melodic move from one C to another C by way of E and G can be quickly charted as follows:

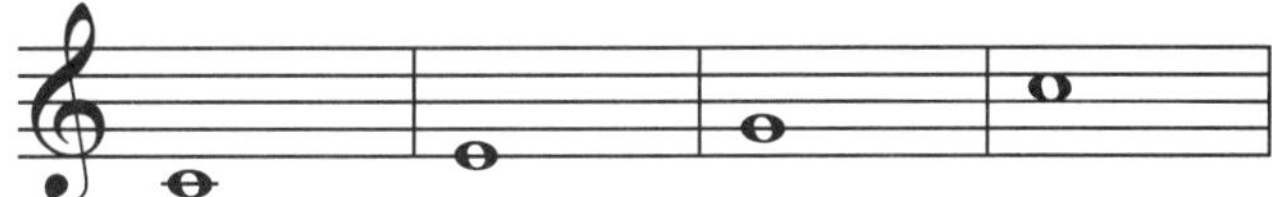

Each path, such as the one above, is simply a phrase made up of defining notes (in this case C–E–G–C). Every time an improvised phrase moves in a purposeful direction, a new path is quickly charted with another set of defining notes. The skilled improviser does this instinctively, moment-by-moment, charting paths that provide interest and direction.

Meandering

Now return to the example of the trip from the kitchen to the bedroom. Imagine that Mrs. Smith has arrived at her upstairs bedroom and now wants her four-year-old son to join her by making the same trip from the kitchen. After she has called him, will he follow her exact path to the bedroom? Not likely. He might take a detour through the dining room before reaching the first hallway. Then, he might slide down the banister rail a couple times before reaching the top of the stairs. On the second level, he might spin around a few times and perhaps stop to get a drink in the bathroom before running down the hall toward his mom's bedroom. Four-year-olds seldom take the direct route—they meander their way to the destination.

Improvising uses the same concept. By using upper/lower neighbors and elaborating notes it is possible to weave in and around the defining notes, gradually meandering toward the destination in a roundabout pursuit of the goal. There are literally hundreds of ways to get from one C to another C by way of E and G. But in an instant, the improviser simply chooses one path.

Charted Path

Meandering Path (arrows show original defining notes)

The earlier concepts—rhythm, dynamics, duration, tone, silence, upper/lower neighbors, and elaborating notes—were more "tactical" in nature. They offered tools and techniques to be used for manipulating specific phrases.

Charting paths and meandering are more "strategic." They take a wider view and force the mind to think in terms of musical destinations (i.e., where the phrases are *going*). The goal should be to become so familiar with the tactical concepts that they become second nature. This frees the mind to chart longer paths that form full and expressive musical paragraphs.

Exercise Series Five: Charting Paths and Meandering

Exercise 5-1: Meandering Examples

1. Play through the examples below to better understand the concept of meandering.
2. After playing the examples, pause to analyze the shape and direction of each path.

Charted Path *Meandering Path*

Exercise 5-2: Creative Meandering

Create a meandering path for each of the charted paths shown below. Always start with short, simple phrases. Then, gradually extend into longer melodic paths.

Exercise 5-3: The Free Ride

1. **Left Hand Rhythm:** So far, only quarter notes have been used in the LH. For this exercise, continue the quarter-note pattern or select one of the alternative patterns below:

Once a LH pattern is selected, repeat it for an extended time to establish a comfort level before beginning to improvise with the RH.

2. **Adding the RH:** While the LH rhythm is playing, use any notes on the keyboard to create ideas with the RH. Feel free to venture in any direction.

   The only firm directive in step 2 is to communicate a meaningful series of musical thoughts. Do not wander without direction. Chart intentional paths and imagine speaking to someone with the notes played.

3. **Trying Different Keys:**
   - Practice this exercise in different keys.
   - Change the bass notes (or rhythm) at any time.
   - Don't forget to utilize dynamics, duration, tone and silence.
   - Practice this exercise regularly for as long as creativity can be sustained.

4. **Conversing with a Partner:** Find a partner and practice switching roles as was done in exercise 4-1 (see pages 19–20).

Exercise 5-4: Be Adventurous

1. Try turning exercise 5-2 upside down (with melodic ideas in LH).

2. Try combining LH rhythms from step 1 of exercise 5-3 to create a more complex pattern. Below is an example of a combination pattern that uses rhythms 4 and 3.

   This example illustrates how rhythm patterns can be connected in a series.

3. Try inserting patterns from Hanon or Czerny into exercise 5-3. Keep in mind that improvisation isn't always the process of creating something completely new. It is often as simple as using familiar patterns in different ways. Play through the "sampler" of Hanon patterns below and then insert them while improvising.

4. Try an even more complex LH pattern from exercise 5-3 that combines many alternate patterns like the example below:

Congratulations! Those who have diligently spent these five chapters "living in the language" and exercising a whole new set of creative muscles should now begin to think of themselves as capable improvisers. When these skills are sufficiently developed, move to the next section entitled *Essential Tools*.

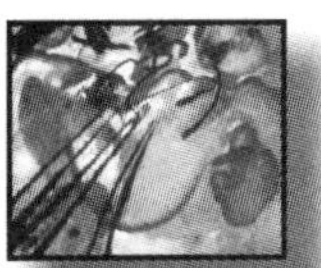

Section 2 *Essential Tools*

Imagine moving to a new country where the language is unfamiliar. In the beginning, only a few words can be picked up from the local citizens. Over time, the rhythms and nuances of the dialect can be heard and then imitated. Eventually, engaging in light conversation with the local people becomes possible as the rudiments of everyday speech are grasped. (This is what happened in the *Foundations* section of this book).

However, to develop a truly solid command of a language, one needs to understand the principles of grammar. Grammar describes the set of guidelines that govern how words relate to one another. It establishes a foundation upon which the words and sentences can be built. A thorough understanding and application of proper grammar makes verbal statements more coherent and eloquent; and allows for confident expression not only in casual conversation, but in any social or academic setting. (Eventually, the rules of grammar can be broken for dramatic effect, but this will be done intentionally, based upon knowledge rather than a lack of skill. This concept will be discussed in later chapters.)

This section is about "musical" grammar. In music, grammar refers to the ways that melody interacts with harmony. It provides a framework upon which coherent, eloquent improvisation can be built. Once the foundational principles of musical grammar are understood, improvising in a variety of musical styles and circumstances will feel comfortable.

In contrast to the first section, this one will base its pedagogical framework on familiar elements that exist in classical music. It assumes that traditional piano repertoire has been explored and that the basic musical "tools" of harmony, scales and rhythm are understood. The section will start with examples that are well known and gradually incorporate the skills acquired in the first section of this book.

Essential Principles

Use the following four basic principles as a guide while progressing through this section:

Principle 1: There are no wrong notes within improvisation, only some that are better than others. One fortunate benefit of improvisation is that the improviser is never locked into only one right way of doing things. As the saying goes, there is always the opportunity to "take lemons and turn them into lemonade." In improvisation, embrace dissonance as an opportunity to create consonance.

Principle 2: Improvisation is not necessarily the process of creating something completely new. More often, it is a process of taking familiar patterns or phrases and applying them creatively to new situations. This idea may be quite liberating to some. Many who have given up on improvisation in the past have done so because they assumed it required them to create new ideas continually. This, of course, is impossible. There is very little an improviser can create that hasn't been played thousands of times before over the course of musical history. While the feeling of creating a truly original phrase or rhythm may be exhilarating, no one (not even the most skilled improviser) can do this continually.

Therefore, remember this—improvisers have full permission to use melodic and rhythmic material they have heard and played before. Of course, well-known melodies will usually be avoided unless they are purposefully chosen for the sake of wit or tribute. But within every notable piece of music, there is an abundance of useful phrases and ideas that can become the "seeds" of any improvisation. They can be played not only as written, but also backwards, spread out, upside down and inside out. Most experienced players probably have enough interesting phrases already stored in their memory to be prolific improvisers. One only needs to know when, where and how to apply this existing arsenal of melodic and rhythmic material.

Principle 3: Knowing the harmonic structure of a musical phrase (or series of phrases) is essential to improvisation. This is where the understanding of music theory will be of immense value. Most improvisation occurs within a distinct context. While it is true that there are no wrong notes in improvisation (see principle 1), there are some that are far better than others. The factor that determines which notes (or entire scales) are better at a given moment is *context*—the harmonic structure of a passage. This section will examine the relationship between melodic notes (scales and patterns) and harmony (structure) and thereby help the player to understand the musical grammar that guides improvisation.

Principle 4: Transposition is power. This is one investment that will yield tremendous dividends over time. Transpose everything (scales, phrases and ideas) into as many different keys as time permits. In doing so, one's melodic vocabulary will grow by leaps and bounds—as will the skill of improvising.

These four principles will be used in this section to develop a set of tools to assist in improvisation. By the end, one should have a complete "toolbox" that will be of great value in any musical situation.

CHAPTER 6 Scales 101

Why start this section with an exercise in scales? It's because scales are essential elements of virtually every improvisation. They help determine the best notes to play at any given moment. They provide melodic material for innumerable patterns and phrases. They connect differing elements to provide continuity and flow. If great improvisers were asked for their best advice for improvising, the most common answer would be, "Learn your scales!" Heed this advice and learn them well.

Below is a well-known excerpt from Mozart's Sonata in C Major, K. 545 (which was originally an improvisation). These four measures will be used to develop a set of scalar exercises and will help start an improvising toolbox. Take a moment to play through them.

There are three components from this excerpt that will become the basis of the next exercise.

1. The melody comes from the notes of the C major scale.

2. The LH accompaniment pattern is also derived from notes found in the C major scale.

3. The basic harmonic structure is in the key of C major.

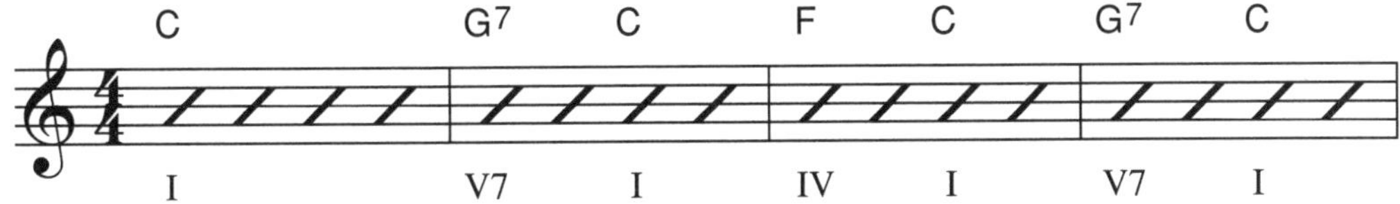

Exercise 6: Scales à la Mozart

1. Memorize the LH (Alberti bass) accompaniment below so that it becomes second nature. (The bar lines have been omitted to help the player think in longer phrases, rather than measure-by-measure.)

2. Repeat the LH accompaniment an octave lower while adding the RH scales below starting with example 1, then example 2, and so on. Complete the LH accompaniment before beginning each new example. Do not stop the LH pattern until all five RH phrases have been played.

   When dissonance occurs, don't be concerned. It will happen naturally as melodic tension is created and released. Practice this exercise until it feels completely comfortable in the key of C major.

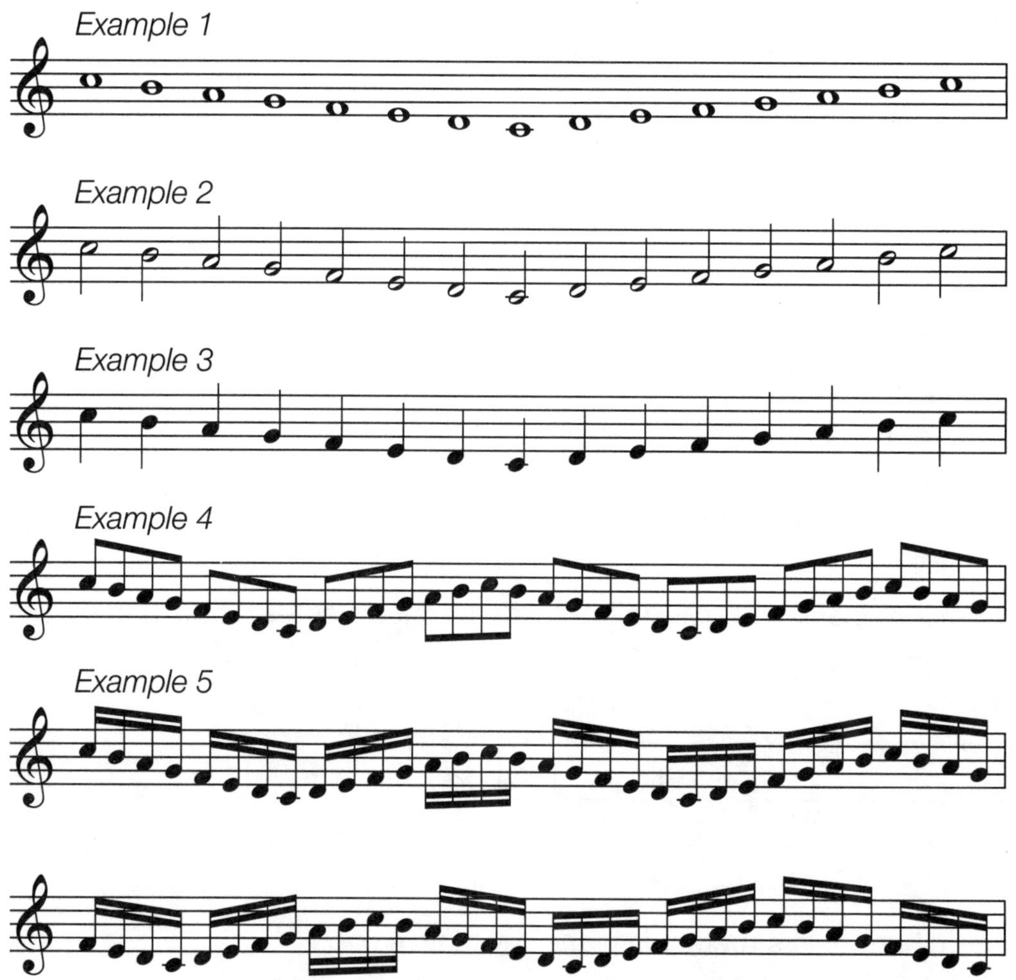

3. When ready, transpose step 2 into different keys. Return to this exercise regularly. The eventual goal is to master it in all 12 keys.

This exercise is not as easy as it first appears. Spend the time required to learn it smoothly. If it seems mindless, remember that pianists don't consider practicing scales to be a waste of time. Keep in mind that this is new territory—putting scales into a new context of improvisation.

Speed as an Improvising Tool

The preceding exercise also shows how scale speed can be an effective tool for improvisation. Note that a scale played at one speed over the accompaniment produces a musical outcome that is vastly different from the same scale played at double or triple the initial speed. The variations of speed bring variety and interest to this exercise.

Key Points from This Chapter

- Scales are important tools of improvisation. They are now officially placed in the improvising toolbox as a key melodic element.
- Melodic tension and release are normal in improvisation (see principle 1 on page 25).
- Scale speed is a valuable tool that can change the character of an improvisation without changing the notes.

CHAPTER 7 Scales 102

Look back at exercise 6 and notice that the scale played did not need to change with every shift in harmony. That is, even though the harmony changed from C major to G major in the 2nd measure (and to F major in the 3rd measure), one didn't have to make a sudden mental shift to a different scale for the melodic material. Apart from a few dissonances, the key of C major was acceptable across the entire passage. This is an important concept to understand in these early stages—improvising is easier when a longer view is taken.

Just Like Driving

Recall the process of learning to drive on a slightly winding highway. Beginning drivers tend to focus on the dividing lines or shoulder markings right in front of the car (within 50 feet). As a result, their driving is often "jerky" as they continually make small adjustments to stay in the lane. But the sage driving instructor would say, "Look farther down the road. Let your destination guide you." By focusing farther down the road, the brain makes the small adjustments automatically—and steering immediately becomes smoother and easier.

The same concept applies to improvisation. With the following exercises, try to look "farther down the road." Where possible, identify the general harmonic intent of a passage and select a scale that allows a smooth ride through the changes. This will make improvising much easier.

Review

Practice exercise 6 (see page 28) again in different keys with this longer-view concept in mind. As the harmony changes, notice how the scale can remain the same—allowing easier navigation through the harmony.

Exercise 7-1: Moving to Minor

This exercise requires the conversion of the LH accompaniment into the minor mode as shown below. Take a moment to play through it.

The chord progression for this passage is as follows:

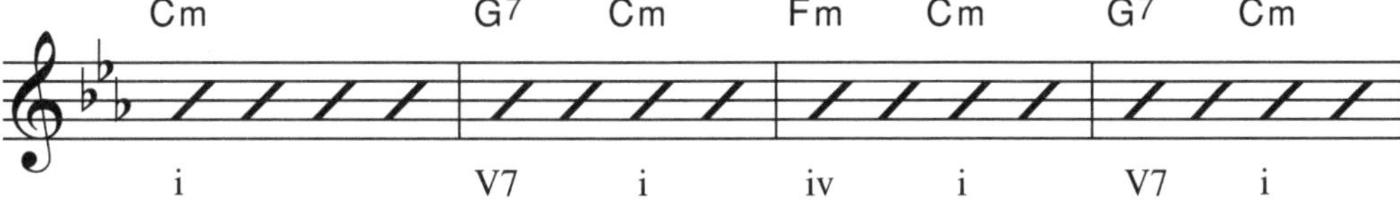

The new harmonic framework requires a different scale for melodic material. In this case, the C natural minor scale is the most appropriate choice. The natural minor scale is based upon the notes of the major scale located a minor 3rd higher. Therefore, the C natural minor scale is based upon the notes of the E♭ major scale as shown below:

1. **Applying the scale to the new harmony:** Play the RH patterns below using this new scale over the Alberti accompaniment in the minor mode. While playing, notice that one scale works with this entire passage despite the changes in harmony.

2. **Transposition:** When step 1 feels comfortable in C minor, transpose it into other minor keys—eventually all 12. Return to this exercise on a periodic basis to practice playing in different keys.

Making Slight Alterations

Sometimes, slight changes in a scale can make an improvisation even better. In the case of exercise 7-1, the B♭ in the C natural minor scale doesn't fit precisely with the G7 chord in the fourth measure. That's because the 3rd scale tone in the key of G major (the B♮ in the LH accompaniment) conflicts with the B♭ in the C natural minor scale.

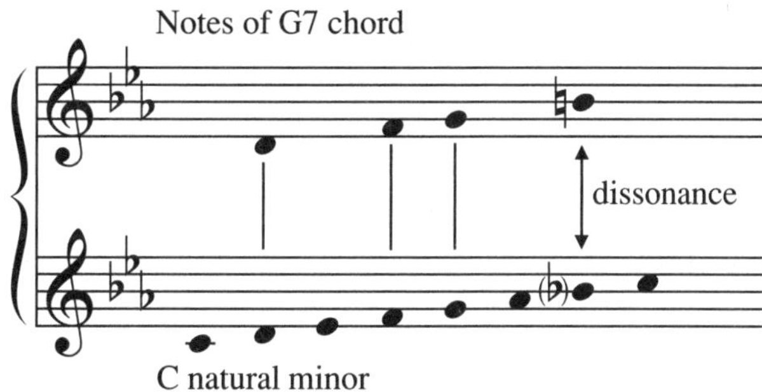

However, a slight modification can remove this dissonance. While playing the G7 chord, switch to the C harmonic minor scale.

The harmonic minor scale uses the same notes as the natural minor scale, except that the 7th tone (in this case, a B♭) is raised a half step (to B♮). The B♮ in the C harmonic minor scale accommodates the 3rd scale tone in the key of G.

Exercise 7-2: Applying the Harmonic Minor Scale

1. Repeat step 1 of exercise 7-1, this time substituting the C harmonic minor scale when appropriate with the G7 in the harmony. Do this until the concept of adapting the scale to suit the harmony feels natural.
2. Periodically return to this exercise and play it in a different key. The ultimate goal is to feel comfortable playing it in all 12 keys.

Note that it only took a slight change to improve the ability to navigate this passage. It will become apparent in later chapters that there are many situations in which a simple one-note change can allow one scale to apply across a range of harmonies.

Key Points from This Chapter

- To select scales for improvisation, first identify the general harmonic direction of a phrase and select one primary scale for that phrase rather than react with a new scale for every chord change.
- Often a slight alteration (sometimes just one note) can allow a scale to adapt to changes in the harmonic structure of a passage.

CHAPTER 8 Which Scale to Choose?

One of the most important questions in the study of musical grammar is, how does an improviser decide which scale is the right one at any given time? Earlier, it was stated that musical grammar is the way that melody interacts with harmony. Just as spoken grammar offers guidelines for the way words and sentences can form coherent statements in the context of language, musical grammar offers similar guidelines for the way notes and scales can speak eloquently in the context of musical harmony.

The Process of Choosing a Scale

For the skilled improviser, the process of choosing the right scale for the right moment may only take a split second. But this skill does not develop overnight. It begins with a fervent desire to understand harmony. This comes easily for some and can be quite challenging for others. However, the good news is that anyone with a reasonable knowledge of chords can learn to identify the harmonic structure of a piece. As the improviser learns to "see" harmony, choosing the right scale becomes easy.

Finding Tonal Focus

Play through the first eight measures of Beethoven's *Für Elise,* WoO 59.

Identify the harmonic structure of this passage. If this seems difficult, here is a series of questions to ask:

1. **What is the primary tonal focus or chord?***

   After examination, it can be concluded that the tonal focus of this passage is A minor. Below are a few clues that may have helped in reaching this conclusion:

   a. The way the passage begins and ends is often a strong indicator of tonal focus. This passage opens with an A minor chord in measure 2 (the previous four beats represent anticipatory upbeats; the passage really begins when the bass enters) and ends with an A minor chord in measure 8. Passages will not always begin and end with the same chord; but when they do, one can be fairly certain that the opening/closing chord is the tonal focus.

* In this example, there are no actual block chords. So, it may be necessary to play the arpeggiated notes together to see what chords they form.

b. The key signature of the piece can sometimes indicate tonal focus, especially when the passage resides near the beginning or end of the piece. But don't rely too heavily on the overall key signature when tonal focus shifts often from passage to passage. In this passage the key signature is A minor.

c. Repeated harmonic resolution can reveal the tonal focus. When various chords continually resolve to one particular chord, that chord is most likely the tonal focus. This passage continually resolves to the A minor chord.

2. **How closely related to the tonal focus are the other chords in the passage?**

   In the *Für Elise* excerpt, the only other chord is an E7. In the key of A minor, E is the dominant chord that seeks resolution to the tonic chord (Am) in a full cadence. Because the two chords are closely related, there is a high probability that one scale can work for both.

From this brief analysis, the harmonic framework for measures 1–8 can be identified as follows:

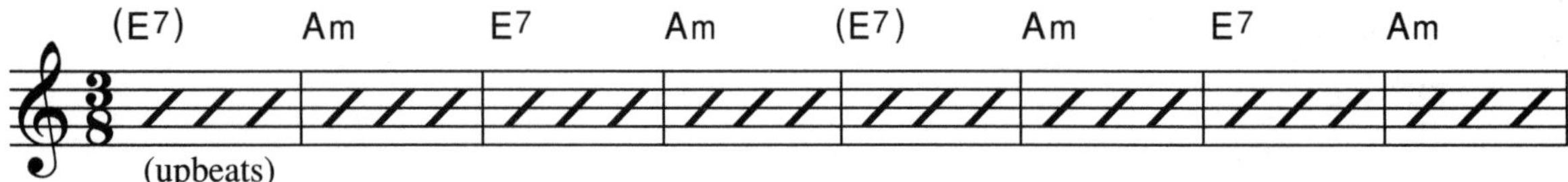

As mentioned earlier, the first four beats are really upbeats to the beginning of the phrase, which starts in measure 2. Also, the E7 chord in measures 1 and 5 are in parentheses, because there is no bass note—the chords are implied.

Now that the overall harmonic structure of the passage and the tonal focus have been identified, return to the critical question: *Is there a scale based on the tonal focus that can generally accommodate all chords in the passage?*

To answer this question, the following exercise will experiment with the scale that best reflects the tonal focus—the A natural minor scale.

Exercise 8-1: Finding the Right Scale

Play the LH part of *Für Elise* (beginning with measure 2) while playing the A natural minor scale with the RH as shown below:

Throughout this passage, the A natural minor scale works fairly well. But there is something not quite right. The G in this scale conflicts with the G♯ in the bass (in measure 2). As in chapter 7, try making one slight change to accommodate the E7 chord. When the G is changed to G♯, the scale becomes the A harmonic minor scale below:

Exercise 8-2: A Better Fit

Repeat the previous exercise using the new harmonic minor scale in the right hand.

Notice how one small adjustment allowed the scale to fit the entire passage. Any notes played within the A harmonic minor scale work perfectly.

Exercise 8-3: Exploration

Play through the following improvisation examples and then spend several minutes improvising the RH part while using the A harmonic minor scale.

Example 1

Example 2

Exploring Further

Now look at the next four measures of *Für Elise*. This passage presents a slightly more difficult challenge for selecting the proper scale. Take a moment to play through it

Identify the harmonic structure of the passage by playing the first four arpeggiated notes of each measure in block form. The four chords are identified below:

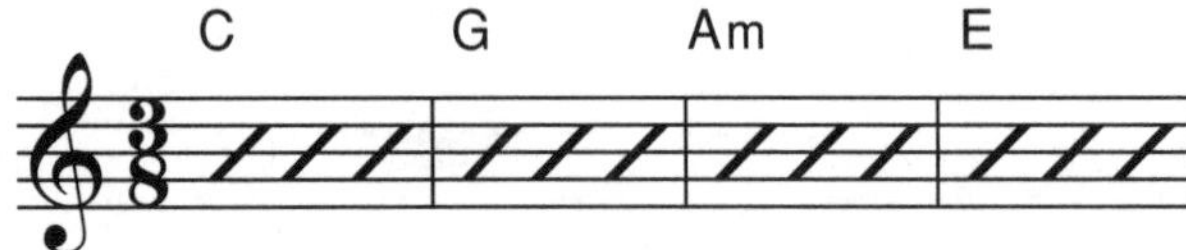

Refer to the question asked earlier, what is the primary tonal focus or chord? In this case, there is no clear tonal focus. Someone skilled in music theory might notice two plagal cadences (subdominant to tonic, i.e., C to G and Am to E); but neither cadence identifies a prime focus for the entire passage. When there is no clear focus, the following two questions may help to determine the right scale:

1. Does the scale associated with the first chord in the passage work well with the subsequent chords?
2. Are there any interrelated chords that indicate a harmonic emphasis?

The answer to the first question is essentially yes—the C major scale will work with the subsequent chords. When the notes of the C major scale are played starting on G (G Mixolydian mode), the resulting scale works well with the G major chord in the second bar.

The answer to the second question confirms the choice of the C major scale. In looking for interrelated chords, notice that the A minor chord in the third measure is the relative minor of the C chord. The fact that these two chords are harmonically related offers further evidence that C major is the tonal focus. It is no coincidence that the C major scale starting on A (the A Aeolian mode) is the A natural minor scale.

Based on these answers to the two questions, the best choice of scale for this passage is C major.

Exercise 8-4: Testing the Process

As before, play the LH part while playing the C major scale over it:

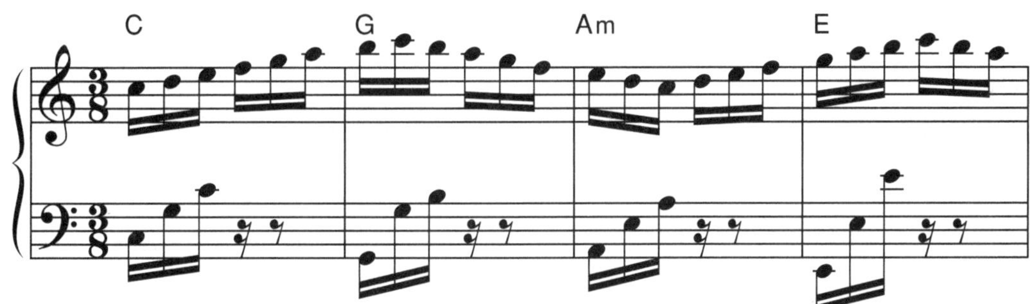

Is C major the best scale to use? Well, almost. In the last measure of this passage, which is harmonized by an E7 chord, Beethoven did not include a G♯ in the LH. So, technically, the C major scale will work. However, had the implied 3rd (G♯) been included in the LH, a one-note adjustment would need to be made by changing the G to a G♯ as shown in the following example:

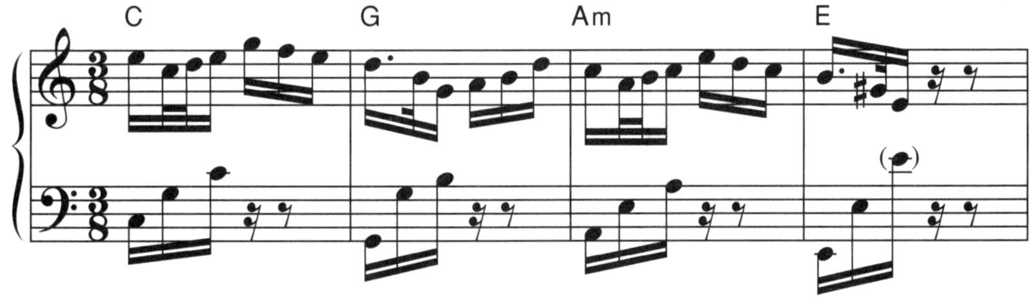

Exercise 8-5: Experimenting

Play through the following example several times and then spend some time improvising:

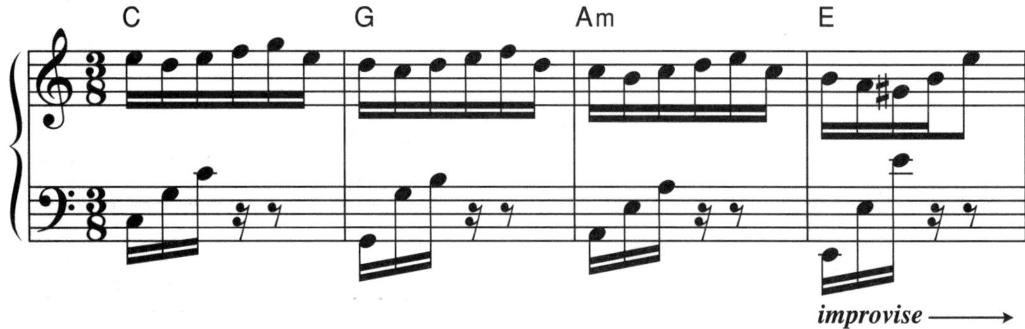

Be sure to make the G♯ adjustment at the E7 chord. Note how slight adjustments allow the improviser to navigate harmonic changes with greater ease.

Scale Choice Questions

The examples in this chapter have helped to identify the key questions to ask in determining scale choice:

1. What is the primary tonal focus of the passage?
    a. Does the way the passage begins and ends suggest a tonal focus?
    b. Does the key signature indicate a tonal focus?
    c. Are there harmonic resolutions that indicate a tonal focus?
2. Is there a scale based on the tonal focus that can generally accommodate all chords in the passage?
3. If there seems to be no clear tonal focus, ask the following:
    a. Will the scale associated with the first chord in the passage work well with the subsequent chords?
    b. Are there any interrelated chords that indicate a harmonic emphasis?

These questions are essential components of a systematic process that will help in selecting the appropriate scale for a given passage.

Scale Choice Guidelines

1. Determine the harmonic structure of a given passage
2. Identify the tonal focus
3. Select a scale that matches this focus
4. Make slight alterations to accommodate other chords in the passage

Exercise 8-6: Minuet in G Major

1. This exercise offers the opportunity to walk through the entire process just described. Play through the following excerpt of Beethoven's "Minuet in G Major" from Sonata Op. 49, No. 2:

2. Using the Scale Choice Guidelines, select a RH scale that will fit over the LH part of the passage. It will be helpful to walk through the same series of questions used for *Für Elise* to determine the appropriate scale. Try to do this without assistance. If the process seems difficult, refer to analysis 8-6 on page 44.
3. Once the proper scale has been determined, use the notes of that scale to improvise with the RH while playing the LH notes of the first eight measures of the minuet.

Exercise 8-7: Folies d'Espagne

Play through the following excerpt of Corelli's *Folies d'Espagne*:

1. Try to identify two related scales that work well through the 16-bar passage. The two scales will differ slightly to accommodate the changing harmony. If difficulty arises in identifying the harmony or scales, refer to analysis 8-7 on pages 45–46.
2. After identifying the two scales, use them to create RH improvisations while playing the written notes in the LH.*

* Afterward, consider studying the score and recordings of Rachmaninoff's *Variations on a Theme of Corelli*, Op. 42 found in Alfred edition #27001.

Exercise 8-8: Gavotte in D Major

Play through the following excerpt of J. S. Bach's "Gavotte in D Major" from the *Sixth Suite for Cello,* BWV 1012:

While this example is more difficult than the previous two, the harmony for this passage is fairly straightforward. Improvisation can be based on two scales. Using the Scale Choice Guidelines, identify the two principle scales that are appropriate for this passage. For assistance, refer to analysis 8-8 on pages 46–48.

Analysis 8-6: Minuet in G Major

1. The harmonic structure consists of two alternating chords D7 and G major.
2. The tonal focus is clearly G major, since the D7 chords continually resolve to G major chords.
3. The G major scale works for both chords. Therefore, one scale fits the entire passage.
4. As with the first 8 measures of the Minuet, a slight alteration can help make the improvisation more pleasing. The strategic use of C♯ with the D7 chord can add color.

Using the G major scale (and the occasional C♯ alteration), here is a sample improvisation that fits this passage:

Analysis 8-7: Folies d'Espagne

1. The harmonic structure of the passage is as follows:

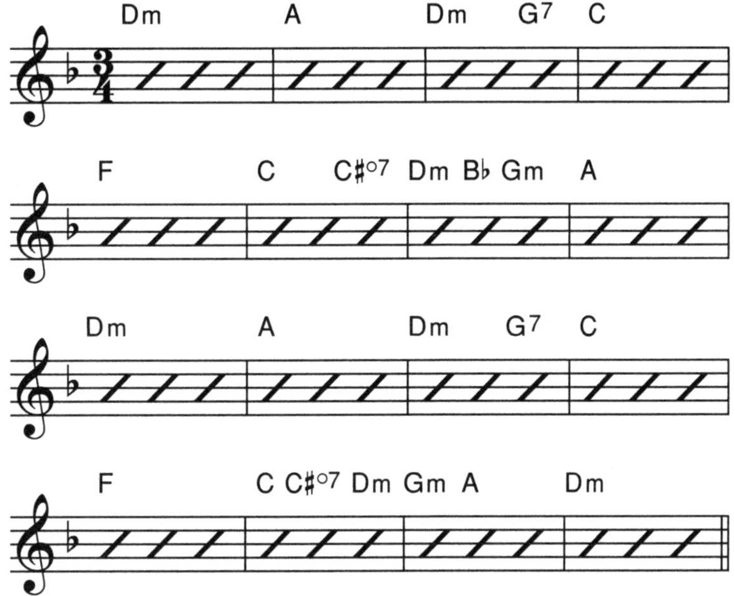

2. There is a clear tonal focus of D minor. The way the passage begins and ends, along with strong dominant to tonic cadences resolving to D minor chords, identifies the tonality. Another clue is the way the restatement in measure 8 begins with a D minor chord.

3. The primary scale is D melodic minor (ascending). It accommodates the D minor, A major and C♯ diminished chords in the passage.

The secondary scale is D natural minor. It accommodates the F, B♭ and C major chords, when they appear.

Notice that these two scales are closely related, which makes it easy to adjust as the harmony changes. This is much easier than trying to adapt to a new scale with each successive chord.

4. Play the LH part as written and use the RH to decide which scale seems most appropriate as the harmony changes. The example below is one way that the scales can be used in this passage:

Analysis 8-8: Gavotte in D Major

1. The harmonic structure of the passage is as follows:

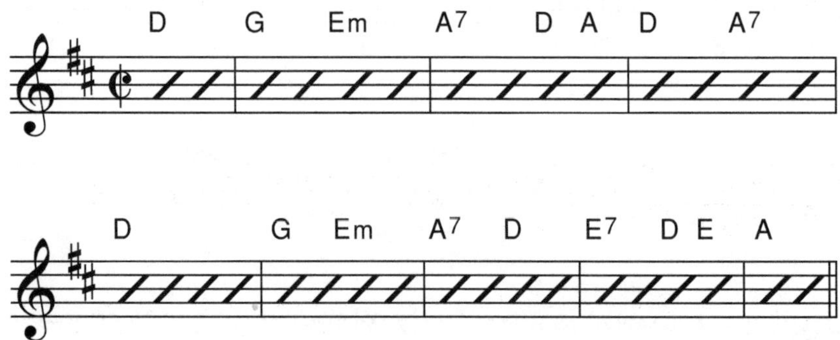

2. The tonal focus is a bit trickier to identify, because the tonic chord does not occur on the downbeat. Two clues suggest that D major is the tonal focus—the key signature and the repeated full cadences (A to D).

3. With a tonal focus in the key of D, the first scale to try over the LH part is D major. It works well until the seventh full measure.

4. The tonal focus changes in measures 7 and 8 to the key of A major (as identified by the full cadence from E to A). At this point, try making a mental shift to the A major scale by making a slight change in the D major scale to accommodate the shift in harmony. This can be done by simply raising the G to a G♯ in the D major scale (D Lydian mode). Again, a slight change of one note allows for easy navigation of the entire passage. Also note that this adapted scale (D Lydian mode) is made up of the same notes as the A Major scale starting on D.*

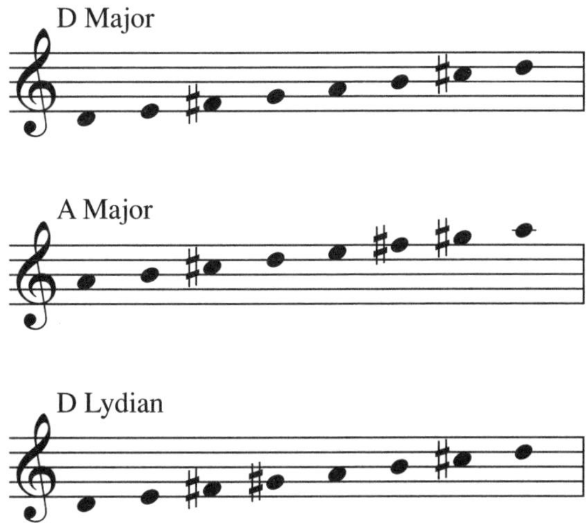

5. Below is an example of the ways the aforementioned scales can be used with the LH part of this Bach passage:

* This concept will be discussed further in later chapters.

6. Sometimes, thinking purely in terms of scales (as in step 5) can create an improvisation that sounds stiff or contrived. As a reminder that improvisation is also about melody, here is another example using the same LH part and a more melodic approach to the RH:

Key Points from This Chapter

- Selecting the right scale requires an understanding of harmony.
- Once the harmonic structure of a passage is clearly seen, selecting a scale for melodic material is relatively easy.
- A single scale (with slight alterations) can often accommodate an entire series of chord changes.

CHAPTER 9 Melodic Manipulation, Part 1: Upside Down & Inside Out

Having learned a basic method of selecting the right scale for a particular passage, the next question will likely be, what should be done with the notes of that scale? After all, no one wants their improvisations to consist only of scales played up and down in the same way every time. Once a player knows which notes are best, the challenge is to use them in creative ways. The next two chapters will introduce some melodic tools that can help the improviser fully utilize the notes of the scale.

Upside Down & Inside Out

At the beginning of this *Tools* section, principle 2 stated that there are many different ways to manipulate the melodic material already in one's memory (see pages 25–26).

Play through the following Mozart sonata excerpt followed by an upside-down version of the melody.

Original Melody

Upside-Down Melody

Notice how the melodic theme stays within the harmonic framework of the Alberti accompaniment despite being turned upside down. Alternate between these two versions a few times to hear the difference.

Melodic themes can also be turned "inside out." Inside out refers to melodic alterations that take inner notes (notes near the center of the melodic range) and move them outward toward the ends of the melodic range and take outer notes and move them toward the center.

In the following example, the rhythm is modified slightly and some ideas are turned inside out while staying within the Alberti framework. Play this example a few times and alternate with the original melody to hear the difference.

Inside-Out Melody

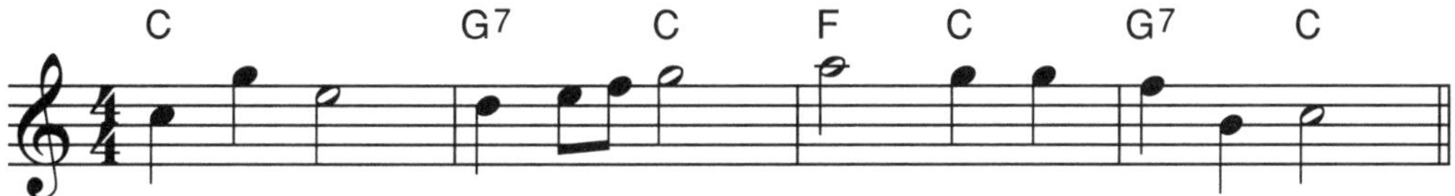

Exercise 9-1: Hearing in Different Keys

Play the preceding upside-down and inside-out Mozart examples several times with the Alberti accompaniment to become familiar with the two manipulation techniques. Then, transpose the examples into different keys to "write" them into memory. (The more melodic material written into memory through transposition, the more options will be available for improvisation.)

Exercise 9-2: A Familiar Song

1. Play the LH Alberti accompaniment with the melody "Twinkle, Twinkle, Little Star."

2. Play through the following examples that turn "Twinkle, Twinkle, Little Star" upside down and inside out:

   Upside-Down Melody

   Inside-Out Melody 1

   Inside-Out Melody 2

   Keep in mind that there are many different ways that an upside-down or inside-out melody can be expressed. It's important not to start out thinking that there is just one right way.

3. Be adventurous by creating several different upside-down and inside-out versions of "Twinkle, Twinkle, Little Star" that follow the harmony.

4. Once several ideas have been developed, transpose steps 1–3 into various keys.

Exercise 9-3: Practicing with Three Famous Melodies

Try turning the following famous melodies upside down and inside out. For examples, see analysis 9-3.

Melody 1: Minuet, BWV Anhang 114 (Attr. to Christian Petzold)

Melody 2: Haydn's Symphony No. 94, "Surprise Symphony"

Melody 3: Beethoven's "Ode To Joy" from Symphony No. 9

Exercise 9-4: Be Adventurous

- Create an original melody and turn it upside down and inside out.
- Try practicing upside-down and inside-out techniques away from the piano. While standing in line at the grocery store or waiting to board a flight at the airport, quietly hum through some well-known melodies (classical melodies, pop tunes, Broadway classics, even nursery rhymes) and try to turn them upside down and inside out. This is a challenging brain exercise that can be done anywhere. It's a great way to grow as an improviser. Use this exercise to occupy downtime in a highly productive way.
- For teachers, try turning this exercise into a game with students. Play or sing a melody and see if they can turn it upside down or inside out.
- Create a simple RH pattern based on the harmony of the Alberti accompaniment and practice creating upside-down and inside-out melodies with the LH.

Analysis 9-3: Three Famous Melodies

Melody 1: Minuet

Original Melody

Upside-Down Melody

Inside-Out Melody

Melody 2: Surprise Symphony

Original Melody

Upside-Down Melody

Inside-Out Melody

Melody 3: Ode to Joy

Original Melody

Upside-Down Melody

Inside-Out Melody

Key Points from This Chapter

- One useful way to manipulate the notes of a scale for improvisation is to turn the original melody upside down or inside out.
- There may be several different ways to turn a melody upside down or inside out. Remember that improvisation is not an exact science—let the ideas flow!

CHAPTER 10 Melodic Manipulation, Part 2: Skipping

This chapter explains another type of melodic manipulation—an interval-based tool called skipping. Skipping refers to the technique of skipping over notes in intervals of 3rds or 4ths. Play through the following example a few times, with the Alberti accompaniment in the LH:

Notice how many of the notes skip in short intervals over the notes of the scale. The phrase above is a good example of separated skipping in which short skipping segments are separated by scale segments.

A Treasury of Skipping Material (Pattern Skipping)

Many of the rudimentary finger exercises practiced by pianists during early years of study are based upon skipping.

Pianists who have played these kinds of exercises regularly in their formative years already have a memory vault filled with skipping patterns that are useful for improvisation.

Exercise 10-1: Using Patterns to Create a Quilt

1. Review some of the rudimentary finger exercises that utilize pattern skipping. Play through the finger exercises previously shown. Take some time to recall as many as possible.
2. Practice step 1 in different keys. This valuable transposition exercise will help the brain and fingers to experience these intervals in a different context. Do this with a variety of different exercises (Czerny, Dohnanyi, etc.).
3. Play steady quarter notes on C with the LH in $\frac{4}{4}$ time. Take segments from the pattern skipping examples in step 1 and patch them together into a "quilt of ideas" played with the RH as shown below. Feel free to insert scale segments and other melodic material at any time.

4. After playing step 3 for a while, let the RH flow into a free-form exploration of skipping intervals. Continue exploring as long as creative ideas flow.
5. Play through steps 3 and 4 in a variety of different keys.

Arpeggiated Skipping

Another familiar form of skipping is the arpeggio. Arpeggios meet the definition of skipping because they move up and down in intervals of 3rds and 4ths. The following example shows how easily arpeggios can flow over harmony. Take a moment to play through it.

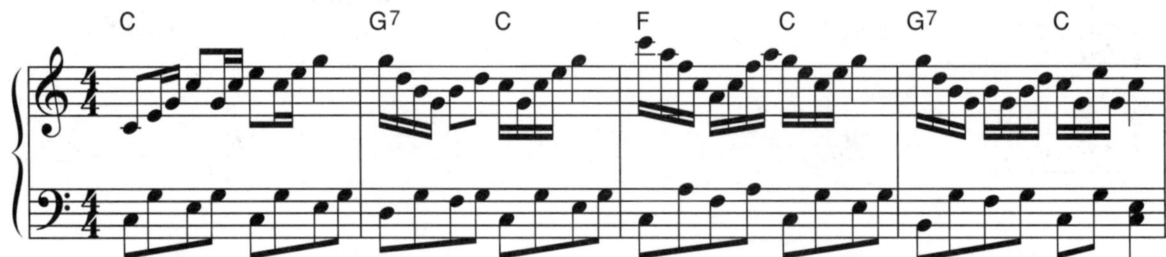

Arpeggios are highly effective tools of improvisation. They can be used virtually anywhere—in short bursts or long, connected phrases. Because they typically follow the harmony (e.g., a G major arpeggio always works over a G major chord), arpeggios are a convenient choice whenever the improviser begins to feel a bit lost and needs to reconnect with the harmony. They are also valuable when the player needs to inject a dose of energy or interest. Bach's Prelude No. 1 in C Major from the *Well-Tempered Clavier, Volume 1,* BWV 846, demonstrates an excellent use of arpeggios to create momentum.

In measures 18–21 of Mozart's Sonata in C Major, K. 545, the composer uses arpeggios to create a connecting passage.

Arpeggios can also be combined with other rhythmic elements and scale segments to create interesting and beautiful hybrid phrases like the following excerpts:

Excerpt from Beethoven's Sonata in C Minor, Op. 13, "Pathétique"

Excerpt from Kuhlau's Sonatina in F Major, Op. 55, No. 4

Suffice it to say that skipping, whether in patterns or arpeggios, is one of the more valuable tools of composition and improvisation.

Exercise 10-2: Improvising with Arpeggios

1. Play through the example below (from page 54). Then, experiment with arpeggios over the Alberti accompaniment. Remember that arpeggios tend to follow the harmony. For example, an F major arpeggio works over an F major chord.

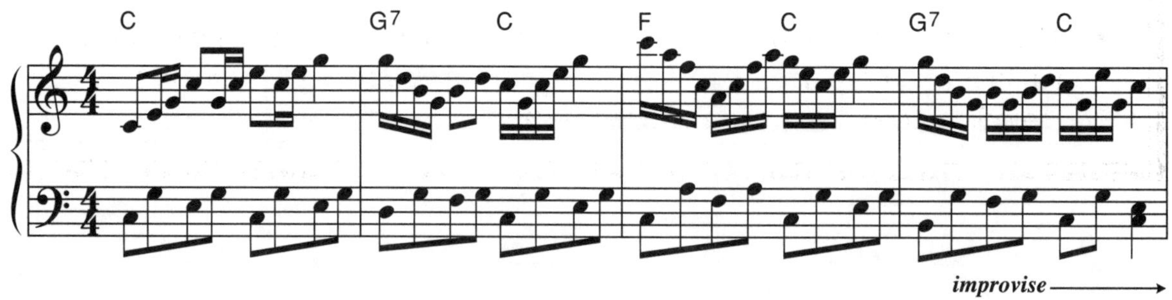

2. The speed of an arpeggio can also be a useful tool for improvisation. The example below illustrates the effect of arpeggio speed in each measure. Take a moment to play through it.

- Practice using arpeggios at various speeds to create different levels of energy. Start slowly, and then increase speed.
- Try mixing arpeggio speed within a measure as in measure 4 of the example.

3. Arpeggios can also be combined with scale segments as shown below. Play through the example, with the Alberti accompaniment, and then try creating other combined phrases:

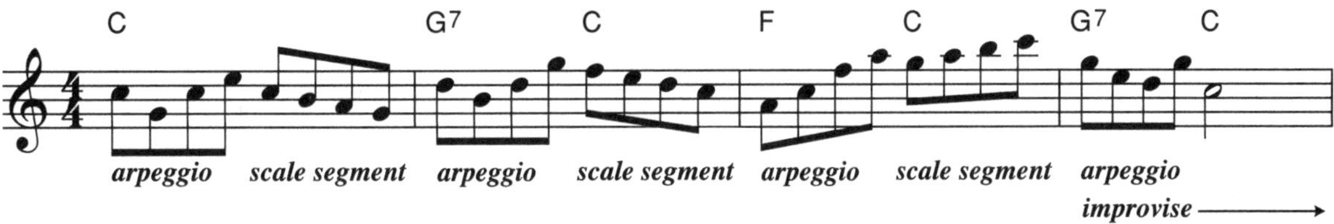

4. As stated earlier, transposition is a powerful improvising tool. Play through steps 1–3 in various keys.
5. Create a simple RH pattern based on the harmony of the Alberti accompaniment and practice creating skipping intervals with the LH.

Key Points from This Chapter

- Skipping is the technique of using intervals of 3rds and 4ths to meander around a melodic line.
- Many rudimentary finger exercises (from Hanon, Czerny, etc.) are based upon skipping patterns. These exercises are a treasury of melodic material that can be a springboard for improvisation
- The most familiar type of skipping is the arpeggio. Arpeggios can be extremely valuable in improvisation. They can be inserted virtually anywhere to create melodic interest, direction and momentum.

CHAPTER 11 Melodic Manipulation, Part 3: Upper & Lower Neighbors

Remember the concept of upper/lower neighbors introduced in the *Foundations* section? That too was a form of skipping, but with a different character and intention.

To see the difference, first envision a grasshopper hopping over notes. That visual image aptly describes the pattern and arpeggiated skipping discussed in chapter 10. In the examples below, the notes seem to "hop" in intervals of 3rds and 4ths:

Pattern Skipping

Arpeggiated Skipping

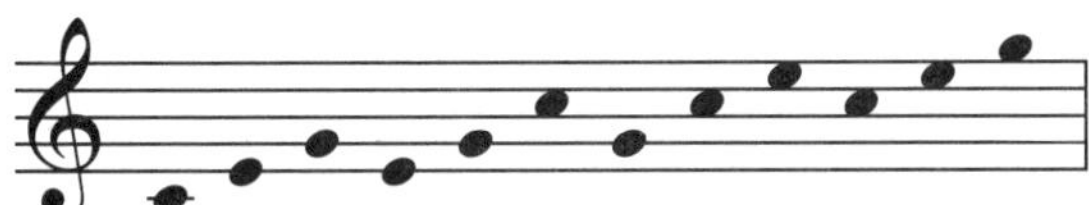

In contrast, the use of upper/lower (or adjacent) neighbors could be described as a snake slithering over and around notes. This can actually be seen on the musical staff. First, imagine a simple defining-note melody using the three notes of the C major triad.

When these defining notes are surrounded with neighboring notes, the following phrase is possible:

See how the expanded melodic line seems to "slither" (or meander) around the three defining notes? The phrase begins to resemble the shape of a snake on the staff. When the melody is extended to include the next C higher, the result is an even more slithery phrase.

These notes form a lyrical, fluid line that is quite different in character from the grasshopper-like skipping phrases discussed in the previous chapter.

Intention of Upper & Lower Neighbors

It was stated earlier that the use of upper/lower neighbors differs from other types of skipping in both character and intention. What was meant by intention? In chapter 10, the skipping intervals were the focus (intention) of each melodic phrase. That is, the use of skipping created the phrases. In this chapter, the opposite is true—the use of upper/lower neighbors creates the skipping.

Look again at the intervals in the previous example. Even though many of those intervals fulfill the definition of skipping (3rds and 4ths), the skips were largely unintentional. They simply happened when the upper/lower neighbors were used to connect the defining notes, and the outcome was engaging lyricism. There is actually a double benefit when using upper/lower neighbors—appealing melodies and skipping intervals.

Choosing Neighboring Notes

What gives these phrases their lyrical quality? It is the neighboring notes that are chosen. Every note has two possible neighbors on either side.

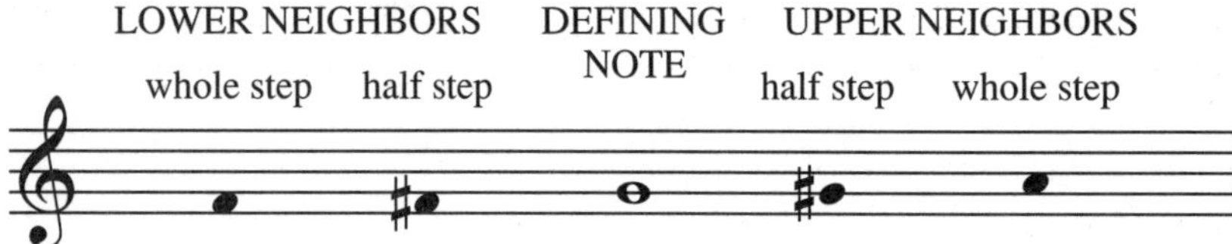

With pattern skipping and arpeggios, the intervals were formed using only tones of the major or minor scale—no chromatic tones were used. The skipping example below illustrates this (notice that every note is part of the C major scale):

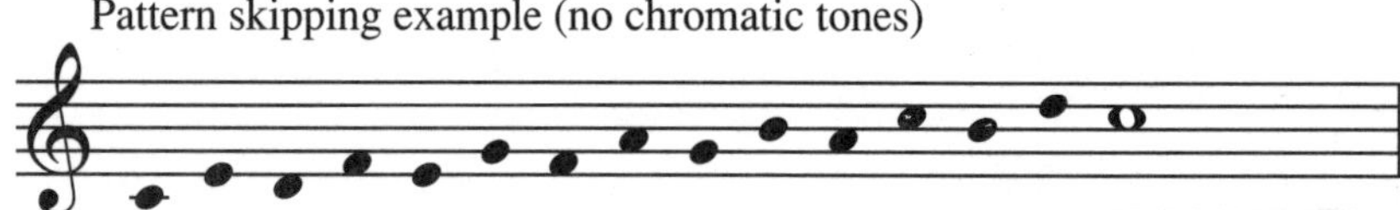

In contrast, upper/lower neighbors are often selected from tones outside the scale. Play through the example below:

Based in the key of C major, this phrase contains two notes that are outside the C major scale (the D♯ and F♯ lower neighbors). These chromatic lower neighbors contribute greatly to the romantic character of the phrase.

Available Choices

There are actually four different sets of adjacent neighbors that can be selected. The following two examples are the most common and appear frequently in all types of musical literature:

whole-step upper neighbor
half-step lower neighbor

half-step upper neighbor
half-step lower neighbor

Below are the two less common combinations.

Note how each of these combinations of adjacent neighbors creates a different melodic and emotional effect. Knowing these differences can help to determine the right combination of neighbors to use at a particular time.

Destinations

Another difference between the skipping in chapter 10 and the use of adjacent neighbors in this chapter is the destination of the phrase. With pattern skipping and arpeggios, the phrase usually has a start point and an end point. The skips all work together to drive toward the end point. That's why these types of skipping are so useful for building energy and momentum.

With upper/lower neighbors, the destination is not always an end point. Rather, each pair of neighbors seeks only to resolve to one defining note (the destination). Adjacent neighbors are essentially "slaves" to the defining notes. The improviser simply decides where the defining notes should go. Once the direction is determined, upper/lower neighbors help to transform those defining notes into an appealing melodic phrase.

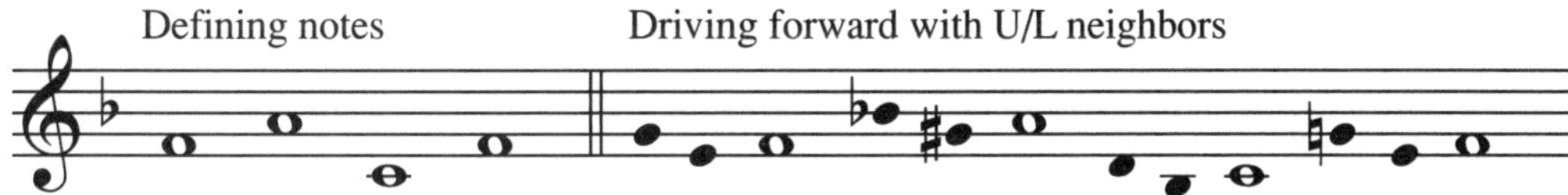

Only when the defining notes are themselves driving toward a destination will the addition of upper/lower neighbors help to build energy and momentum, as shown below:

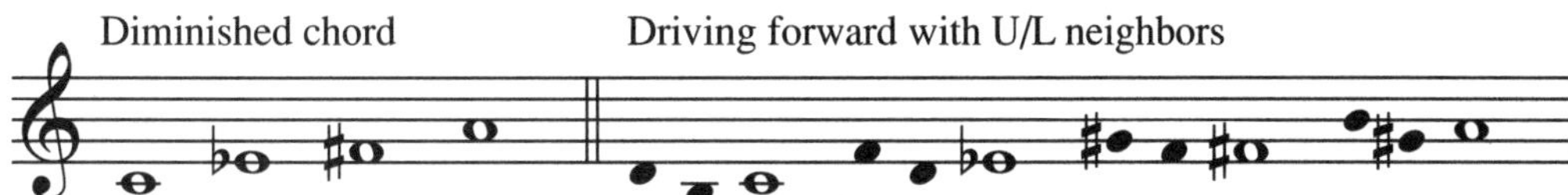

Passing Tones and Chromatic Tones

One final use of upper/lower neighbors is their common application as passing tones in both major and chromatic scales. Assuming that C–E–G–C are the defining notes, the following examples below show how adjacent neighbors can operate as connecting tones that help create scalar phrases:

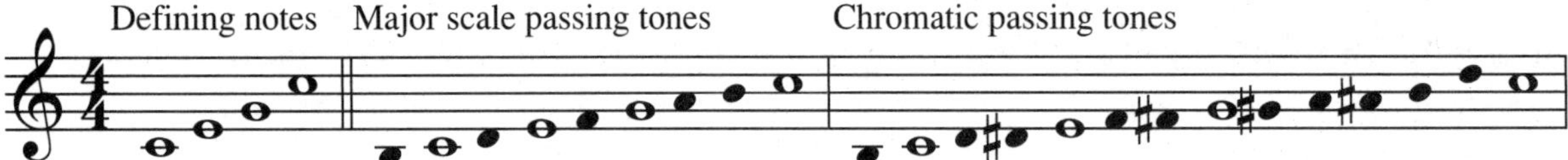

Exercise 11-1: Building Phrases

1. **Upper Neighbor First:** Connect the following sets of defining notes with adjacent neighbors to create interesting melodies. When circling each defining note, use an upper neighbor first, then a lower neighbor (like the first example below).

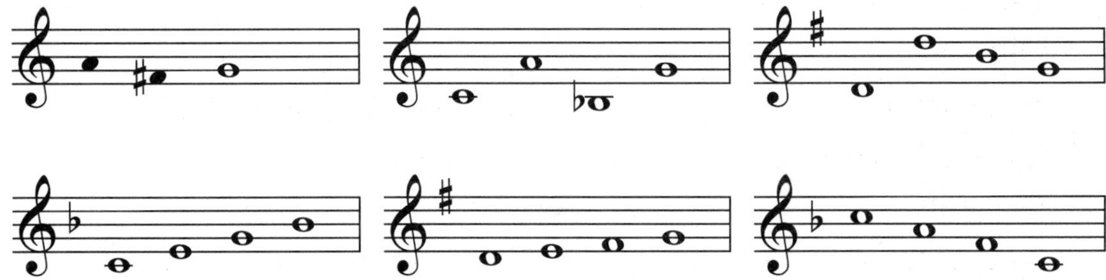

2. **Lower Neighbor First:** Repeat step 1, but play the lower neighbor first and then the upper neighbor, like the following example:

3. **Random Selection:** Repeat step 1, but this time alternate. Use the upper neighbor first for some defining notes and the lower neighbor first for others. Notice how easily this adds variety to the phrases.
4. **New Defining Notes:** Spontaneously decide upon a series of 4–5 defining notes and connect them using upper/lower neighbors as above.
   - Do this several times with different notes.
   - Change keys when this process becomes comfortable in a particular key.
5. **Engaging the Left Hand:** Play through steps 1–4 using the LH.

Exercise 11-2: Transposition

Transposition helps to drive a concept into the mind. Below are two extended phrases that combine the various applications of upper/lower neighbors and skipping:

Phrase 1

Phrase 2

1. Play through both phrases several times to internalize the patterns.
2. Once they have been played into memory, transpose them into several different keys.
3. Play through steps 1 and 2 using the LH.
4. Return to these two exercises periodically. The ultimate goal should be to master both phrases in all 12 keys.

Key Points from This Chapter

Patterns and arpeggios are different from upper/lower neighbors in the following ways:

1. **Pattern Skipping and Arpeggios**
    - The skipping is intentional.
    - The skipping intervals move together in sequence toward a common destination where resolution occurs.
    - The beginning and ending of the phrase are the defining notes.
    - Best Use: For creating direction, energy and momentum.
2. **Upper and Lower Neighbors**
    - The skipping is unintentional. Skipping intervals simply happen when upper/lower neighbors are used.
    - The skipping intervals do not necessarily work together in sequence.
    - Upper/lower neighbors desire to resolve to one defining note only. The improviser determines the series of defining notes.
    - Best Use: For connecting defining notes in a way that creates melodic interest through engaging melodies and skipping intervals.

CHAPTER 12 Melodic Manipulation, Part 4: Jumping

The difference between skipping and jumping is in the size of the interval. While skipping utilizes shorter intervals of 3rds and 4ths, jumping involves intervals equal to or larger than a perfect 5th. Here is an example that features jumping (indicated by arrows):

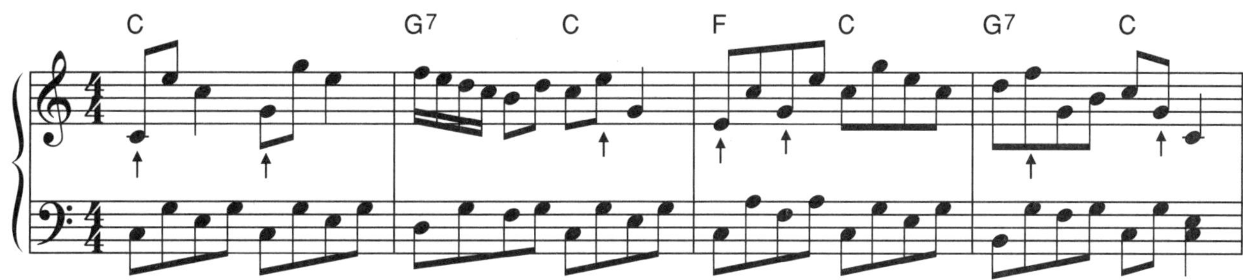

Jumping can occur within the context of any melodic line. Below are some other examples:

Transposed excerpt from Mozart's Sonata in F Major, K. 332

While skipping tends to be a useful technique for meandering to a destination in a deliberate and disciplined way, jumping—especially in wide intervals—tends to open up an improvisation by expanding the melodic palette. Whenever an improvisation seems too confined, use jumping to provide more room to be creative.

Jumping can also help to avoid predictability. A well-placed melodic jump (or series of jumps) can be "just what the doctor ordered" to surprise the listener and revive interest in an improvised passage that doesn't seem to be going anywhere.

However, jumping intervals are not typically extended into long phrases. Too many jumps in a given passage can become tiresome to the listener, as in the following passage:

At a certain point, one's ears long for a break from incessant jumping. A few well-placed scale segments can help to provide variety and create a better flow to the same passage as in the following example:

Pedal Point Jumping

A simple technique for creating jumps is to utilize a familiar melody and insert an upper or lower pedal point between the notes of the melody. The most common pedal points are the root tone and the 5th in any given key. Play through the following examples that use Beethoven's *Ode to Joy*:

Original Melody

Lower Pedal Point Melody

Upper Pedal Point Melody

Exercise 12-1: Pedal Point Jumping

1. Use the upper and lower pedal point technique with the following melodies. The most logical pedal note for both examples is G, the 5th of C major.

   Melody 1: Mary Had a Little Lamb

   Melody 2: Hail to the Victors

   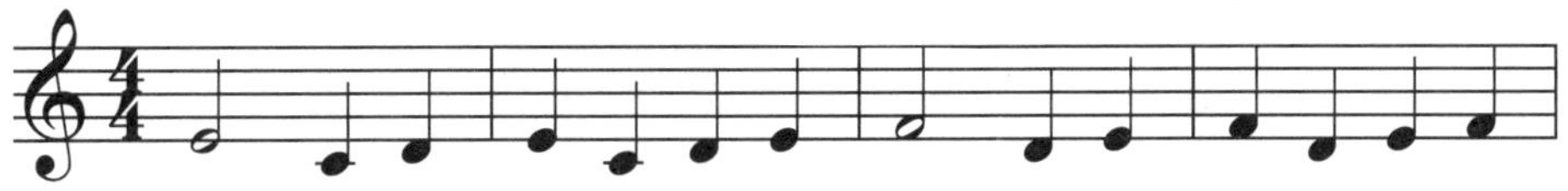

2. Periodically return to this exercise until all 12 keys have been explored.

Parallel Jumping

Another useful technique is to establish fixed interval jumps that move in tandem with a melodic line. The most common intervals for parallel jumping are 6ths and octaves. The examples below demonstrate "Mary Had a Little Lamb" with parallel intervals:

Jumping in 6ths

Jumping in Octaves

Exercise 12-2: Parallel Jumping

1. Play through melody 2 of exercise 12-1 using parallel jumps.
2. Select any familiar melody and experiment with parallel jumps.
3. Periodically return to this exercise until all 12 keys have been explored.

Arpeggiated Jumping

As stated in the last chapter, arpeggios fit the definition of skipping by moving in intervals of 3rds and 4ths. However, when every other note of an arpeggio is played, the result automatically satisfies the definition of jumping (i.e., moving in intervals of a perfect 5th or more). Here is an example:

Arpeggios provide a framework for even larger intervals when the player jumps over three or more notes of the arpeggio as shown below:

Exercise 12-3: Arpeggiated Jumping

1. Play steady quarter notes on C with the LH.
2. While playing the LH notes, experiment with longer arpeggio jumps as described above. Feel free to insert scale segments whenever necessary.
3. Return to exercises 12-1 and 12-2 and experiment with longer jumps while playing quarter notes in the LH.
4. Transpose steps 1–3 into different keys.
5. Periodically return to this exercise until all 12 keys have been explored.

Jumping through Octave Switching

Interesting jumps occur when the player makes a decision to switch octaves in the middle of a phrase. Consider the following example that contains only skipping intervals:

By changing the octave of selected individual notes (or pairs of notes), the resulting jumps can make the passage more interesting:

Exercise 12-4: Jumping through Octave Switching

1. Play the following examples that create jumps through octave switching:

2. Use octave switching to alter the following examples. Don't be afraid to switch the octave of a note (or notes) in the middle of a phrase. Try experimenting with wild intervals to see how they sound.

Example 1

3. Periodically return to this exercise until all 12 keys have been explored.

Free Form Jumping

Each of the previous exercises have focused on a particular type of jumping. When improvising, however, one doesn't have time to stop and think about which type to use. The player simply chooses to jump spontaneously when the moment seems right. Exercise 12-5 encourages this type of spontaneity.

Exercise 12-5: Free Form Jumping

During this exercise, don't forget to utilize many of the tools developed in the *Foundations* section—dynamics, tone, duration and silence. Improvisations will be far more interesting when these elements are integrated.

1. Play steady quarter notes on C with the LH.
2. Use all of the various methods introduced in the previous exercises (pedal points, parallel intervals, arpeggios and octave switching) to create interesting phrases that include jumping and other melodic material (scale segments and some skipping to provide balance and flow). The canvas is blank—start "painting" with intervals.
3. Switch to quarter notes in the RH and experiment with step 2 using the LH.
4. Periodically return to this exercise until all 12 keys have been explored.

Key Points from This Chapter

- Jumping is the technique of using intervals that are a perfect 5th or larger. New melodic material can be created by manipulating existing melodies with jumping intervals.
- Jumping too often or too long in a series can be tiresome to a listener. Be sure to interject other melodic elements to create a more natural flow in a passage.
- Interesting interval jumps can be created by switching octaves in the middle of a phrase.

CHAPTER 13 Repetition as a Creative Tool

So far, several important tools for manipulating scales and melodic material have been explored:

- Scalar Speed (chapter 6)
- Upper/Lower Neighbors (chapters 2 and 11)
- Turning Melodies Upside Down or Inside Out (chapter 9)
- Intervals: Skipping and Jumping for Melodic Interest (chapters 10 and 12)
- Octave Switching to Create New Patterns (chapter 12)

This chapter will add one more element to the improviser's toolbox—repetition.

The *Foundations* section challenged the player to begin "speaking" in sentences and paragraphs rather than short phrases. Citing verbal communication as an example, it described the difficulties of listening to someone speaking in short, unrelated sentence fragments. Imagine a stranger speaking in the following way:

Why don't we go to the mall? Hit the ball now. Let's dance! I like soda.
Do you have a computer? I'm hungry. Piano playing is fun. Who let the dogs out?

After a few moments of someone speaking in such a random way, one would likely conclude that very little meaningful conversation could take place. That's because meaningful communication requires a convergence of related thoughts—or coherence. A more coherent conversation might proceed as follows:

Why don't we go to the mall? If you like, I can drive. Be sure to bring your credit card.
The stores are having big sales this weekend. I'm planning to get some new shoes.
We can stop for lunch at my favorite restaurant.

See how all the thoughts move in a common and consistent direction? Clearly, this presents a more coherent flow of communication. The direction of the conversation may eventually change, but not until all information related to the shopping trip has been expressed. To be regarded as a clear verbal communicator, one must make the message coherent. This also applies to the improviser.

Beginning improvisers sometimes have trouble "speaking" coherently. They tend to connect unrelated ideas together into a long series of individual phrases that fails to communicate a unified thought. Below is an example:

In this intentionally schizophrenic example, the individual ideas are good, but the overall improvisation seems clumsy and disconnected.

To solve this problem and develop coherence, utilize repetition. Composers throughout the ages have used repetition to establish melodic/rhythmic themes and infuse a passage with purposeful energy and direction. The recurrence of familiar elements connects ideas and brings a sense of unity to a written passage (or an entire work). Similarly, repetition will bring coherence to improvisation.

This chapter will discuss two major types of repetition—sequential and recurring.

Sequential Repetition (Melodic and Rhythmic Patterns)

Examine the following excerpt from Beethoven's Sonata in C Minor, Op. 13, "Pathétique":

One can easily see the rhythmic motif repeated four times in the first three measures. Beethoven used this rhythmic series to firmly establish his thematic point. The notes changed with each restatement of the rhythm, but there is no doubt that Beethoven was trying to say something specific and compelling to the listener with this opening passage. The improviser has the same goal—to say something specific and compelling to the listener.

Sequential Patterns

A sequential pattern is a series of contiguous repeated melodic or rhythmic patterns that creates a dramatic effect. If not overused, this type of repetition can provide a clear sense of direction and momentum to an improvisation. Many types of sequential patterns may already be quite familiar.

Type 1: Repetitive Scalar Patterns

These are patterns based on a series of scale segments connected to provide momentum toward a destination.

Scalar Pattern

Notice that the four sixteenth-note scale segments in the first measure are unified in driving toward the middle C at the beginning of the second measure. While this pattern focuses on the use of scale elements, it also involves rhythmic repetition (the sixteenth-note motif). Most scalar patterns incorporate a repeated rhythm.

Sometimes, complete scales can be used in repetition. In the following excerpt, the cascading scales create the feeling of undulating musical "waves":

Scalar Pattern (from Kuhlau's Sonatina in A Minor, Op. 88, No. 3)

At other times, the use of scales and scale segments can be less predictable. Scalar patterns are not required to move in the same direction, nor must they share the same scale. In the following excerpt the scale segments follow the harmonic changes and switch direction as necessary:

Scalar Pattern (from Kuhlau's Sonatina in C Major, Op. 55, No. 3)

The listener may feel tossed around by the frequent changes in direction, but the overall outcome is a beautifully lilting passage that captures interest.

Type 2: Repetitive Non-Scalar Melodic Patterns

Non-scalar patterns are made up of repeated melodic material that is not built upon a scale. Most non-scalar patterns are based on the skipping and jumping tools discussed in chapters 10–12. Notice how each of the following examples use repetitive patterns to provide melodic direction and create energy within the passage:

Skipping Pattern (from Bach's Sinfonia No. 15, BWV 801)

Jumping Pattern (from Beethoven's Rondo a capriccio, Op. 129)

Arpeggiated Pattern (from Beethoven's Rondo a capriccio, Op. 129)

Type 3: Repetitive Rhythmic Patterns

Rhythmic patterns rely upon the repetition of rhythm only for their commonality. The Beethoven "Pathétique" excerpt demonstrated this type of repetition as the harmony and notes changed, but the rhythmic pattern repeated sequentially. Below is another example by Beethoven that repeats a two-measure rhythmic phrase:

Rhythmic Pattern (from Beethoven's Six Variations on a Duet by Paisiello, WoO 70)

Notice that both the scales used and the direction of the phrases differ (when comparing measure 1 to measure 3 and measure 2 to measure 4), but the rhythmic pattern in measures 1–2 is nearly the same as in measures 3–4.

While all of the previous examples were composed rather than improvised, the concepts they illustrate are fundamental tools of the improviser. It is possible that many of these examples began as improvisations that eventually found their way to paper.

When to Use Sequential Repetition

As stated earlier, any verbal communicator wants to be perceived as coherent—one who expresses thoughts clearly and in a well-ordered manner (to do otherwise is to be perceived as scatterbrained or confusing). Whether conversing or improvising, it is important to speak in extended patterns of related thoughts. Each stream of related ideas should flow to its natural conclusion before moving on to the next.

That is why repetition is important. It is part of the glue that holds ideas together in a coherent direction and allows musical statements to be clearly understood by the listener. Below are situations in which repetition will be most valuable:

- **To establish a theme:** Use repetition to ingrain a melodic or rhythmic idea in the listener's mind.
- **To establish direction:** Use repetition to point a phrase in a particular direction. For example, a continually ascending or descending pattern can indicate strong direction toward a defining note or chord.
- **To build energy or tension:** Use repetition to create momentum and cause the listener to anticipate the next phrase leading toward a conclusion. Repetition can be like a tension spring that captures the listener's interest as it is wound up. When the tension is finally released, the energy of the moment can be exhilarating.
- **To connect ideas:** Use repetition to provide a helpful segue between one series of musical ideas and another. It can give the mind a momentary mental break while contemplating alternative ideas or directions.

But beware, one can overdo repetition. In most cases, sequential patterns can only be sustained for short periods. Continuing too long may overstate the point and perhaps tire the listener. Therefore, it is better to use repetition continually rather than continuously. Integrate it into a varied and balanced palette of tools that allows ideas to be expressed fluidly and coherently.

Melodic and Rhythmic Contour

In writing, there is a certain contour to any well-crafted paragraph or essay. The ideas rise and fall, ebb and flow with a certain balance that the reader perceives as elegance. One can especially hear this in a speech that is delivered well. The speaker captures both the mind and heart with a tapestry of crescendos, diminuendos, thundering exhortations, long pauses, alliteration, conceptual repetition and variation—all tools utilized to engage the listener's attention and emotions, and create a bond with the audience. These are the primary goals of the improviser—to create musical statements that possess contour and elegance by employing all the creative tools described so far, and to create a bond with the listener.

Play through the simplistic improvisation below of sequential repetition over a revised Alberti accompaniment:

Notice how repetition gives a sense of logic and order to this example.

- The rhythm of measures 1–3 is mirrored in measures 5–7.
- The eighth-note pattern in measure 9 is repeated in measure 10 (and part of measure 11).
- The identical rhythmic patterns in measures 4 and 12 serve as rhythmic markers that communicate a sense of structure.
- The ascending arpeggios in measure 13 are repeated in measures 14 and 15.
- The sixteenth-note pattern builds energy from measure 13 to the end of the passage.

Perhaps the most important point of this example is that each new idea is not introduced until the previous idea is fully stated. Repetition helps each idea find completion. Furthermore, the gradually increasing speed of the notes in each idea (from quarter notes to eighth notes to sixteenth notes) gives the overall improvisation a sense of momentum and direction.

Exercise 13-1: Practicing Sequential Patterns

In this exercise, use sequential repetition with the set of motifs below to create complete statements. Play through each of the motifs below before beginning step 1:

1. Play the following Alberti accompaniment with the LH:

2. Play through the following example that combines motifs 1 and 2 into a repetitive phrase. Notes can be changed to fit the changing harmony.

3. Repeat step 2 using the same rhythms but different notes. Play through the following example and then experiment.

4. Use motif 4 (in measures 1 and 3) and motif 2 (in measures 2 and 4) to create a different phrase and then experiment with different notes based on these rhythms.

5. Using the same LH accompaniment, build a new phrase with motifs 6 and 7. Then, experiment with different notes based on these rhythms.
6. Mix and match the various motifs to build repeating patterns.

7. Use the alternative LH accompaniment below to create a series of new phrases:

8. Move the accompaniment from step 1 to the RH. Then proceed with steps 2–5 while creating phrases with the LH.

Recurring Repetition

The previous section discussed one type of repetition that occurs in a continuous sequence. But repetition can often be distributed more sparingly across a passage. This is called recurring repetition. The third movement of Clementi's Sonatina in C Major, Op. 36, No. 1, offers a good example of this technique.

Note the sixteenth-note rhythm in measure 7 that resolves to an eighth note in measure 8. This two-bar motif reappears throughout this short piece, but never in a contiguous series. It is essentially Clementi's signature rhythm to end each phrase. The motif appears again in measures 15–16, 23–24, 27–28, 41–42, 49–50, 53–54, 57–58, 61–62, and 65–66. As a recurring element, it provides the glue that holds this piece together. This same technique can be used in improvisation.

Exercise 13-2: Creating Recurring Phrases

1. Play steady quarter notes on C with the LH.
2. With the RH, begin with the simple dotted-eighth and sixteenth recurring rhythm shown below. Play this motif every few bars over the LH quarter notes.

3. Play through the following example that utilizes this recurring motif and then spend several minutes exploring this concept further:

Although the recurring pattern tends to appear at the end of each phrase, placing it there isn't necessary. It can appear at the beginning or middle. In this case, placing it at the end provides a persistent finality that holds the entire passage together. Recurring repetition can serve as a reminder to the listener that the improvisation has direction. It also provides a sense of unity to a longer passage.

Exercise 13-3: Practicing Recurring Repetition

Continue the LH quarter notes and use the motifs shown below to create passages that include recurring rhythmic repetition. Be strategic about the placement of these motifs. Use them as markers to pull ideas together.

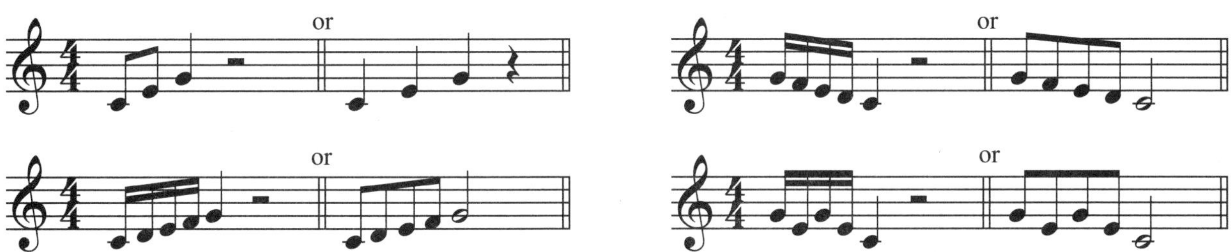

Key Points from This Chapter

- Repetition is a valuable tool that can add direction and continuity to improvisation.
- A sequential pattern can create strong direction and momentum.
- Recurring repetition can provide a periodic reminder to the listener that the improvisation has overall direction and unity.

CHAPTER 14 Borrowing Inspiration

It is well known that Johann Sebastian Bach was one of the most gifted improvisers of all time. Is it possible that he might have played the same melodic or rhythmic passage more than once as he improvised? Of course he did. In fact, he repeated those phrases over and over again. Surely, Bach did not perceive that improvisation required him to be spontaneously original at every moment. His creative use (and reuse) of existing material contributed to his greatness.

Now explore this idea even further. Is it possible that Mozart was influenced by Bach and used many of Bach's phrases and ideas in his own music and improvisations? The answer is yes. Look at the LH phrase in the excerpt below from Bach's English Suite in G Minor, BWV 808:

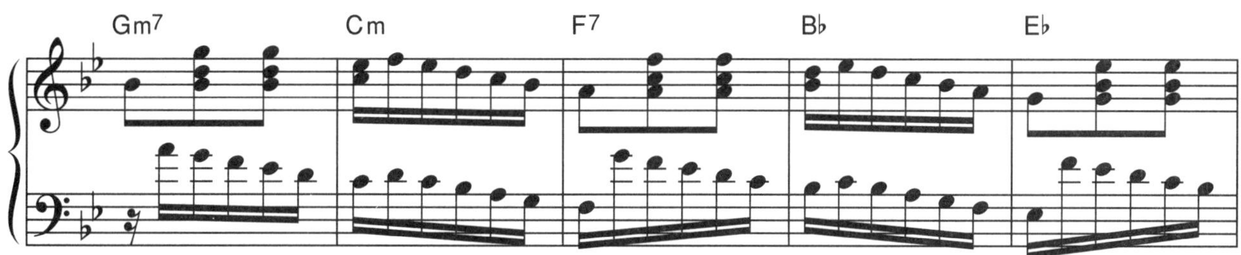

Now look at the RH in the first and third measures of the excerpt below from Mozart's Sonata in D Major, K. 311:

Notice the similarity between the LH part in the Bach example and the RH part in the Mozart example? Improvisers and composers in every period and musical genre have always borrowed from and built upon the ideas of their contemporaries and predecessors.

At the beginning of this section, principle 2 stated the following:

> Improvisation is not necessarily the process of creating something completely new. More often, it is a process of taking familiar patterns or phrases and applying them creatively to new situations.

The following exercise will encourage the player to borrow ideas from the masters.

Exercise 14: Creative Borrowing

1. Play through the following transposed phrases from Mozart's Sonata in B♭ Major, K. 333:

Phrase 1

Phrase 2

2. Play through the following example that applies the phrases from step 1 to the Alberti accompaniment:

Note that the process of applying borrowed phrases to a new harmony may require modification of a phrase or selected notes to fit the changing harmony (as in the second and fourth measures above). Relax and change whatever needs alteration along the way. Remember, this is improvisation.

3. Chapter 9 focused on the concept of turning melodies upside down and inside out. It's time to apply this concept at a more advanced level. Play through the following example in which some of the patterns from step 1 have been inverted, and then experiment with new phrases:

4. Chapters 10 and 12 focused on the application of jumps, skips and scale segments to add melodic interest. Since the example in step 3 already has a great deal of jumping, the following version mixes in some skipping and scale segments. Play through the example below to see how skipping and scale segments can add contour and variety to the passage:

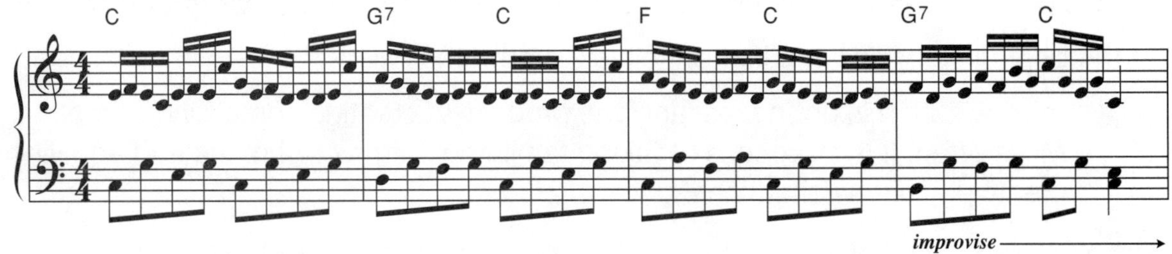

5. Select some favorite pieces by Bach or Mozart and play through them with a different mindset. While playing, look for melodic and rhythmic material that can be borrowed for improvising. Keep in mind that Bach was so prolific that much of his compositional work is made up entirely of improvisations that he had time to write down. Here is an opportunity to learn from the best.

    - From the selected pieces, borrow phrases or ideas that seem especially interesting and useful for improvising within the Alberti accompaniment.
    - For ease of use, transpose these phrases into the key of C major.
    - Apply and adapt these phrases to fit the Alberti accompaniment as in steps 2–4.
    - Turn the melodies inside out and upside down; add skips, jumps and scale segments where appropriate.

    Below are some interesting phrases and ideas borrowed from well-known works. Try starting with a few of them if it is difficult to find pieces for step 5.

Excerpt from Scarlatti's Sonata in E Major, K. 380

Excerpt from Mozart's Sonata in B♭ Major, K. 333

Excerpt from J. S. Bach's Invention No.1, BWV 772

Excerpt from J. S. Bach's Invention No. 3, BWV 774

Excerpt from Chopin's Ballade in A♭ Major, Op. 47

Excerpt from Beethoven's Sonata in C Minor, Op. 13, "Pathétique"

6. Transpose the ideas from step 5 (phrases and accompaniment) into various keys.

Key Points from This Chapter

- Improvisers throughout the ages have routinely borrowed ideas from predecessors, contemporaries and even their own past work.
- There is great creativity in applying these borrowed ideas to new harmonic settings and manipulating them to discover new material.
- Most players already have a treasury of melodic and rhythmic material committed to memory that can become part of the improviser's toolbox.

CHAPTER 15 Putting the Tools to Work

The toolbox has now been filled with a valuable array of improvising tools:

- Scalar Speed
- Dynamics, Tone, Duration and Silence
- Upper/Lower Neighbors
- Charting Paths and Meandering
- Turning Phrases Upside Down and Inside Out
- Skipping and Jumping
- Octave Switching
- Sequential and Recurring Repetition
- Borrowing Motifs from Existing Works

This capstone chapter of the *Essential Tools* section will assess how well these skills have been learned and how well they can be applied in a standard musical setting.

In the early stages of improvisation, the temptation is to utilize many tools at the same time, which often results in chaos. But the maturing improviser realizes the value of knowing what tools to apply and when to apply them (less is often more). With practice, these tools will become second nature, and the brain will instinctively know how to employ the right ones at the right time—this is the ultimate goal.

The exercises in this chapter will revisit the three pieces from chapter 8 and allow for the application of new tools learned from chapters 9–14.

Exercise 15-1: Beethoven's Minuet Op. 49, No. 2

1. Play through the Beethoven passage below as written.
2. Repeat the LH part and apply upper/lower neighbors to the melody. After experimenting with the melody for a while, create new defining notes (within the harmonic structure) and meander in and around them. Try turning these melodies upside down and inside out.
3. Practice with skipping, jumping and octave switching with the RH.
4. Experiment with sequential and rhythmic repetition of ideas, and apply some of the borrowed motifs that were acquired in chapter 14.
5. Build an improvisation using any of the above tools. Start simply and gradually build upon any new ideas. Be sure to utilize dynamics, tone, duration and silence.

Exercise 15-2: Corelli's Folies d'Espagne

Repeat steps 1–5 from exercise 15-1 using the Corelli passage below:

Exercise 15-3: J. S. Bach's "Gavotte in D Major" from the *Sixth Suite for Cello,* BWV 1012

Repeat steps 1–5 from exercise 15-1 using the Bach passage below:

Exercise 15-4: Engaging the Left Hand

1. Select any of the preceding exercises.
2. Create a simple RH accompaniment based on the harmony of the selected passage.
3. Try improvising through the passage with the LH.

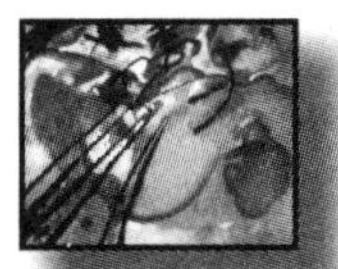

Section 3 *Advanced Tools*

The first two sections of this text explored a great deal of musical territory. The *Foundations* section experimented with the fundamental elements of improvisation—creativity and expression. The purpose was to introduce the concept of "talking" with musical notes and help the player realize that improvising is as easy as conversing with another person. Once ideas began to flow, it was possible for the process of improvisatory expression to become natural and often effortless.

The *Essential Tools* section offered guidelines for musical grammar—a framework for selecting the best notes to play and some valuable ways to organize and manipulate those notes to create interesting melodic statements.

The *Advanced Tools* section will delve deeper into these concepts and explore more complex ways to view the above framework. It will also examine what to do in situations when the framework needs to bend. Finally, the player will step beyond melody and have an opportunity to improvise with harmony. With these more complex tools, one can begin to "paint the sky a different color."

CHAPTER 16 When One Scale Won't Work, Part 1: Transitional Thinking

The last few chapters have explored situations in which one or two related scales work well across an entire passage. But there are many circumstances in which the harmonic movement is too rapid or diverse to work with so few scales. This chapter will address these situations.

Chopin's Prelude in C Minor Op. 28, No. 2, is a piece that most everyone has either played or heard. It is simultaneously simple and complex. Take a moment to play through it, and notice that the harmony shifts too often to work with just one or two scales.

Most of the earlier examples in this text have demonstrated slow harmonic movement with the chords changing gradually. This piece demonstrates faster harmonic movement with the chords changing more rapidly—in fact, with every beat. Also, the harmonic movement is less predictable, making the piece more difficult for improvisation.

Improvising through this prelude without considerable forethought might seem quite treacherous—like trying to steer a kayak through swift rapids with shifting currents. But, in extending that analogy, the skilled kayaker would advise that rough waters can be navigated more easily when one first takes time to study the intricate nuances of the river. Similarly, the best way to navigate a difficult musical passage is to first study its harmonic nuances measure-by-measure.

Analysis of Measure 1

Play through the first measure of the prelude again. Before reading further, try to determine the tonal focus of this measure.

The harmony is as follows:

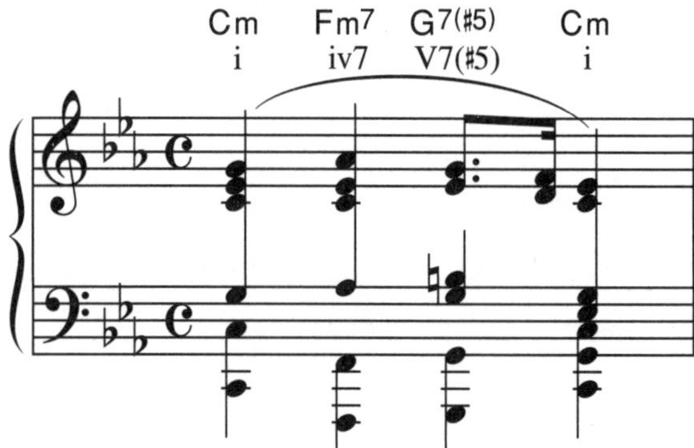

It should be fairly clear that the tonal focus of this measure is C minor. The key signature is a strong clue. Also, the full cadence (G7(♯5) to Cm) in beats 3 and 4 confirms the C minor focus. What scale is best for improvising through this measure? The logical choice is the C minor scale, but which one—the natural minor, harmonic minor or melodic minor (ascending)?

The two interior chords help to determine the best C minor scale to use. First, look at the Fm7 chord on beat 2. The notes F and C in this chord are found in all C minor scales. But the A♭ eliminates the C melodic minor (ascending) scale, which contains an A♮.

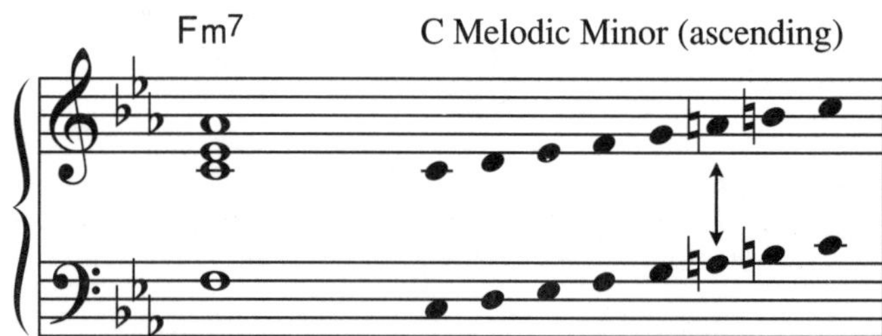

Now, consider the G7(♯5) chord on beat 3.* The notes G and E♭ in this chord are found in all C minor scales. However, the B♮ offers the final clue in selecting the right scale for this measure.

Since the B♮ would clash with the B♭ in the C natural minor scale, there is only one scale that fits the entire measure. The C harmonic minor scale contains both the A♭ from the Fm7 chord and the B♮ from the G7(♯5) chord. That makes C harmonic minor the best scale for measure 1.

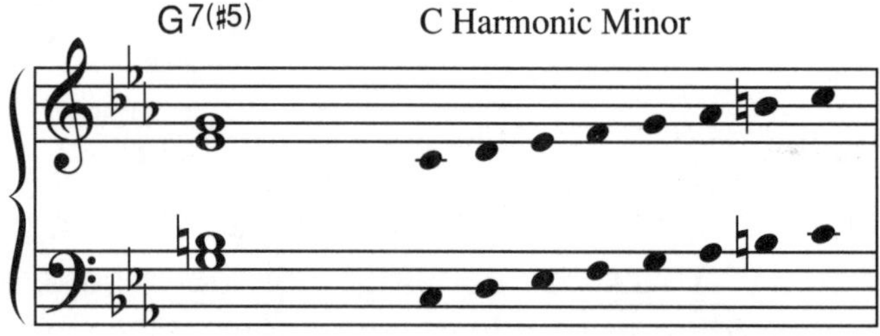

For those who find the C harmonic minor scale to be too exotic for beats 1 and 2, an alternative method is to use the C natural minor scale for the entire measure and make the adjustment to B♮ for beat 3. While not as simple as using just one scale, this method (and its tonal result) may be preferred by many players. The examples in this chapter will focus on using the C harmonic minor scale.

* Technically, the augmented 5th in the G7(♯5) chord is D♯. However, this analysis will use its enharmonic equivalent (E♭) for the sake of simplicity.

Exercise 16-1: Navigating Measure 1

1. Repeat the following simplified LH chord pattern of measure 1:

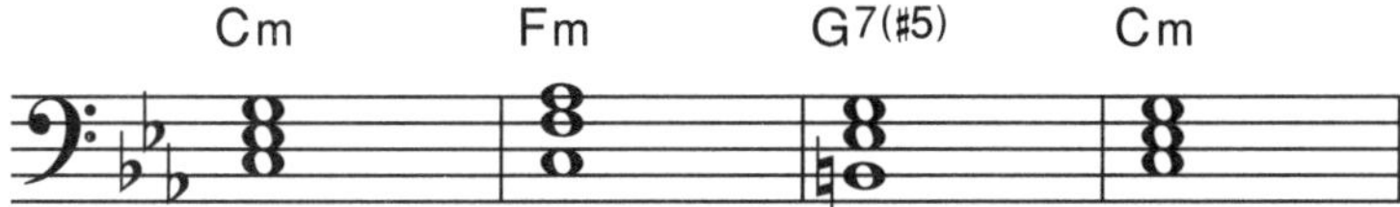

2. Play the C harmonic minor scale over this LH harmony. Notice that there are no conflicting notes when using this scale.

3. Next, play the C harmonic minor scale over the LH harmony. Play the harmony twice as fast (half notes).

4. Now double the speed of the C harmonic minor scale in the RH (sixteenth notes).

5. Continue the sixteenth notes in the RH while doubling the harmonic speed of the LH (quarter notes).

6. Now that the scale is comfortable, begin to improvise over the LH harmony (at any speed) utilizing the various improvising tools discussed earlier (upper/lower neighbors, skipping, jumping, patterns, etc.).

Analysis of Measure 2

Play through the second measure of the prelude again.

The harmony is as follows:

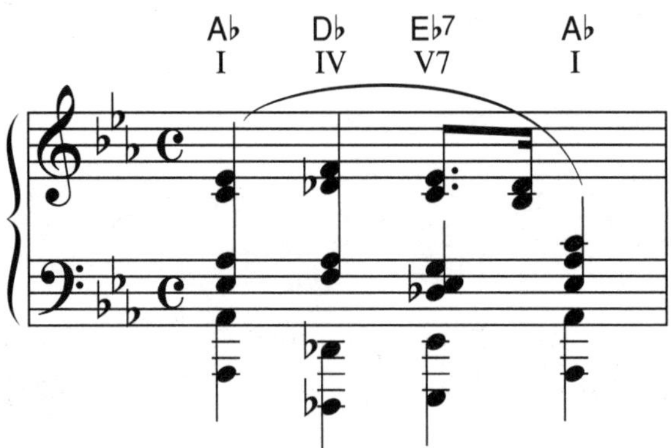

The tonal focus is clearly A♭ as seen by the way the measure begins on the A♭ major chord and ends with the full cadence in the last two beats. The A♭ major scale will certainly work well with the A♭ major chords on beats 1 and 4, but what about the two interior chords?

When the A♭ major scale is played over the D♭ major chord on beat 2, there is no dissonance, because all the notes of this chord are found within the A♭ major scale.

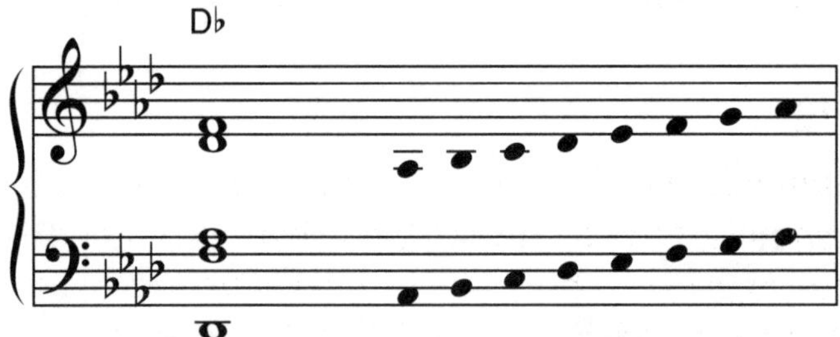

Similarly, all the notes of the E♭7 chord on beat 3 are found within the A♭ major scale.

Because there is no strong dissonance when the A♭ major scale is played over the four chords, this is the best scale for measure 2.

Exercise 16-2: Navigating Measure 2

1. Repeat the following simplified chord pattern with the LH:

2. As was done in exercise 16-1, play the A♭ major scale over the LH harmony (in whole notes, half notes, and quarter notes).

3. After playing the scale over the harmony in several different ways, begin to improvise with the notes of the scale using the various improvising tools discussed earlier (upper/lower neighbors, skipping, jumping, patterns, etc.).

Transitional Thinking

While reflecting on the first two measures of the Chopin prelude, it may be easier for some players to make a quick mental transition from the C harmonic minor scale to the A♭ major scale. This thought process will now be referred to as *literal transition*. Using this method, the player identifies a change of tonal focus and literally moves from one scale to the next as the harmony shifts. This is the easiest mental approach when the harmonic movement is slow and there are only a few scales to consider.

But when the tonal focus and associated scales are changing rapidly through a passage, literal transition may be too cumbersome, and one's improvisation may become choppy and disconnected. There is an alternative approach that may be easier for some.

Recall a technique from chapter 8 that utilized one primary scale for a given passage and made slight note alterations to improvise through changing harmonies. This alternative thought process will now be referred to as *incremental transition*. The first two measures of the Chopin prelude will help to illustrate this concept.

Notice the relationship between the C harmonic minor scale used for measure 1 and the A♭ major scale for measure 2. For comparison, both scales are shown below starting on C:

Table 16-1: Incremental Transition for Measures 1–2

Measure	Scale	Scale Notes
1	C Harmonic Minor	C **D** E♭ F G A♭ **B(♮)** C
2	A♭ Major	C **D♭** E♭ F G A♭ **B♭** C

The scales differ by only two notes—D (or D♭) and B (or B♭). Using incremental transition, one would navigate through measures 1 and 2 thinking in terms of just *one* scale (C harmonic minor). Then, while improvising, the player would make incremental changes to the scale (for the notes D♭ and B♭) to adapt to the changing harmony in measure 2.

There are two benefits to incremental transition: 1) it allows for consolidation of one's thinking into scale groups rather than shifting direction with each scale; and 2) it may bring about smoother, more elegant phrasing. Incremental transition does require careful analysis before starting an improvisation, but it can greatly simplify navigation through a difficult passage.

Exercise 16-3: Practicing Both Transition Methods

Play the following condensed LH harmony of measures 1–2:

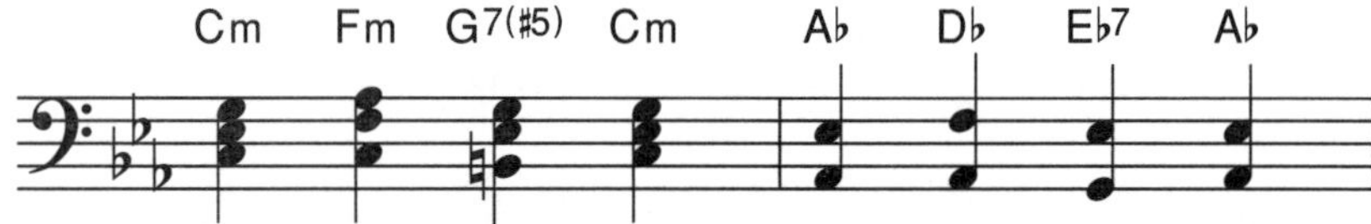

1. Use literal transition to improvise through the two measures. That is, make the mental shift from the C harmonic minor scale to the A♭ major scale while moving from measure 1 to measure 2.

2. Use incremental transition to improvise through the two measures. That is, think in terms of the C harmonic minor scale only, but make incremental changes to the D and B notes when necessary.

After trying both methods several times, which one seems easier? Since all minds think differently, a given player may discover that one method is clearly easier, or find that both are equally valuable (and that the choice depends on musical circumstances). Keep both methods in mind while pressing forward into more difficult harmony.

Analysis of Measure 3

Measure 3 is somewhat complex. The harmony is as follows:

Before reading further, try to determine the tonal focus and appropriate scales.

The tonal focus is basically C major, as indicated by the full cadence in beats 1–2 and the plagal cadence in beats 3–4. But choosing the appropriate scales is difficult. Alterations are necessary with every beat to accommodate the harmonic movement.

Using literal transition (thinking chord-by-chord), the player may want to think in terms of four separate scales. The table below shows that there are only two conflicting notes among these scales (A/A♭ and B/B♭). (Also notice that the altered lowered 7th scales accommodate the lowered 7th tone in the dominant chords.)

Table 16-2: Literal Transition for Measure 3

Chord	Appropriate Scale	Scale Notes
G7	G Major with lowered 7th	G A B C D E F(♮) G
C7	C Major with lowered 7th	C D E F G A B♭ C
Fm	F Melodic Minor (ascending)	F G A♭ B♭ C D(♮) E(♮) F
C	C Major	C D E F G A B C

Despite the similarities among the four scales, the process of changing the scale with every beat (using literal transition) may be too cumbersome, and the result may be an improvisation that is choppy and disjointed.

Incremental transition can be a valuable tool in this case. Since the tonal focus is C major, the table below shows each of the four scales starting on C:

Table 16-3: Incremental Transition for Measure 3

Chord	Appropriate Scale	Scale Notes
G7	G Major with lowered 7th	C D E F(♮) G **A** **B** C
C7	C Major with lowered 7th	C D E F G **A** **B♭** C
Fm	F Melodic Minor (ascending)	C D(♮) E(♮) F G **A♭** **B♭** C
C	C Major	C D E F G **A** **B** C

It should now be easier to see the two notes (A/A♭ and B/B♭) that require alteration to navigate through measure 3 with the notes of the C major scale. With incremental transition, the improviser uses C major as the primary scale for the entire measure and makes incremental changes as the harmony requires.

Exercise 16-4: Navigating Measure 3

1. Play the following condensed LH harmony of measure 3:

2. Using incremental transition, navigate through the harmony with the notes of the C major scale and strategic alterations on the C7 and Fm chords. Play through the example below and then experiment.

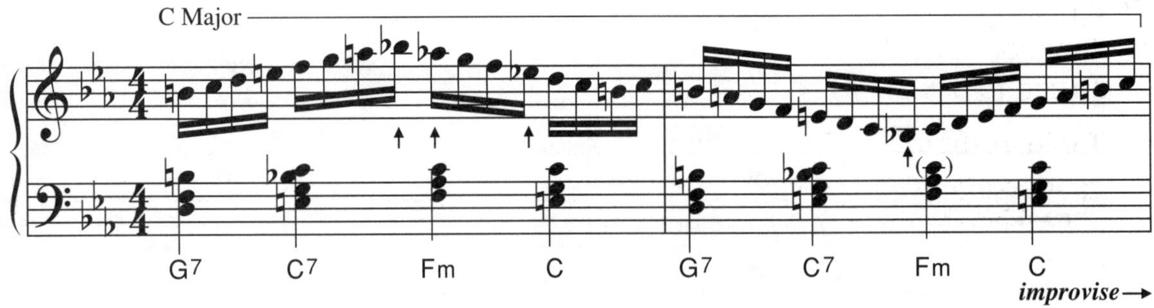

3. For comparison, try navigating measure 3 using literal transition and the four scales identified earlier.

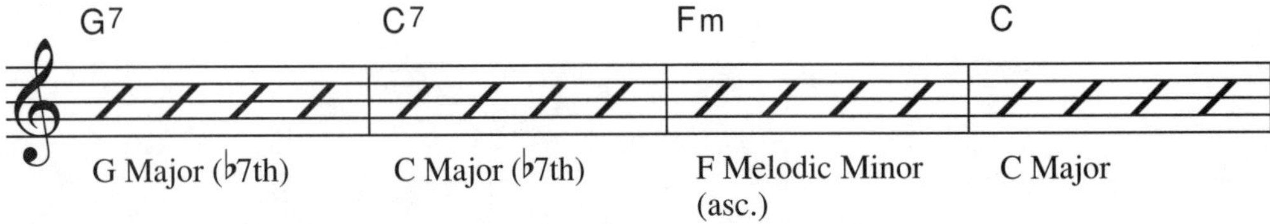

With either transition method, the notes played will likely be the same. But the way a player thinks about the chord transitions can make one method simpler than the other.

Analysis of Measure 4

The focus of measure 4 is clearly G major, with its two full cadences. The G major scale is the obvious choice for improvisation.

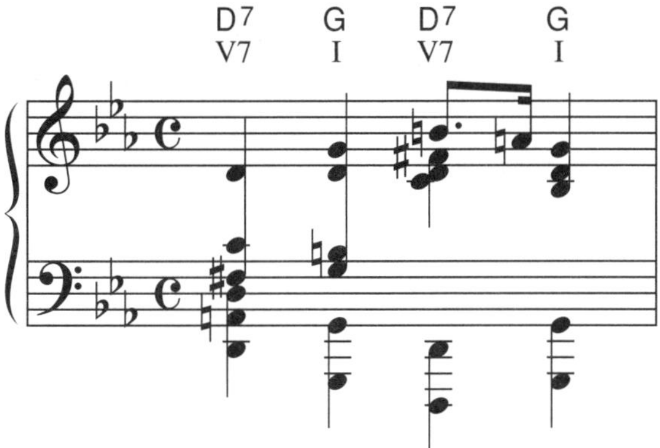

The D major scale with a lowered 7th works well with the D7 chord; but since the notes of that scale are identical to the G major scale (see table below), it isn't necessary to think in terms of two separate scales.

Table 16-4: Incremental Transition for Measure 4

Chord	Scale Description	Scale Notes
D7	D Major with lowered 7th	D E F♯ G A B C(♮) D
G	G Major (starting on D)	D E F♯ G A B C D

Take a moment to play the notes of the G major scale over the harmony of measure 4.

Combining Measures 3 and 4

When measures 3 and 4 are combined, the G major scale used for measure 4 presents another conflict that requires alteration. Below are the scales for the two measures organized for literal transition:

Table 16-5: Literal Transition for Measures 3–4

Measure	Chord	Appropriate Scale	Scale Notes
3	G7	G Major with lowered 7th	G A B C D E F(♮) G
	C7	C Major with lowered 7th	C D E F G A B♭ C
	Fm	F Melodic Minor (ascending)	F G A♭ B♭ C D(♮) E(♮) F
	C	C Major	C D E F G A B C
4	D7	D Major with lowered 7th	D E F♯ G A B C(♮) D
	G	G Major	G A B C D E F♯ G
	D7	D Major with lowered 7th	D E F♯ G A B C(♮) D
	G	G Major	G A B C D E F♯ G

The previous table should illustrate why literal transition becomes more difficult as the player takes a wider view. In just two measures, there are six different scales to keep in mind. In this case, however, the solution is not overwhelming. The improviser simply makes the mental shift from the C major scale to the G major scale for measure 4 and adjusts for the F♯ when necessary.

On the other hand, incremental transition may offer an easier way to navigate measure 3. The player would think in terms of just one primary scale (C major) and make incremental adjustments to address the A/A♭, B/B♭ and F/F♯ dissonances as they appear. For greater clarity, here are the notes of the six scales starting on C:

Table 16-6: Incremental Transition for Measures 3–4

Measure	Chord	Appropriate Scale	Scale Notes
3	G7	G Major with lowered 7th	C D E **F(♮)** G **A B** C
	C7	C Major with lowered 7th	C D E **F** G **A B♭** C
	Fm	F Melodic Minor (ascending)	C D E **F** G **A♭ B♭** C
	C	C Major	C D E **F** G **A B** C
4	D7	D Major with lowered 7th	C(♮) D E **F♯** G **A B** C
	G	G Major	C D E **F♯** G **A B** C

Exercise 16-5: Navigating Measures 3–4

1. Play the following condensed LH harmony of measures 3–4:

2. **Literal Transition:** Navigate through measures 3 and 4 using literal transition and the six appropriate scales:

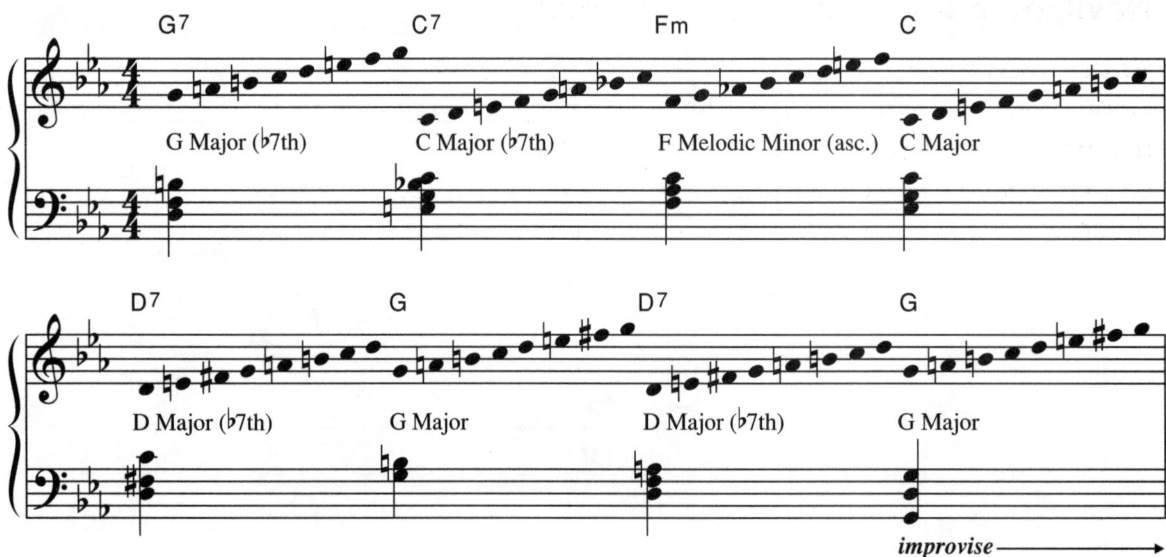

3. Once the scales feel comfortable, try navigating through measures 3 and 4 using only the chord symbols below:

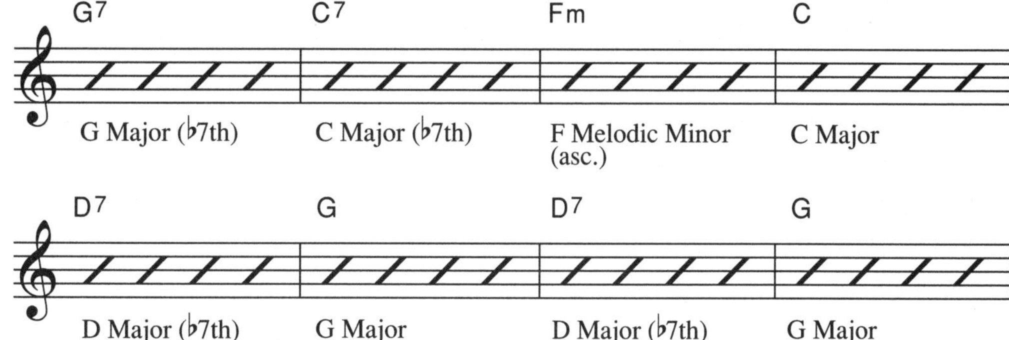

4. **Incremental Transition:** Navigate through the harmony using the notes of the C major scale and strategic alterations to accommodate specific chords. The following steps may be helpful:

   a. Visualize only the notes of the C major scale before playing.

   b. Start improvising with those notes over the LH harmony.

   c. Make alterations (shown below in the treble clef) when needed.

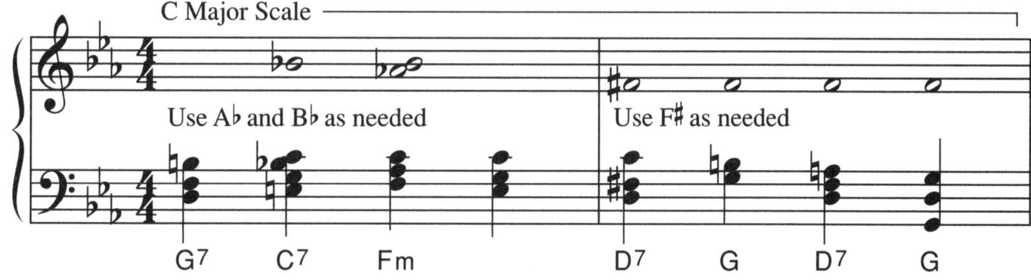

5. After trying both methods of transition, decide which one works better for this particular passage.

Navigating the First Four Measures

Having studied the nuances thoroughly, the process of navigating measures 1–4 of the Chopin prelude should not seem as daunting as it first appeared. The best scales to use have now been identified—and two different ways of thinking through the harmonic changes have been examined. Improvising through all four measures should now help to determine which method of transitional thinking one prefers.

Literal Transition

Using literal transition in its purest sense, the number of scales the improviser should use for navigating through the passage is quite intimidating.

Table 16-7: Literal Transition for Measures 1–4

Measure	Chord	Appropriate Scale	Scale Notes
1	Cm	C Harmonic Minor	C D E♭ F G A♭ B(♮)C
	Fm7	F Natural Minor	F G A♭ B♭ C D♭ E♭ F
	G7(♯5)	C Harmonic Minor	C D E♭ F G A♭ B(♮)C
	Cm	C Harmonic Minor	C D E♭ F G A♭ B(♮)C
2	A♭	A♭ Major	A♭ B♭ C D♭ E♭ F G A♭
	D♭	D♭ Major	D♭ E♭ F G♭ A♭ B♭ C D♭
	E♭7	E♭ Major with lowered 7th	E♭ F G A♭ B♭ C D♭ E♭
	A♭	A♭ Major	A♭ B♭ C D♭ E♭ F G A♭
3	G7	G Major with lowered 7th	G A B C D E F(♮) G
	C7	C Major with lowered 7th	C D E F G A B♭ C
	Fm	F Melodic Minor (ascending)	F G A♭ B♭ C D(♮)E(♮) F
	C	C Major	C D E F G A B C
4	D7	D Major with lowered 7th	D E F♯ G A B C(♮)D
	G	G Major	G A B C D E F♯ G
	D7	D Major with lowered 7th	D E F♯ G A B C(♮)D
	G	G Major	G A B C D E F♯ G

In the analyses of measures 1, 2 and 4, the scales were consolidated to make navigation easier, as shown in the following abridged table:

Table 16-8: Consolidated Literal Translation for Measures 1–4

Measure	Chord(s)	Appropriate Scale	Scale Notes
1	Cm–Fm7–G7(♯5)–Cm	C Harmonic Minor	C D E♭ F G A♭ B C
2	A♭–D♭–E♭7–A♭	A♭ Major scale	A♭ B♭ C D♭ E♭ F G A♭
3	G7	G Major with lowered 7th	G A B C D E F G
	C7	C Major with lowered 7th	C D E F G A B♭ C
	Fm	F Melodic Minor (ascending)	F G A♭ B♭ C D E F
	C	C Major	C D E F G A B C
4	D7–G–D7–G	G Major	G A B C D E F♯ G

Exercise 16-6: Navigating Measures 1–4 with Literal Transition

1. Improvise through the first four measures using the seven identified scales.

C Harmonic Minor
A♭ Major
Cm Fm G7(♯5) Cm
A♭ D♭ E♭7 A♭

G Major (♭7th) C Major (♭7th) F Melodic Minor (asc.) C Major
G Major
G7 C7 Fm C
D7 G D7 G

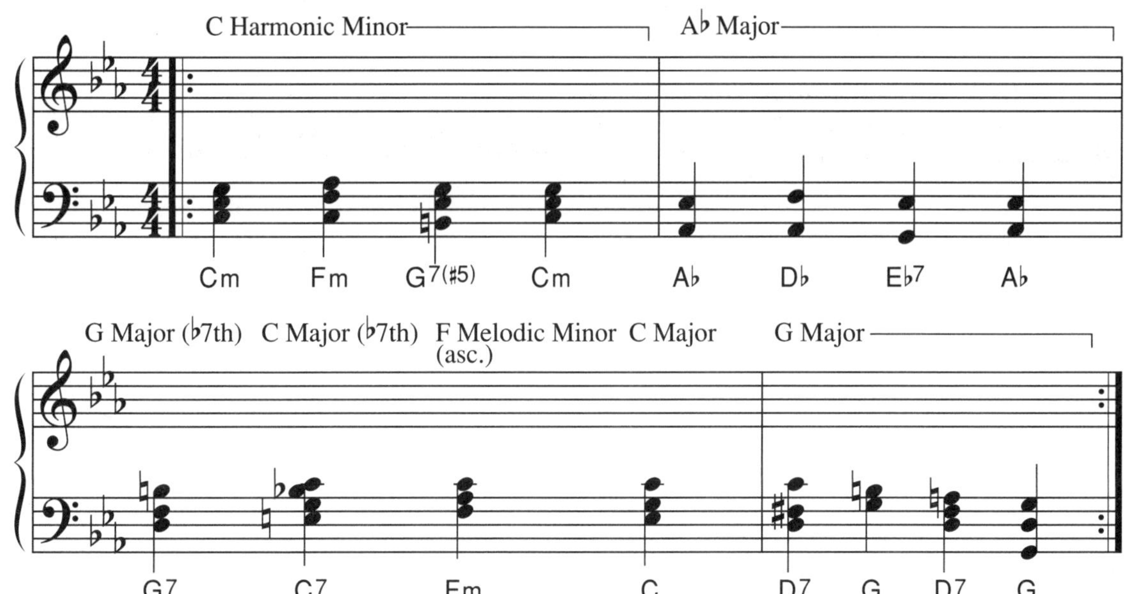

2. After improvising with basic scales, begin to utilize other tools (upper/lower neighbors, skipping, jumping, etc.). Try the examples below and then experiment:

Example 1

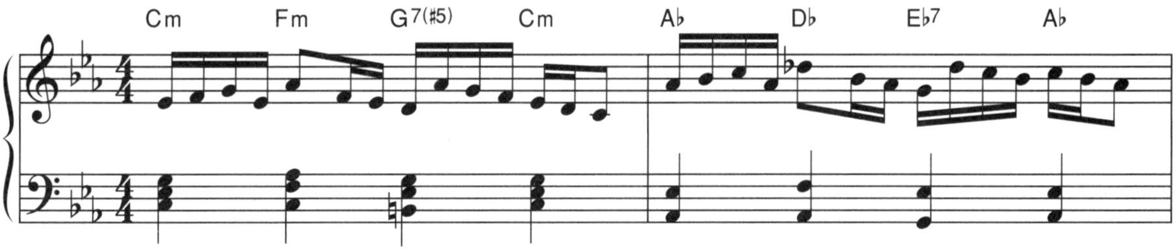

Cm Fm G7(♯5) Cm
A♭ D♭ E♭7 A♭

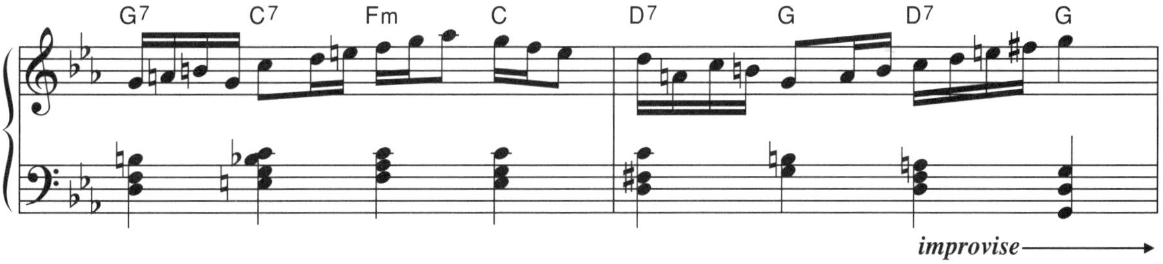

G7 C7 Fm C
D7 G D7 G
improvise

Example 2

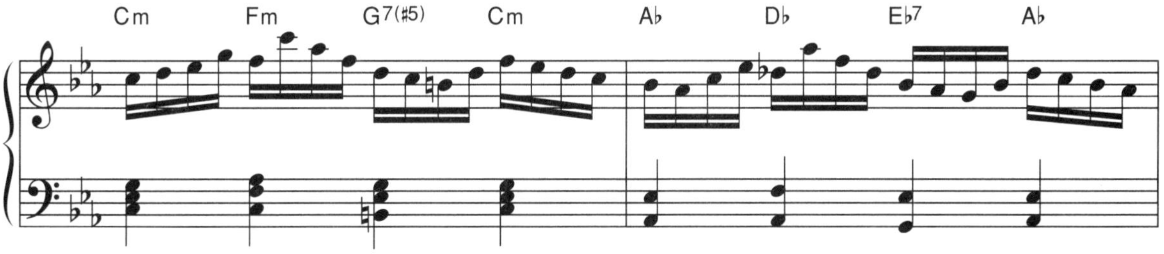

Cm Fm G7(♯5) Cm
A♭ D♭ E♭7 A♭

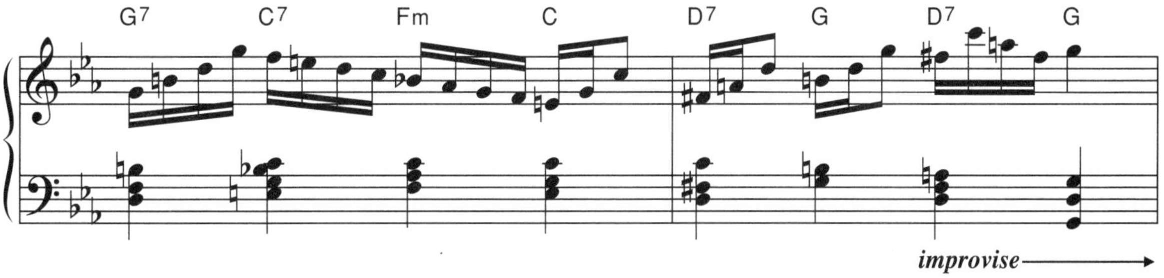

G7 C7 Fm C
D7 G D7 G
improvise

3. Move the harmony to the RH and try steps 1 and 2 while creating phrases with the LH.

Incremental Transition

Now use incremental transition to think in broader "brush strokes." Separate the four-measure phrase into two sections, each with its own primary scale.

Table 16-9: Incremental Transition for Measures 1–4

Measures	Primary Scale	Scale Notes	Alterations (When Needed)
1–2	C Harmonic Minor	C D E♭ F G A♭ B C	D/D♭ and B/B♭
3–4	C Major	C D E F G A B C	F/F♯, A/A♭ and B/B♭

Exercise 16-7: Navigating Measures 1–4 with Incremental Transition

1. Improvise through the first four measures using the two primary scales from table 16-9, making incremental adjustments as necessary.

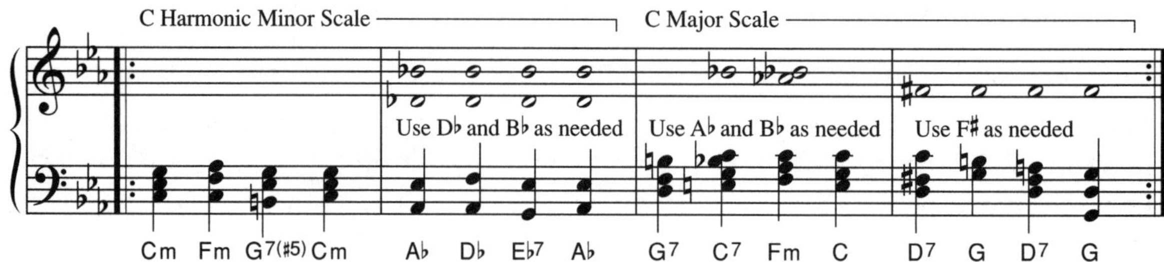

2. After improvising with basic scales, begin to utilize other tools (upper/lower neighbors, skipping, jumping, etc.). Play the example below and then experiment:

3. Move the harmony to the RH and try steps 1 and 2 while creating phrases with the LH.

Key Points from This Chapter

- There are two mental approaches for dealing with harmonic transition—literal transition and incremental transition.
- The choice of transition method will vary from person to person and from one musical situation to another.

CHAPTER 17 Scales à la *Mode*

Before tackling the next four measures of Chopin's Prelude in C Minor, it will be helpful to explore a valuable scalar concept called modality. Most traditional study of harmony focuses on only a few basic scales in each key that all begin on the root tone. For example, the scales related to the key of C would be the following:

- C Major
- C Natural Minor
- C Melodic Minor (ascending)
- C Harmonic Minor

These are all highly useful scales that can help to navigate most types of music. But modality—an alternative way of thinking about scales—can open up a whole new world of improvisational opportunity and make the process of improvising easier.

To understand modality, begin with a C major scale: C–D–E–F–G–A–B–C

In traditional thinking, these notes form just one scale. However, when thinking in terms of modality, these notes form seven different scales (referred to as modes of the major scale). For example, if one uses the notes of the C major scale but starts on D instead of C, the resulting scale would be the following: D–E–F–G–A–B–C–D

Take a moment to play through these notes. They actually comprise a unique scale of their own, called the Dorian scale, which takes the notes of the C major scale and puts them in a new context. The Dorian scale has great application for improvisation. At first, it may seem difficult to identify the seven scale modes; but, with practice, the improviser will see them quickly and understand the unique value of each one.

Table 17-1: Modes of the C Major Scale

Mode	Name	Scale Note
1st mode	C Ionian	C D E F G A B C
2nd mode	D Dorian	D E F G A B C D
3rd mode	E Phrygian	E F G A B C D E
4th mode	F Lydian	F G A B C D E F
5th mode	G Mixolydian	G A B C D E F G
6th mode	A Aeolian	A B C D E F G A
7th mode	B Locrain	B C D E F G A B

There are two ways to visualize each mode—the derivative method and the altered method. The derivative method sees each mode in terms of the scale from which it was derived. Using the derivative method, one would visualize the D Dorian scale as the C major scale starting on D (with C major being the origin scale). The altered method provides another way of visualizing modes by showing how they are created through the modification of major or natural minor scales. The following table explains how each method can be used to create all seven modes:

Table 17-2: Identifying the 12 Scale Modes

Mode	Derivative Method	Altered Method
Ionian	Same as a major scale	No alteration is required
Dorian	Starts on the 2nd scale degree of the major scale D Dorian uses the C major scale	Major scale with a lowered 3rd and 7th D Dorian is the D major scale with F♮ and C♮
Phrygian	Starts on the 3rd scale degree of the major scale E Phrygian uses the C major scale	Natural minor scale with a lowered 2nd E Phrygian is the E natural minor scale with F♮
Lydian	Starts on the 4th scale degree of the major scale F Lydian uses the C major scale	Major scale with a raised 4th F Lydian is the F major scale with B♮
Mixolydian	Starts on the 5th scale degree of the major scale G Mixolydian uses the C major scale.	Major scale with a lowered 7th G Mixolydian is the G major scale with F♮
Aeolian	Starts on the 6th scale degree of the major scale A Aeolian uses the C major scale	Same as the relative natural minor scale A Aeolian is the A natural minor scale
Locrian	Starts on the 7th scale degree of the major scale B Locrian uses the C major scale	Natural minor scale with a lowered 2nd and 5th B Locrian is the B natural minor scale with C♮ and F♮

The table below offers one more perspective by describing all modes that start on C:

Table 17-3: Modes Starting on C

Mode	Scale Notes	Origin Scale
C Ionian	C D E F G A B C	C Major
C Dorian	C D E♭ F G A B♭ C	B♭ Major
C Phrygian	C D♭ E♭ F G A♭ B♭ C	A♭ Major
C Lydian	C D E F♯ G A B C	G Major
C Mixolydian	C D E F G A B♭ C	F Major
C Aeolian	C D E♭ F G A♭ B♭ C	E♭ Major
C Locrian	C D♭ E♭ F G♭ A♭ B♭ C	D♭ Major

Each mode has a unique application for improvisation. A complete study of modes would occupy an entire volume of its own. For now, it is important only to become acquainted with the concept of modality and establish a foundation for later study. This chapter will explore two of the seven modes—Dorian and Mixolydian.

The Dorian Mode

The Dorian scale is created using the notes of the major scale found one whole step (a major 2nd) below its root tone. For example, the D Dorian scale utilizes the notes of the C major scale (the scale that starts one whole step below the root tone D). Many players may prefer to use the altered method and visualize the Dorian scale as a major scale with a lowered 3rd and 7th. But, over time, the goal should be to see the Dorian scale as a unique scalar pattern of its own, rather than an altered version of a major scale.

Exercise 17-1: Practicing the Dorian Scales

Play through each of the Dorian scales shown in the table below. While practicing, use the two different ways of perceiving the scale. (The "LH Chord" column will be used for exercise 17-2.)

Table 17-4: The 12 Dorian Scales

Dorian Scales	Scale Notes	Origin Scale	LH Chord
C Dorian	C D E♭ F G A B♭ C	B♭ Major	Cm(7)
C♯ Dorian	C♯ D♯ E F♯ G♯ A♯ B C♯	B Major	C♯m(7)
D Dorian	D E F G A B C D	C Major	Dm(7)
E♭ Dorian	E♭ F G♭ A♭ B♭ C D♭ E♭	D♭ Major	E♭m(7)
E Dorian	E F♯ G A B C♯ D E	D Major	Em(7)
F Dorian	F G A♭ B♭ C D E♭ F	E♭ Major	Fm(7)
F♯ Dorian	F♯ G♯ A B C♯ D♯ E F♯	E Major	F♯m(7)
G Dorian	G A B♭ C D E F G	F Major	Gm(7)
A♭ Dorian	A♭ B♭ C♭ D♭ E♭ F G♭ A♭	G♭ Major	A♭m(7)
A Dorian	A B C D E F♯ G A	G Major	Am(7)
B♭ Dorian	B♭ C D♭ E♭ F G A♭ B♭	A♭ Major	B♭m(7)
B Dorian	B C♯ D E F♯ G♯ A B	A Major	Bm(7)

1. **Derivative Method:** Visualize each Dorian scale as a series of notes starting on the second tone of the origin scale. Practice all 12 scales using the example below as a guideline:
   a. For D Dorian, the origin scale is C major.
   b. Play the C major origin scale first.
   c. Then, begin on the second tone (D) and play the D Dorian scale using the same notes of the C major scale (adjusting fingering as necessary).
   d. D Dorian is derived from the C Major scale.
2. **Altered Method:** Visualize each of the 12 Dorian scales as a major scale with a lowered 3rd and lowered 7th. Practice all 12 scales with this mental approach.
3. **Pattern Practice:** Play each Dorian scale using the exercise patterns below:

Dorian Skipping

Applying the Dorian Scale

Every mode can be applied to a specific harmony. Dorian scales work best with minor and minor 7th chords. For example, the D Dorian scale will always work well with Dm and Dm7 chords. Play through the example below:

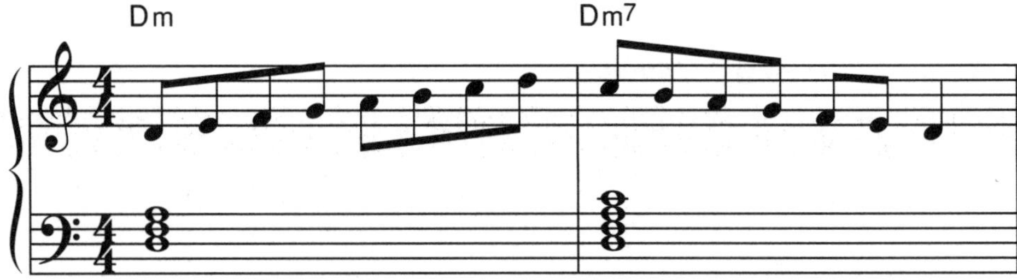

The 6th tone of the Dorian scale may sound a bit unusual to an experienced player after playing natural and harmonic minor scales for so long. But eventually, one may find it to be somewhat more exotic than the others—a colorful addition to the improvising toolbox.

Exercise 17-2: Applying the Dorian Scales

Use the table in exercise 17-1 to play the appropriate Dorian scale in the RH over the appropriate chord in the LH.

1. Play all 12 Dorian scales several times over their corresponding minor chords as shown in the example below of the C Dorian scale over the Cm7chord:

2. After playing each Dorian scale in its root form, try using the scale notes to improvise. Be sure to utilize the tools described in earlier chapters (upper/lower neighbors, skipping, jumping, etc.). Feel free to use the Alberti accompaniment in the LH as shown below:

The Mixolydian Mode

The Mixolydian scale is created using the notes of the major scale found a perfect 5th below its root tone. For example, the C Mixolydian scale is created with the notes of the F major scale (the scale that starts a perfect 5th below the root tone C). There are 12 Mixolydian scales, as shown below:

Table 17-5: The 12 Mixolydian Scales

Mixolydian Scale	Scale Notes	Origin Scale	LH Chord
C Mixolydian	C D E F G A B♭ C	F Major	C(7)
C♯ Mixolydian	C♯ D♯ E♯ F♯ G♯ A♯ B C♯	F♯ Major	C♯(7)
D Mixolydian	D E F♯ G A B C D	G Major	D(7)
E♭ Mixolydian	E♭ F G A♭ B♭ C D♭ E♭	A♭ Major	E♭(7)
E Mixolydian	E F♯ G♯ A B C♯ D E	A Major	E(7)
F Mixolydian	F G A B♭ C D E♭ F	B♭ Major	F(7)
F♯ Mixolydian	F♯ G♯ A♯ B C♯ D♯ E F♯	B Major	F♯(7)
G Mixolydian	G A B C D E F G	C Major	G(7)
A♭ Mixolydian	A♭ B♭ C D♭ E♭ F G♭ A♭	D♭ Major	A♭(7)
A Mixolydian	A B C♯ D E F♯ G A	D Major	A(7)
B♭ Mixolydian	B♭ C D E♭ F G A♭ B♭	E♭ Major	B♭(7)
B Mixolydian	B C♯ D♯ E F♯ G♯ A B	E Major	B(7)

Remember playing the C major scale with a lowered 7th over the C7 harmony in chapter 16 (see page 97–98)? That was the C Mixolydian scale. Mixolydian scales generally work well over major and dominant 7th chords. Some players may find it easiest to use the altered method and visualize the Mixolydian scale as a major scale with a lowered 7th. Again, the goal is to see it as a unique scalar pattern of its own.

Exercise 17-3: Practicing the Mixolydian Scales

Use the table above to play the appropriate Mixolydian scale in the RH over the corresponding dominant 7th chord in the LH:

1. Play through all 12 Mixolydian scales over their corresponding dominant 7th chords as shown in the example below:

2. Once a given Mixolydian scale feels comfortable, use the scale notes to improvise. Be sure to utilize the tools described in earlier chapters (upper/lower neighbors, skipping, jumping, etc.).

Exercise 17-4: Applying the Dorian and Mixolydian Scales

Corelli's *Folies d'Espagne*, from chapters 8 and 15, provides an easy way to apply the two scales just explored. Play through it slowly to become reacquainted with the harmony.

The general harmonic structure for the passage is found below. Note that some of the major chords have been changed to dominant 7th chords to help illustrate the use of modes.

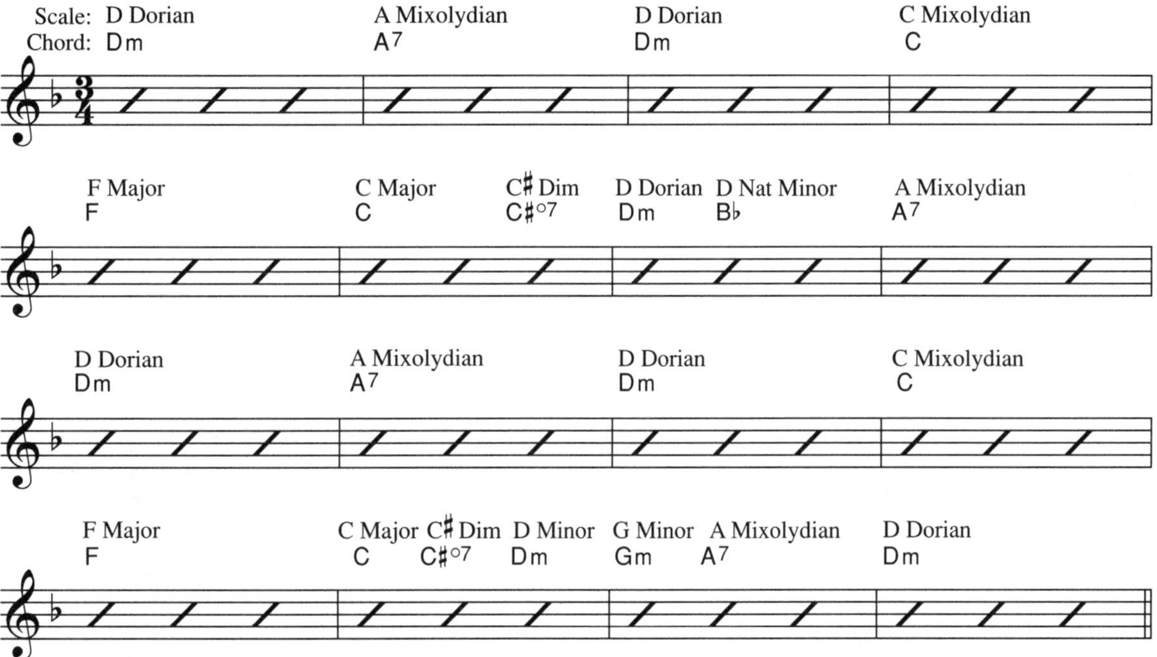

1. Play through the following example of measures 1–8 that uses a condensed version of the LH and scale segments in the RH. Then continue to use the appropriate scales to improvise through the passage.*

* For the C♯ diminished chords, either the notes of the chord (C♯–E–G–B♭) or the A Mixolydian scale can be used. Navigate measures 6–7 with short scale segments that follow the harmony.

2. Play through the following example that combines scales with skipping and jumping. Then explore further by adding tools learned in earlier chapters (upper/lower neighbors, repetition, borrowed phrases, etc.)

Other Modal Applications

Using the first two tables of this chapter (see pages 105–106) and the one below, explore the other modal scales in the same way that the Dorian and Mixolydian scales were practiced in the preceding exercises. As mentioned earlier, each modal scale works best with a particular harmony. The table below offers a list of their primary applications. As each mode grows more comfortable, another valuable tool for improvisation is acquired.

Table 17-6: Applying the Remaining Modes

Mode	Application	Examples
Ionian	Major, Major 7th chords	C Ionian works with Cmaj and Cmaj7
Dorian	Minor, Minor 7th chords	D Dorian works with Dm and Dm7
Phrygian	Minor 7th ♭9 chords	E Phrygian works with Em7$^{(\flat 9)}$
Lydian	Major 7th, Major 7th ♯11 chords	F Lydian works with Fmaj7, Fmaj7$^{(\sharp 11)}$
Mixolydian	Dominant 7th chords	G Mixolydian works with G7
Aeolian	Minor, Minor 7th chords	A Aeolian works with Am and Am7
Locrian	Half-Diminished chords	B Locrian works with Bm7$^{(\flat 5)}$ (B^{ø}7)

Key Points from This Chapter

- Each major scale tone can become the starting point for a modal scale.
- Modal scales can provide helpful tools to navigate particular harmonies.
- Understanding modes will provide a new musical vocabulary for expression.

CHAPTER 18 When One Scale Won't Work, Part 2: Navigating by Chord Pairs

With an understanding of modes, a player will be better prepared to tackle the intricacies of the next four measures (5–8) of Chopin's Prelude in C Minor. Take a moment to play through the passage below:

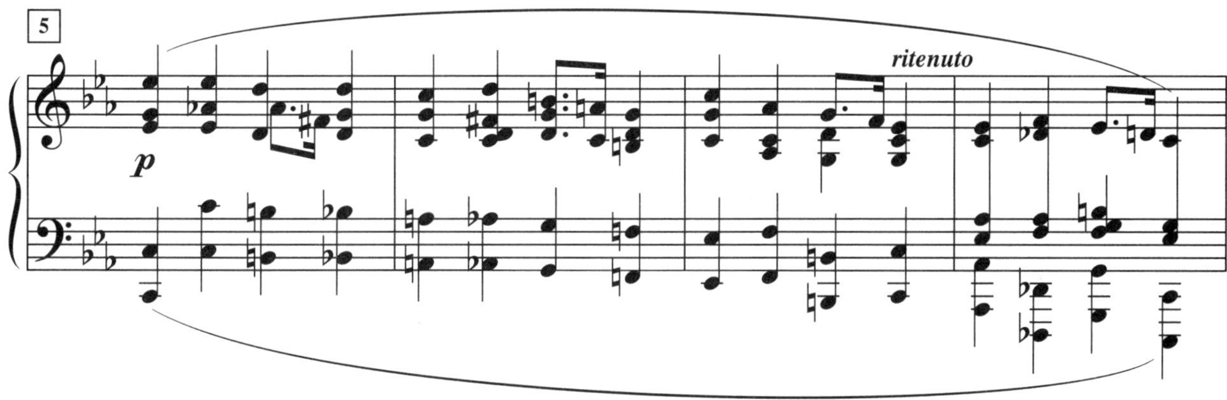

Analysis of Measures 5–6

Notice how difficult it is to identify a tonal focus in measures 5–6. That's because both measures are moving toward an external focal point. The theme of measures 5–6 is the descending bass that resolves to the C minor chord on the first beat of measure 7. Without a clear focus for each individual measure, it is difficult to select a primary scale for this passage. In this situation, a practical strategy is to divide and conquer. Divide the measures into "chord pairs" and determine which scales provide the best fit with each pair. The general harmony for measures 5–6 can be outlined as follows:*

* For simplicity, ignore the movement of the inner voices on the third beat of measure 5.

Navigating the First Chord Pair (Measure 5)

Study the first chord pair. Based on earlier exercises, the two best scales for these chords are C natural minor and A♭ major.

Table 18-1: Scales of the First Chord Pair

Chord	Best Scale	Scale Notes
Cm	C Natural Minor	C D E♭ F G A♭ B♭ C
A♭/C	A♭ Major	A♭ B♭ C D♭ E♭ F G A♭

Only one alteration (D/D♭) is needed to navigate these two chords. But could there be an even easier way to handle both chords? Notice that the note D♭ is only implied in the A♭ chord on beat 2. Since this note does not actually appear in the score, the D♭ alteration may not be necessary. The following exercise will help explain this reasoning.

Exercise 18-1: Navigating the First Chord Pair

1. Play the two scales (C natural minor and A♭ major) with the RH over the alternating LH whole-note pattern below:

2. Play step 1 again using only the C natural minor scale (without the D♭) in the RH.

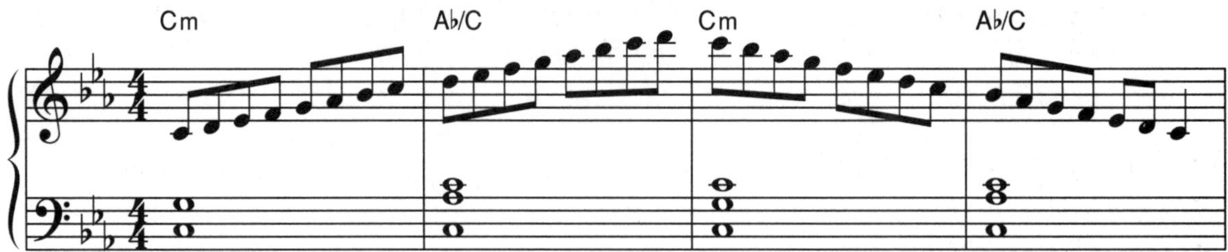

After playing this exercise, one can see that the C natural minor scale not only simplifies navigation, but also sounds better.

3. Use the notes of the C natural minor scale to improvise through the two chords until it feels comfortable. Play through the example below and then experiment:

Exercise 18-1 suggests that the improviser should not rely solely on harmonic analysis to decide on the proper scales. Be flexible and use common sense. Experimentation can often lead to an easier way of accommodating any set of chords.

Navigating the Second Chord Pair (Measure 5)

The second chord pair presents a great deal of creative opportunity for the improviser.

The G major chord on beat 3 offers either of the following scale choices:

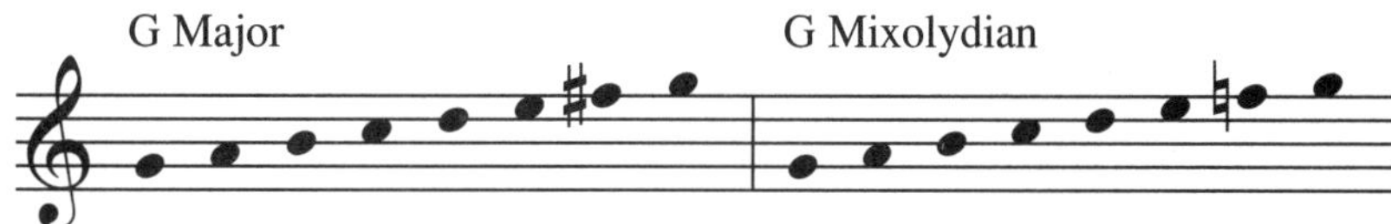

The Mixolydian scale is always a consideration for major and dominant 7th chords. To accommodate the movement of the inner voices on beat 3 (particularly the F♯), use the G major scale. When improvising, however, one has a choice of either scale.

For beat 4, the G minor chord works with any of the minor scales.

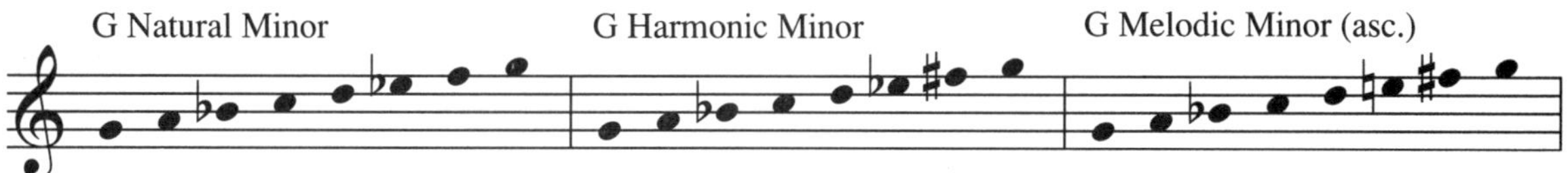

With many available scale choices, there is no "right way" to navigate these two chords—only a myriad of very good options. The following exercise will offer the freedom to mix and match scales with the harmony.

Exercise 18-2: Navigating the Second Chord Pair

1. Play the LH harmony and experiment with each of the following scale options:

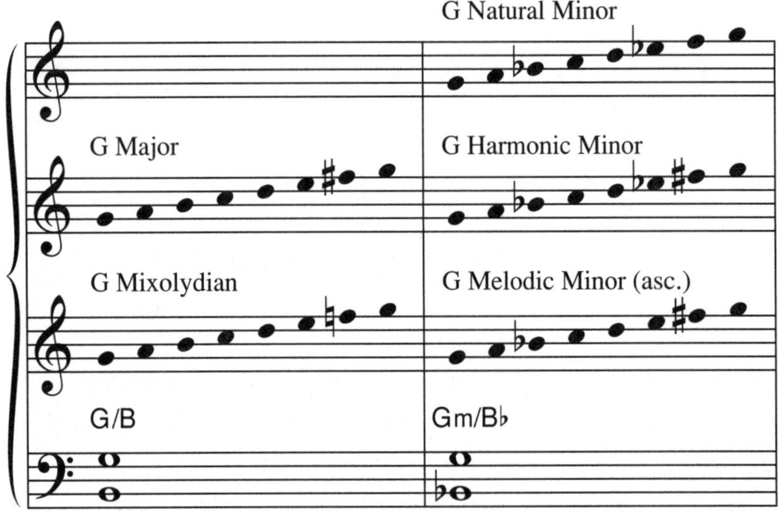

2. While playing the LH pattern, mix and match the scales by playing through the following example. Try to determine which scale combinations sound the best. Continue the LH pattern throughout this step.

3. Now improvise through the chord pair using the improvisatory tools learned in earlier chapters.

Improvising through Measure 5

Based upon exercises 18-1 and 18-2, the following framework can be used to improvise through measure 5. Take a moment to improvise through this framework below:

Based on the example above, the first chord pair is navigated with incremental transition—using one primary scale across multiple chords. The second chord pair is navigated with literal transition—changing scales with each chord. This two-fold way of approaching the measure does work. But the theme of this chapter is to continually ask the question, Could there be an easier way? In this case, would incremental transition work for the entire measure?

Exercise 18-1 showed that a change of harmony did not always demand a change of scale. Because the D♭ was only implied on beat 2 (the A♭ major chord), the C natural minor scale (with D♮) worked quite well. This concept captured the essence of incremental transition. It allowed the player to focus on one primary scale and make incremental changes only when necessary.

Following this line of thinking, could C natural minor serve as the primary scale for all of measure 5? If so, what incremental changes are required? To answer these questions, try playing the C natural minor scale through the entire harmony of measure 5.

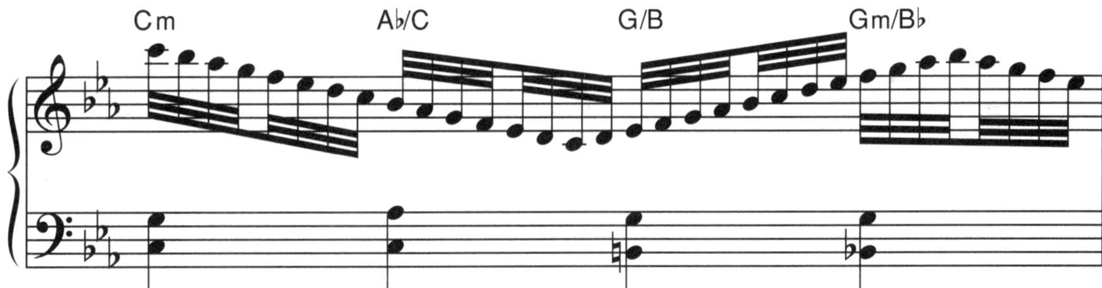

Notice that it works quite well except for beat 3 (the G major chord) when the B♭ in the scale conflicts with the B♮ in the bass. Try the example again with the B♮ substitution in beat 3.

Incremental transition is clearly the easier way to approach measure 5. The C natural minor scale works throughout the measure, with only one slight alteration. Note that incremental transition works best when there is some ambiguity in the chords (i.e., implied notes). This lack of harmonic clarity offers great freedom for selecting scales.

Exercise 18-3: Improvising through Measure 5

1. Repeat the LH harmony from the previous example and use incremental transition (with the C natural minor scale) to improvise with the various tools acquired in previous chapters (upper/lower neighbors, skipping, jumping, etc.). Play through the example below and then experiment:

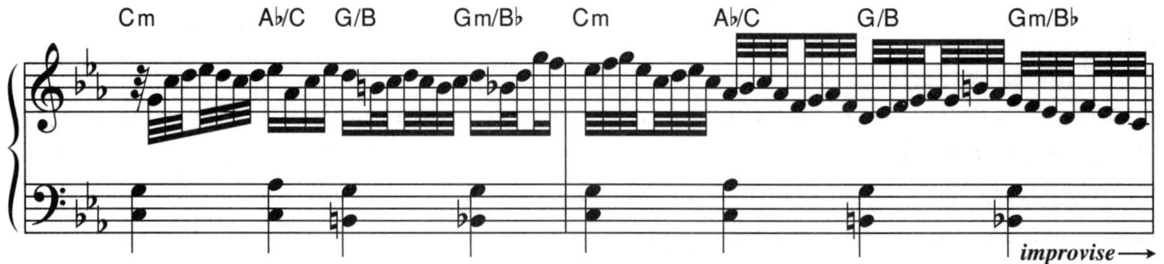

2. For comparison, use the framework below to improvise with literal transition:

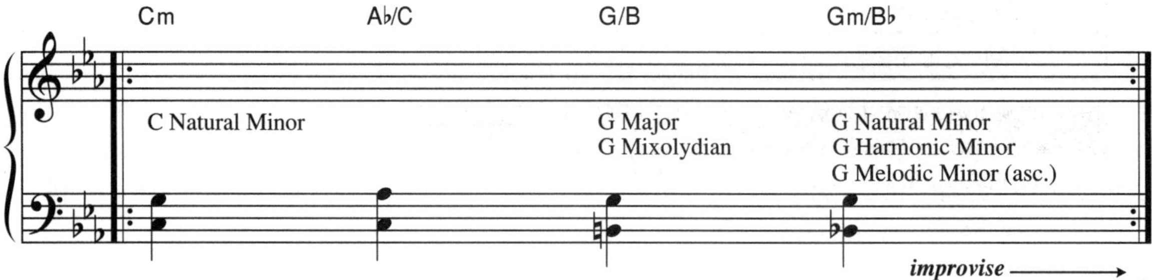

Navigating the Third Chord Pair (Measure 6)

The third chord pair provides an opportunity to experiment with a liberating concept—when the right scale can't be found, create one!

Take a moment to play through measure 6 below:

The two chords at the beginning of the measure are Am7 and A♭7(♭5). The Am7 chord is usually associated with one of the A minor scales. The best choice for this chord is the A natural minor scale because of the lowered 7th (G).

The A♭7(♭5) chord, however, presents some problems. The root component (A♭) and lowered 7th (F♯/G♭) of this chord suggests the use of the A♭ Mixolydian scale:

A♭–B♭–C–D♭–E♭–F–G♭–A♭

But the lowered 5th (D♮) conflicts with the D♭ in the Mixolydian scale. To solve this problem, one could try the A♭ Lydian scale (which has a raised 4th) to accommodate the D♮:

A♭–B♭–C–**D**–E♭–F–**G**–A♭

But then the G♮ in the A♭ Lydian scale conflicts with the lowered 7th (F♯/G♭) in the A♭7(♭5) chord. Therefore, a dilemma occurs—there appears to be no commonly-used scale that can accommodate the A♭7(♭5) chord. In this circumstance, the player should do what improvisers have done throughout the ages—invent a scale that fits. The challenge is to construct a scale that incorporates the D♮ of the A♭ Lydian scale and the G♭ of the A♭ Mixolydian scale. The solution is a hybrid scale that could be called the Lydian flat-7th scale. As the name implies, this new scale is a Lydian scale with a lowered 7th.

Table 18-2: Creating the Lydian Flat-7th Scale

Original Scales	Scale Notes
A♭ Lydian	A♭ B♭ C **D** E♭ F G A♭
A♭ Mixolydian	A♭ B♭ C D♭ E♭ F **G♭** A♭

Hybrid Scale	Scale Notes
A♭ Lydian Flat-7th	A♭ B♭ C **D** E♭ F **G♭** A♭

This altered scale works very well with the A♭7(♭5) and provides yet another tool for improvisation. The following exercises will explore the Lydian and Lydian flat-7th scales.

Exercise 18-4: Becoming Familiar with the Lydian Scale

In addition to its use with major chords, the Lydian scale also works well whenever a lowered 5th or raised 11th occurs. It may sound exotic at first, but know that the Lydian scale can bring valuable color and purposeful tension to improvisation. It can be a key element that keeps one's playing from becoming tiresome to the listener.

1. Spend some time playing through the various Lydian scales using tables 18-3 and 18-4. Play the chord in the LH and the scale with the RH.

Table 18-3: Identifying the Lydian Scale

Derivative Method	Altered Method
Starts on the 4th scale degree of the major scale	Major scale with a raised 4th
A♭ Lydian uses the E♭ major scale	A♭ Lydian is the A♭ major scale with a D♮

Table 18-4: The 12 Lydian Scales

Lydian Scales	Scale Notes	Origin Scale	LH Chord
C Lydian	C D E F♯ G A B C	G Major	C Major
C♯ Lydian	C♯ D♯ E♯ F× G♯ A♯ B♯ C♯	G♯ Major	C♯ Major
D Lydian	D E F♯ G♯ A B C♯ D	A Major	D Major
E♭ Lydian	E♭ F G A B♭ C D E♭	B♭ Major	E♭ Major
E Lydian	E F♯ G♯ A♯ B C♯ D♯ E	B Major	E Major
F Lydian	F G A B C D E F	C Major	F Major
F♯ Lydian	F♯ G♯ A♯ B♯ C♯ D♯ E♯ F♯	C♯ Major	F♯ Major
G Lydian	G A B C♯ D E F♯ G	D Major	G Major
A♭ Lydian	A♭ B♭ C D E♭ F G A♭	E♭ Major	A♭ Major
A Lydian	A B C♯ D♯ E F♯ G♯ A	E Major	A Major
B♭ Lydian	B♭ C D E F G A B♭	F Major	B♭ Major
B Lydian	B C♯ D♯ E♯ F♯ G♯ A♯ B	F♯ Major	B Major

2. Play an A♭ major chord with the LH and spend some time improvising with the A♭ Lydian scale with the RH. Use skipping, jumping, upper/lower neighbors and other essential tools to experiment with this scale. Don't stop until the A♭ Lydian scale feels comfortable.

3. Play the A♭7(♭5) chord (from beat 2 of measure 6) and spend some time improvising with the notes of the A♭ Lydian flat-7th scale. Again, use a range of improvising tools.

Exercise 18-5: Navigating the Third Chord Pair (Measure 6)

Now knowing the appropriate scales for the first two beats of measure 6, improvise over the chord pair.

1. Play the LH chords in whole notes and improvise with the two scales with the RH.

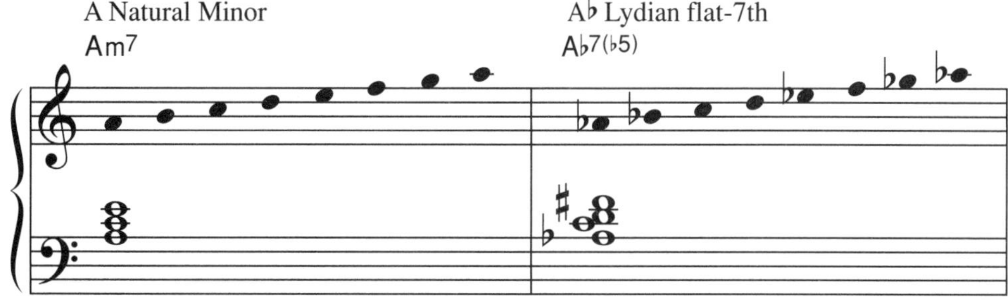

2. Play through the following example that uses several improvising tools and then experiment:

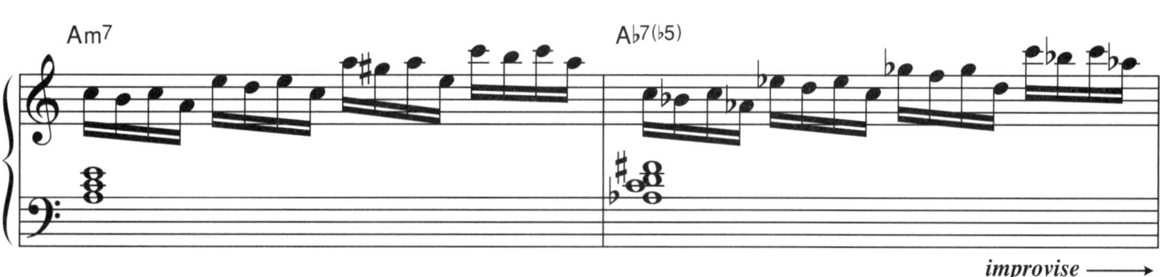

3. This time, play the LH chords in quarter notes. Because the chords change quickly, it may only be possible to use scale segments while improvising. Play through the following example and then experiment:

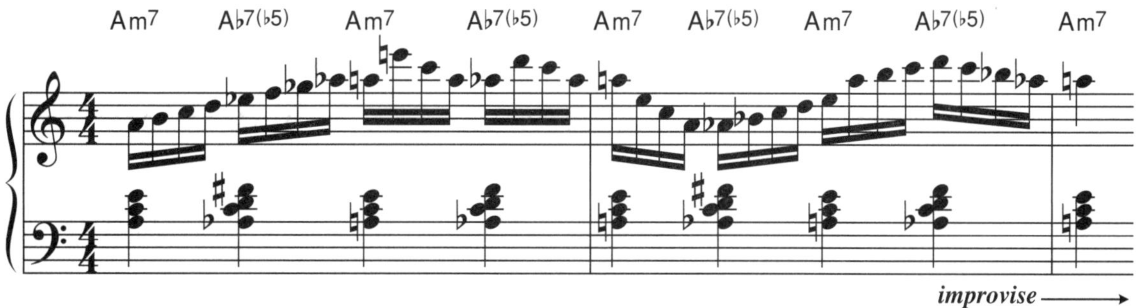

Navigating the Fourth Chord Pair (Measure 6)

Navigating the fourth chord pair will be easy, since both the G and G7 chords are quite similar:

As discussed in the previous chapter, the G Mixolydian scale works well across both chords. Take a moment to play this scale over the two chords.

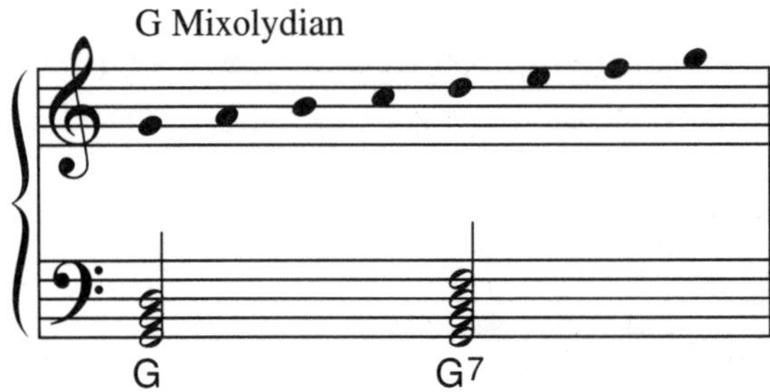

Creative Transition

Measures 5–6 provide an interesting test passage for the application of a new concept called *creative transition*.

To review, the word "transition" refers to the way the improviser thinks through chord changes. With literal transition, the player looks at each individual chord (or tonal focus) and reacts with an appropriate scale. With incremental transition, the player takes a wider view, selecting one general scale for a particular measure (or series of measures) and making incremental adjustments to adapt to the transitions from chord to chord.

To understand creative transition, think back to the analogy of the rapids. Imagine spending several hours studying the nuances of a treacherous spot along the river. After intense analysis, the flow of the changing currents is understood, and ways to navigate each perilous segment of the rapids have been devised. When entering the rapids with the kayak, there will be little time to think—only moments to react with the help of past experience and the specific knowledge just acquired.

Creative transition uses the same mental approach as navigating the rapids. It is most useful in situations when the harmony is changing rapidly and there is no clear harmonic emphasis (as in measures 5–6). In these situations, the improviser has little time to think—only moments to react with a short scale segment before it transforms into another scale. In essence, creative transition is a reactive technique that draws upon existing experience with harmony and scales to navigate smoothly through a changing harmony. To say it more plainly, "Scales are created as they are played."

Below is an example of creative transition through measures 5 and 6:

Note that creative transition doesn't require the player to think in complete scales. A passing listener might not be able to identify any particular scale (as in the descending notes above). But with practice, improvising can become a tapestry of scalar content that will speak with eloquence.

Exercise 18-6: Creative Transition

1. Practice the example of creative transition (shown again below) until it feels comfortable and a smooth flow from one scale segment to the next is established:

2. Play the following inverted example until it feels comfortable:

3. Once the previous steps are completely comfortable, begin to use the other tools acquired earlier (skipping, jumping, upper/lower neighbors, etc.) to improvise through the passage. Play the example below and then experiment:

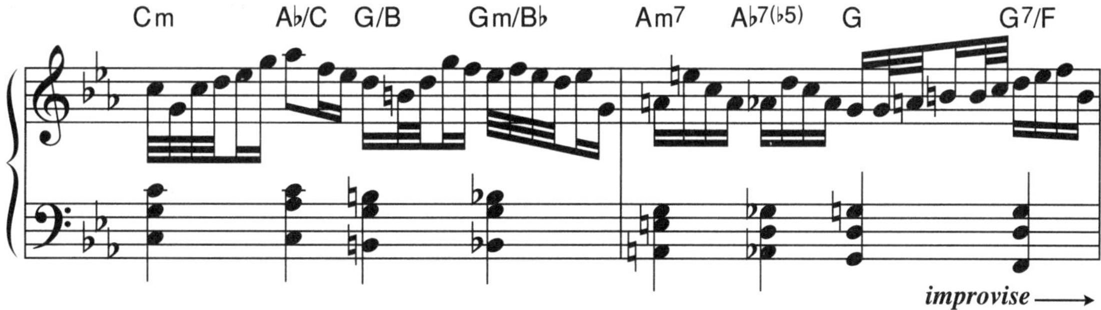

Exercise 18-7: Applying Creative Transition to Measures 1–4

Try to apply creative transition to the first four measures of the Chopin prelude.

1. Play through the following scalar example and then experiment with different scalar patterns:

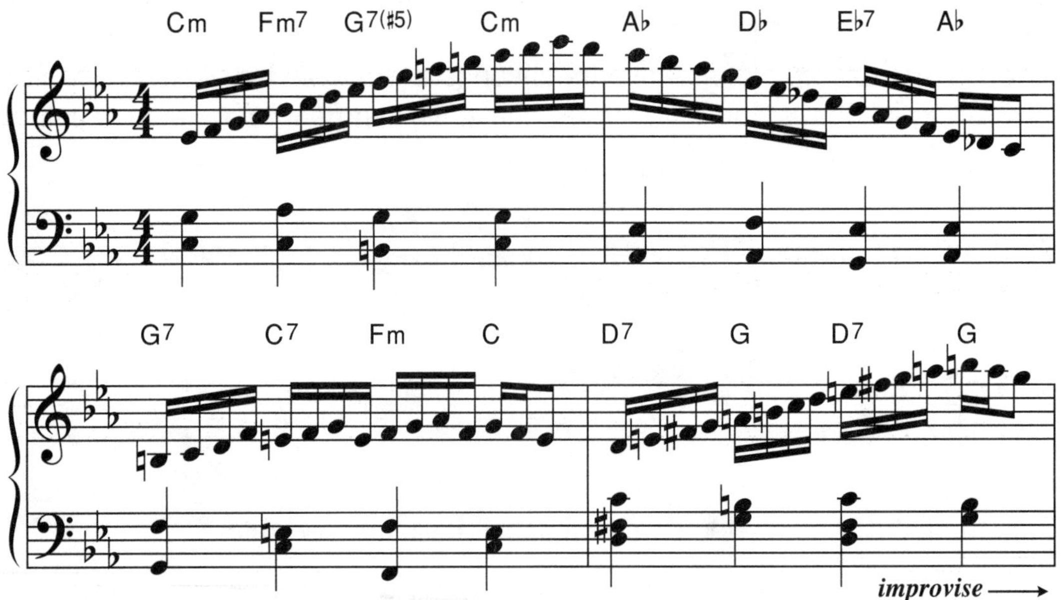

2. Play through the following non-scalar example and then experiment using the various tools acquired earlier:

3. Move the accompaniment into the RH (in an appropriate octave) and try to employ creative transition while building phrases in the LH.

Exercise 18-8: Applying Creative Transition to Other Pieces

Find another passage with fast harmonic rhythm that lacks tonal focus and apply the following methodology for improvisation:

1. Break the passage into manageable segments for harmonic analysis.
2. Determine the appropriate scales for improvising over the harmony.
3. Once the scales feel comfortable, use creative transition to navigate smoothly through the passage.

If an alternative passage is hard to find, analyze the traditional hymn below entitled "Praise to the Lord, the Almighty." While it does have a tonal focus, it will provide experience in navigating a passage with a more rapid harmonic rhythm.

Creative transition becomes easier as the player matures in the knowledge of scales and their applications. A player who can apply creative transition to a variety of harmonic circumstances can be considered an advanced improviser.

Key Points from This Chapter

- Always ask the question, could there be an easier way?
- When the harmony in a passage is changing too quickly, break the passage into smaller increments (as small as chord pairs) to determine the appropriate scales.
- When an appropriate scale can't be found, create a new one.
- Creative transition can help to navigate difficult harmony in which there is no tonal focus.

CHAPTER 19 Additional Tools

Before leaving measure 6 of Chopin's prelude, consider the following: What if Chopin had added an E♭ to the chord on the first beat of measure 6? Would that affect the way one improvises through that measure?

The chord on beat one of measure 6 is somewhat ambiguous. It includes an A♮ (the root tone), C (the minor 3rd) and G (the minor 7th). But the 5th is implied. That tone could be either an E♮ (the perfect 5th) or an E♭ (the diminished 5th). In the earlier analysis, the E♮ was assumed. However, the general descending character of this passage would suggest that the E♭ is more appropriate, since it strongly desires to resolve downward to the D on beat 2. The use of E♭ transforms this chord into an Am7(♭5) (or half-diminished) chord, which is sometimes notated as Aø7.

Why such intense scrutiny? The half-diminished chord allows the introduction of another valuable mode called the Locrian scale, which can be identified as follows:

Table 19-1: Identifying the Locrian Scale

Derivative Method	Altered Method
Starts on the 7th scale degree of the major scale	The natural minor scale with a lowered 2nd and 5th
The A Locrian scale uses the B♭ major scale	The A Locrian scale is the A natural minor scale with B♭ and E♭

The derivative method may be the easier method for locating Locrian scales. Use the next exercise to become acquainted with Locrian scales and their use with half-diminished chords.

Exercise 19-1: Practicing the Locrian Scale

Play the half-diminished chords with the LH and play through the corresponding Locrian scales with the RH.

Table 19-2: The 12 Locrian Scales

Locrian Scale	Scale Notes	Origin Scale	LH Chord	LH Chord Notes
C Locrian	C D♭ E♭ F G♭ A♭ B♭ C	D♭ Major	Cm7(♭5)	C–E♭–G♭–B♭
C♯ Locrian	C♯ D E F♯ G A B C♯	D Major	C♯m7(♭5)	C♯–E–G–B
D Locrian	D E♭ F G A♭ B♭ C D	E♭ Major	Dm7(♭5)	D–F–A♭–C
D♯/E♭ Locrian	D♯ E F♯ G♯ A B C♯ D♯	E Major	D♯m7(♭5)	D♯–F♯–A–C♯
E Locrian	E F G A B♭ C D E	F Major	Em7(♭5)	E–G–B♭–D
F Locrian	F G♭ A♭ B♭ C♭ D♭ E♭ F	G♭ Major	Fm7(♭5)	F–A♭–C♭–E♭
F♯ Locrian	F♯ G A B C D E F♯	G Major	F♯m7(♭5)	F♯–A–C–E
G Locrian	G A♭ B♭ C D♭ E♭ F G	A♭ Major	Gm7(♭5)	G–B♭–D♭–F
G♯ Locrian	G♯ A B C♯ D E F♯ G♯	A Major	G♯m7(♭5)	G♯–B–D–F♯
A Locrian	A B♭ C D E♭ F G A	B♭ Major	Am7(♭5)	A–C–E♭–G
A♯/B♭ Locrian	A♯ B C♯ D♯ E F♯ G♯ A♯	B Major	A♯m7(♭5)	A♯–C♯–E–G♯
B Locrian	B C D E F G A B	C Major	Bm7(♭5)	B–D–F–A

Applying the Locrian Scale

When the Locrian scale feels comfortable, return to the first chord pair in measure 6 with the following revised harmony:

Using the Locrian scale for the Am7(♭5) chord, the following two scales can now be used to navigate the first chord pair:

Table 19-3: Scales of the Revised Chord Pair

Scale Type	Scale Notes	LH Chord
A Locrian	A B♭ C D E♭ F G A	Am7(♭5)
A♭ Lydian Flat-7th	A♭ B♭ C D E♭ F G♭ A♭	A♭7(♭5)

Notice the similarity between the two scales? Adjustments are required for only two notes (A/A♭ and G/G♭), which makes improvising much easier than in exercise 18-5 when the original harmony was used and four notes needed alteration. The lesson is this: a slight change in harmony can sometimes simplify improvisation. When the harmony permits alternative chords, use the ambiguity to make improvising easier.

Exercise 19-2: Navigating the Revised Chord Pair

Use the process from exercise 18-5 (see page 123) to improvise over the revised chord pair from measure 6. Because the scales have more notes in common than those used in exercise 18-5, improvising should be easier.

1. Play the LH chords in whole notes and experiment with the two scales with the RH.

2. Play through the following scalar example and then explore further:

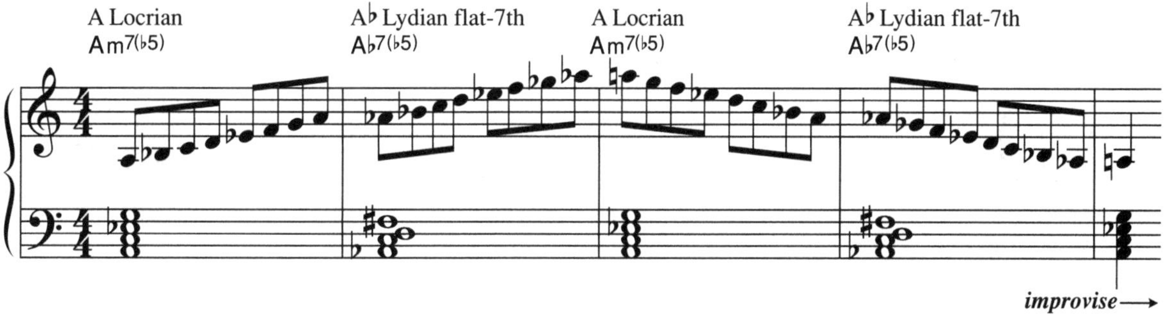

3. This time, play the LH chords in quarter notes. Because the chords change more quickly, it may only be possible to use scale segments while improvising. Play through the following example and then experiment:

Because half-diminished chords are quite common in all styles of music, the Locrian scale should become an important element of one's improvising toolbox.

Analysis of Measures 7 and 8

Since all of measure 7 and the first chord pair of measure 8 (shown below) are harmonically identical to the beginning of the prelude, no analysis is required. The same scales and thought processes can be used. The third chord of measure 8, however, offers another opportunity to add resources to the improviser's toolbox. The G7(♯5) is made up of four notes: G (the root), B♮ (the major 3rd), D♯/E♭ (the augmented 5th) and F (the minor 7th). No scale used so far can accommodate this chord. The G Mixolydian scale works with G7 chords, but is not compatible with the augmented 5th tone. Once again, the solution is to create a new scale.

Since the G Mixolydian scale requires the least modification, use it as the starting point. Then, search for a single alteration that will solve the conflicting tone. The table below shows that an E♭ (instead of E♮) on the 6th tone will make the scale compatible with the chord:

Table 19-4: Scale Modification for the G7(♯5) Chord

Scale Type	Scale Notes	Chord
G Mixolydian	G A B C D E F G	G7
G Mixolydian Flat-6th	G A B C D E♭ F G	G7(♯5)

This new scale, which will be called the Mixolydian flat-6th scale (tradition has favored "flat 6th" in the scale name over the enharmonic "sharp 5th"), works well with the G7(♯5) chord and also allows an easy flow into the Cm chord on beat 4 of measure 8.* If the C melodic minor (ascending) scale is selected for the Cm chord on beat 4 of measure 8, no alterations are necessary to navigate the final chord pair. The notes are exactly the same, as shown below:

Table 19-5: Scale Comparison for the G7(♯5) Chord

Scale Type	Scale Notes	Chord
G Mixolydian Flat-6th	G A B C D E♭ F G	G7(♯5)
C Melodic Minor (ascending)	C D E♭ F G A(♮) B(♮) C	Cm

* There is one additional scale that will work with the G7(♯5) chord. It is the whole tone scale, built entirely on whole steps. The G whole tone scale consists of G–A–B–C♯–D♯–F–G. Give it a try in the following exercise.

Exercise 19-3: Applying the Mixolydian Flat-6th Scale

1. Use the G Mixolydian flat-6th and C melodic minor (ascending) scales to improvise through the last chord pair of measure 8. Note that both scales utilize the same notes.

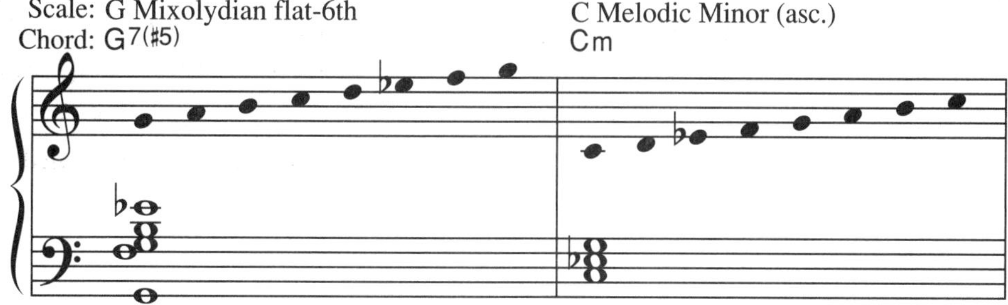

2. Play through the following examples of concluding phrases and then experiment:

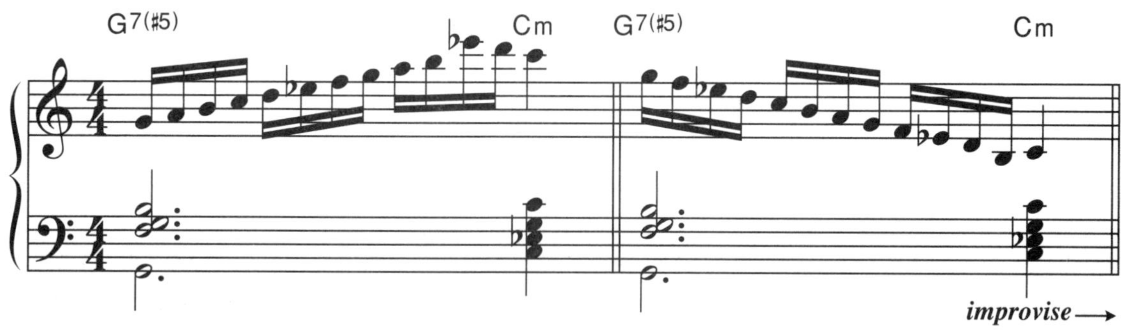

3. Play the LH chords in quarter notes and use the notes of the scales to improvise. Play the example below and then experiment:

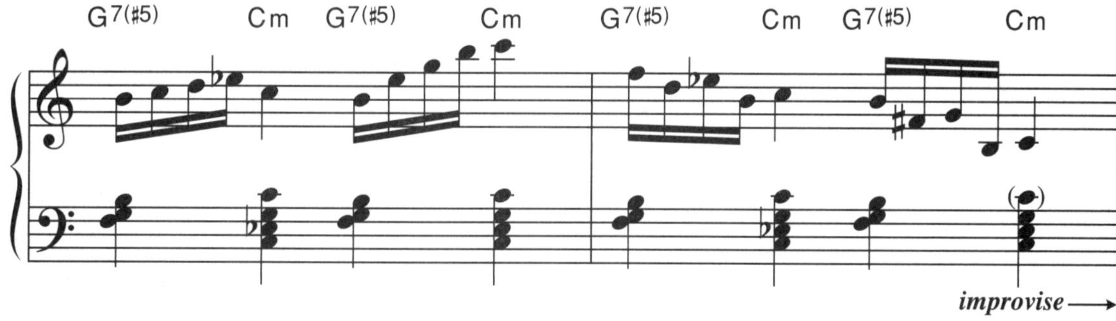

Key Points from This Chapter

- The Locrian scale is useful for all half-diminished chords.
- The Mixolydian flat-6th scale works well with any dominant 7 ♯5 chord.
- If the right scale can't be found, create a new one.

CHAPTER 20 Putting It All Together

After four challenging chapters on Chopin's Prelude in C Minor, it is now time to engage the entire work. Note that measures 5–8 and 9–12 are harmonically identical, providing two exciting opportunities to navigate the rough waters. The player should now have all the tools necessary to improvise successfully through all 13 measures of the piece.

Exercise 20: Navigating the Entire Prelude

The complete prelude is shown below with corresponding harmony:

1. **Slow and Easy:** For the first improvisation through the complete prelude, proceed slowly. Take whatever time is necessary with this first step. Don't move on until improvising at this slower speed feels very comfortable.
   - Play each LH chord for four beats (as though the chords were whole notes).
   - Use mostly ascending and descending scales.
   - At this slower pace, literal transition is possible.
2. **Increasing the Pace:** Think in longer phrases and use incremental transition to limit the number of scales utilized.
   - Play each LH chord for two beats.
   - Gradually begin to utilize all other acquired tools in addition to scalar material.
   - Use incremental transition wherever possible.
3. **As Written:** At normal tempo, there will be less time to react to each chord change. Creative transition will allow the player to react instinctively to the changes in harmony using the knowledge gained in previous chapters.
   - Play the LH chords as written (one chord per beat).
   - Use scalar material and other acquired tools to improvise (don't forget silence).
   - Use creative transition if possible.
4. **Sample Improvisation:** Play through the example of creative transition below that uses a condensed LH harmony; then, continue exploring.
5. **Engaging the Left Hand:** Create a simplified version of the harmony in the RH and try to improvise through the prelude using the LH.

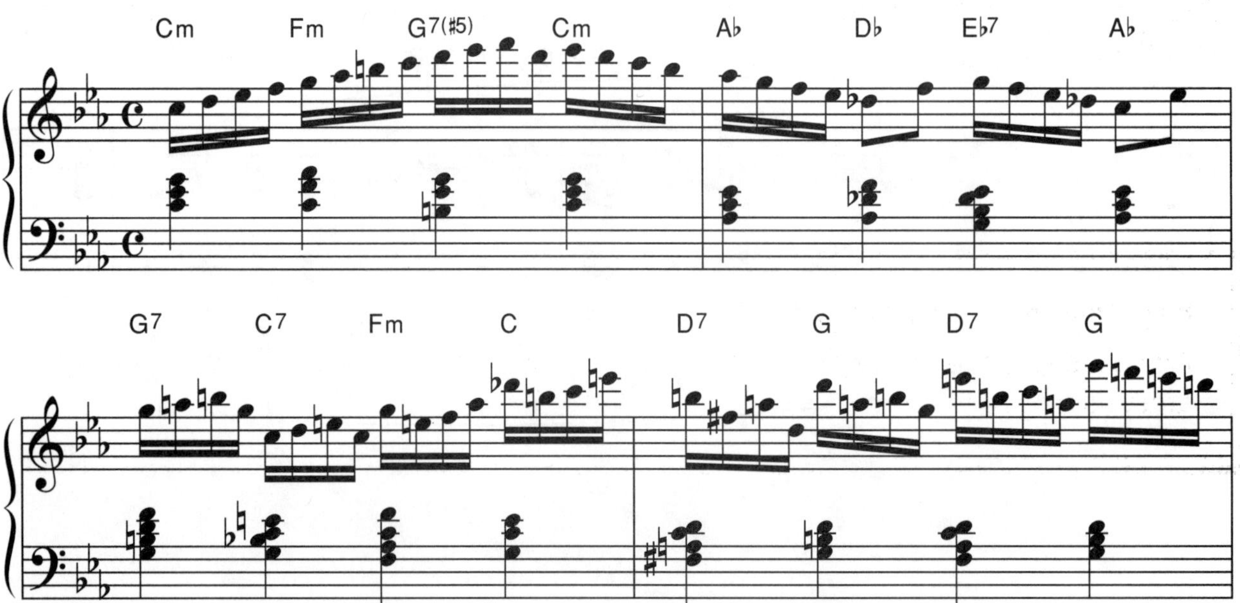

Key Point from This Chapter

Any passage, even a very difficult one, can be successfully navigated with careful analysis and preparation.

CHAPTER 21 Does a Wrong Note Exist?

This chapter raises an interesting question: when improvising, is there such a thing as a wrong note? The simple answer is no. As stated earlier, some notes are certainly better than others in any given situation. But one of the great joys of improvisation is discovering that every supposedly wrong note is an opportunity to create something compelling—a chance to "turn lemons into lemonade."

Intentional Dissonance

Keep in mind that "wrong" notes are sometimes used purposefully to create interest or tension. This is referred to as appoggiatura, a musical ornament that takes attention away from a main note. See the excerpt below of Robert Schumann's "Vogel als Prophet" from *Waldscenen*, Op. 82:

In this example, the "wrong" note (the C♯ used on the upbeat and again in the first two measures) is used on primary beats to establish initial tension that quickly resolves. When used in this way, the C♯ is not a wrong note at all. In fact, it is the "right" note to accomplish the composer's intention.

One can use dissonance in improvisations to accomplish the same goal. The improviser has the freedom to move in any direction at any time. Therefore, any given note, no matter how dissonant, has the potential to become a "right" note. Mozart's Sonata in C Major, K. 545 (from previous chapters) can be employed once again to illustrate this concept. Play through the following unusual revision of the melody:

Dissonant Melody

This melody could be aptly characterized as one of the worst of all time. Eight of the thirteen notes are intentionally dissonant, resulting in a horrendous cacophony of seemingly wrong notes. One might expect that this passage has absolutely no hope of becoming an enjoyable musical phrase.

But remember that every supposedly wrong note is an opportunity to create something compelling. With that in mind, play through the following improvisation based on the previous example:

Neighboring-Note Melody

With only a few added notes, lemonade is made. Notice that all the notes from the previous dissonant melody are in exactly the same position in the neighboring-note melody. The only difference is the addition of neighboring notes that provide context for the dissonant notes. The resulting passage of appoggiatura (and resolution) is not only consonant, but also quite lyrical.

The lesson is this—any note played, whether intentional or accidental, can be a right note. By having the freedom to turn dissonance into consonance at any moment, every apparently wrong (dissonant) note can be seen as an opportunity to create new and interesting melodic phrases.

Exercise 21-1: Making Lemonade

Play the dissonant passage below and then add neighboring notes to create a more pleasing melodic line:

Dissonant Melody

Try experimenting with the dissonant melody above before playing the following neighboring-note melody.

Neighboring-Note Melody

Exercise 21-2: Creating Appogiatura

1. Play through the following segment of Beethoven's Minuet in G Major:

2. While playing the LH part of the passage, use the RH to improvise a new melodic line using appoggiatura on most of the primary beats. Improvise through the passage several times, continually creating dissonance and resolution.

Exercise 21-3: Finding Consonance

Play through the following passage of dissonant notes and then try inserting additional neighboring notes to create a better melodic line:

Dissonant Melody

Try experimenting with the dissonant melody above before playing the neighboring-note melody on the following page.

Neighboring-Note Melody

Key Points from This Chapter

- There is no such thing as a wrong note in improvisation.
- View every dissonant note as an opportunity to create something new and exciting.

CHAPTER 22 Harmonic Improvisation and Borrowing

This final chapter of the *Advanced Tools* section will focus on the left hand. A new bass pattern will help demonstrate the flip side of previous chapters where the harmony defined the appropriate scale. In the first part of this chapter, the scale will define the harmony.

Start by using the following modified bass progression from C. P. E. Bach's *Essay on the True Art of Keyboard Playing, Volume 2*, published in 1762:

Renaissance and early baroque musicians based their improvisations on bass lines like the one above. Their technique was to establish a harmonic framework over the figured bass first, and then improvise with melodic lines that fit this combination of bass and harmony. The job of the keyboardist was to select from various available harmonies with the LH and improvise with the RH based upon the harmonies selected. This process is quite similar to jazz, where the players establish a walking bass line and chord changes, and then improvise melodies and patterns over that foundation.

Because the figured bass shown above is composed around the A natural minor scale, a tonal focus of A minor can be assumed. But the next logical question is, where is the harmony? This element (or lack thereof) is what makes this chapter different from previous ones. The answer is that there is no harmony—at least not yet. In this chapter, the harmony must be created.

But where should one start in developing harmony? Common sense dictates starting with the only notes available—the figured bass. Notice that the bass contains just four notes: A, G, F and E. These notes are used repeatedly to form the phrase. The first step in creating harmony is to determine which chord options are available with these bass notes.

Because the range of possible chords for the harmony is so immense, one must first establish some parameters:

1. The chords must contain notes from the A natural minor scale.
2. The bass note must be contained within any selected chord.
3. The chords must be built in thirds (since much of the harmony in Western music is based upon the interval of a third).

Using these parameters, the following chord (harmony) choices are available for each of the four bass notes:

Table 22-1: Chords Containing the Bass Notes

Bass Note	Chord Notes	Chord
A	**A**–C–E	A Minor
	F–**A**–C	F Major
	D–F–**A**	D Minor
G	**G**–B–D	G Major
	E–**G**–B	E Minor
	C–E–**G**	C Major
F	**F**–A–C	F Major
	D–**F**–A	D Minor
	B–D–**F**	B Diminished
E	**E**–G–B	E Minor
	C–**E**–G	C Major
	A–C–**E**	A Minor

The chords in the above table would appear on the grand staff as follows (with the bass note shown in black):

Following the prescribed parameters, all of the above chords contain the bass note, are built in thirds and use the notes of the A natural minor scale.

Some of the bass notes share the same chords. For instance, the A–C–E triad is shared between the bass notes A and E. Similarly, the C–E–G triad is shared between the bass notes G and E. After the duplicates are removed from the twelve chord choices above, there are actually only seven distinct chords available—one for each tone of the A harmonic minor scale.

Table 22-2: Available Chords for the A Harmonic Minor Scale

Scale Note	Chord Notes	Chord
A	A–C–E	A Minor
B	B–D–F	B Diminished
C	C–E–G	C Major
D	D–F–A	D Minor
E	E–G–B	E Minor
F	F–A–C	F Major
G	G–B–D	G Major

This illustrates an essential point that can add depth to one's understanding of improvisation: While it is true that harmony typically governs the choice of scale, it is also true that the choice of scale can govern harmony. Any given scale will present a complete set of chords that complement it. Seeing both sides of this equation will help a player more fully understand musical grammar (defined earlier as the way melody interacts with harmony). The best improvisers can think in both directions.

Establishing Chord Choices

Having determined the range of available chords, the next step is to decide which chords should be used with each bass note. The table below shows the root triad for each note of the A natural minor scale and the two inversions associated with that note. It offers an even wider assortment of available chords.

Table 22-3: Inversions of the Available Chords

Base Note	Root Triad	First Inversion	Second Inversion	Chord
A	A–C–E	C–E–A	E–A–C	A Minor
B	B–D–F	D–F–B	F–B–D	B Diminished
C	C–E–G	E–G–C	G–C–E	C Major
D	D–F–A	F–A–D	A–D–F	D Minor
E	E–G–B	G–B–E	B–E–G	E Minor
F	F–A–C	A–C–F	C–F–A	F Major
G	G–B–D	B–D–G	D–G–B	G Major

To make chord selections easier, the next table reorganizes these root triads and inversions by grouping together only the chords that feature the bass note as the lowest note. All other chords are eliminated.

Table 22-4: Chord Inversions Containing Bass Notes as the Root

Bass Note	Chord Notes	Chord	Inversion
A	A–C–E	A Minor	Root
	A–C–F	F Major	1st
	A–D–F	D Minor	2nd
G	G–B–D	G Major	Root
	G–B–E	E Minor	1st
	G–C–E	C Major	2nd
F	F–A–C	F Major	Root
	F–A–D	D Minor	1st
	F–B–D	B Diminished	2nd
E	E–G–B	E Minor	Root
	E–G–C	C Major	1st
	E–A–C	A Minor	2nd

Below is a notated example of table 22-4:

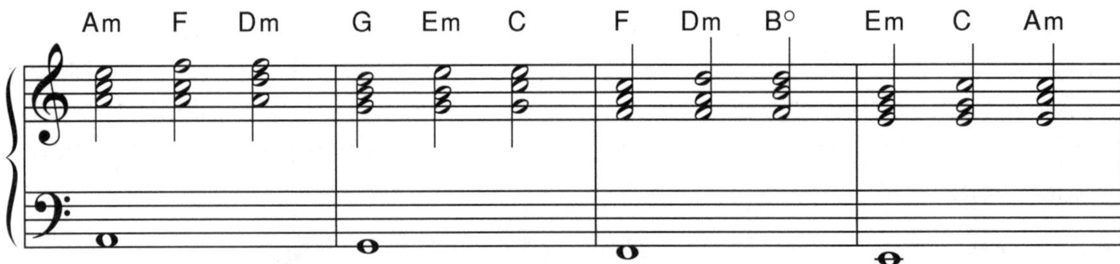

The notated example above will serve as a guide for the following exercise. It will help to quickly identify the chords that can be selected for each note of the figured bass.

Exercise 22-1: Harmonic Improvisation

With this exercise, the player will be mixing and matching chords with bass notes; in other words, improvising a harmony.

1. **Memorization and Transposition**
    a. Memorize the C. P. E. Bach figured bass below:

    b. Once this line is well memorized, transpose it into all 12 keys. This will allow the bass to become second nature.

2. **Bass and Harmony**
    a. Play the figured bass with the LH, holding each note for two beats.
    b. With the RH, match the LH pulse while playing one of the three chord choices that correspond with each bass note.

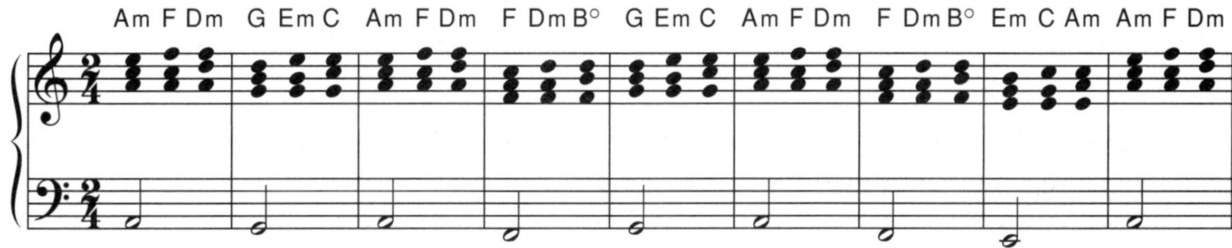

c. Continue to experiment with various chords until the process feels comfortable.

3. **Improvising Harmony and Melody (as a Duet)**

   a. Ask a friend to play the figured bass (if no one is available, the exercise can still be played).

   b. Move the chord selection to the LH and select chords as desired. The chord choices are shown below:

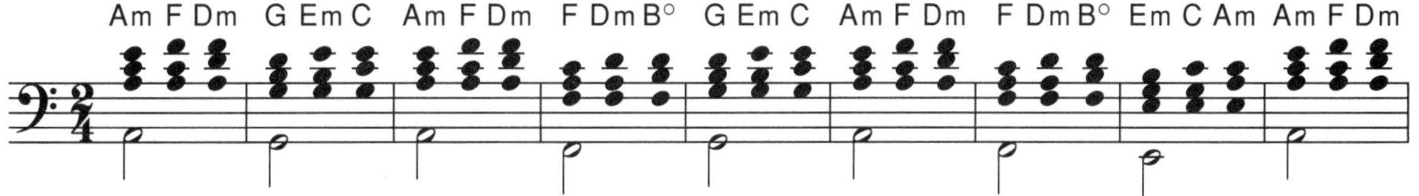

   c. When the LH feels comfortable selecting chords, begin improvising with the A natural minor scale with the RH. The chords that are selected with the LH will determine the direction of improvisation with the RH. Use all available tools to create interesting melodic lines. Play through the following example and then experiment:

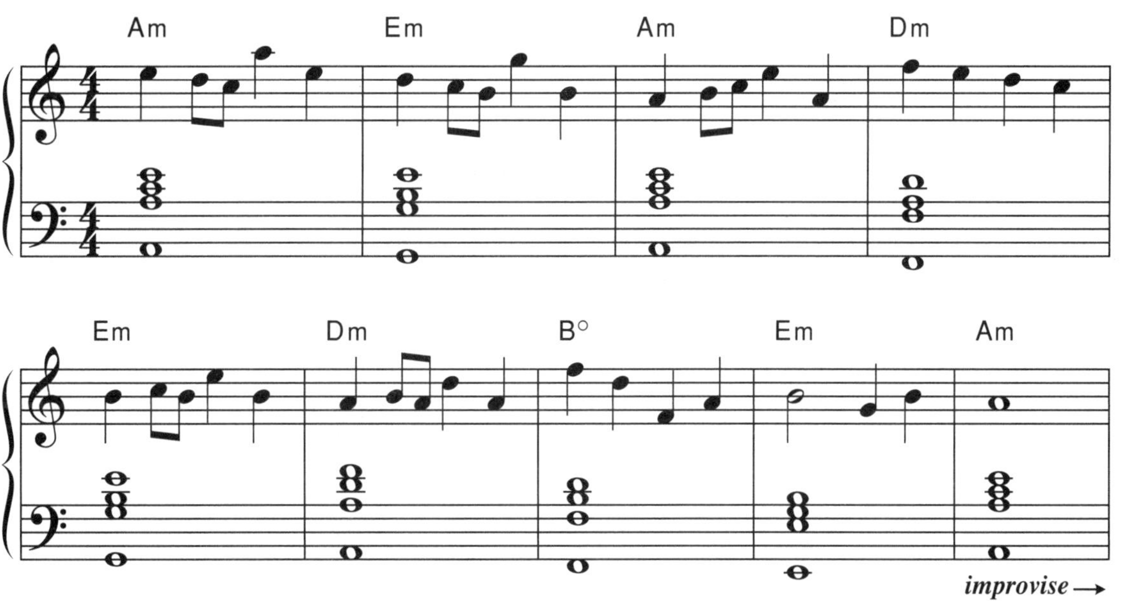

4. **Transposition**

   a. Once steps 1–3 feel comfortable, transpose this exercise into different keys.

   b. Over time, try to play this exercise in all 12 keys.

Borrowing Harmony

Chapter 14 gave permission to borrow melodic material from the masters for use in improvisation. That permission also applies to harmony. As the beneficiary of experimentation by centuries of great composers, why shouldn't today's improviser utilize this treasury of harmonic material when improvising?

Literal Borrowing

One of the most renowned and certainly most important composers of piano music was Frédéric Chopin. His pieces are some of the most revered in all of musical history for their beauty and construction. Chopin's Waltz in D♭ Major, Op. 64, No. 1 ("The Minute Waltz") is the most famous of his waltzes. Take a moment to play through the first 20 measures below:

Since the waltz was a standard compositional form in the nineteenth century, the LH progression was one that Chopin himself had borrowed from other composers of the period. Memorize the following progression taken from measures 5–12:

Exercise 22-2: Improvising Over a Borrowed Harmony

Choosing a scale to improvise over this progression is quite easy. The D♭ major scale works well with the D♭ major chord and the A♭ Mixolydian scale works best with the A♭ dominant 7th chord. Since both scales are composed of the same notes, improvising through the passage with the D♭ major scale is simple.

Play the following example that uses rhythmic repetition and appoggiatura. Then, use all available tools with the D♭ major scale to improvise over the harmony borrowed from Chopin's waltz.

D♭

A♭7

D♭

A♭7

improvise ⟶

Revising a Borrowed Harmony

Gymnopédie No. 1 by Erik Satie is a modern-sounding piece that provides a simple harmonic framework that can be borrowed and revised. Take a moment to play through the first 12 measures below. Notice that the harmony is composed of only two chords—Gmaj⁷ and Dmaj⁷.

For the following exercise, play the LH notes as written, but (with apologies to Satie) change the time signature to 4/4. This allows the player to break free from the strong 3/4 pulse and the compelling melodic line presented by the composer.

Exercise 22-3: Borrowing Satie's Harmony

1. Play through the following revised LH harmony in 4/4 time:

2. Choosing a scale for RH improvisation is quite simple for this harmony. The D major scale works beautifully over both chords. Play through the following example below and then use all improvising tools to create new melodies:

Creating Representative Harmony

One of the many composers of beautiful, lush harmonies is Alexander Scriabin. Play through the first eight measures of his Prelude in E Major, Op. 11, No. 9.

Within this lovely passage is a rich harmony waiting to be borrowed. But the literal LH notes do not offer a simple harmonic backdrop for RH improvisation. Consequently, it is helpful to adapt a "representative" harmony for this purpose. To do this, it is important to understand the harmonic structure of the passage first. The melody and harmony can be written as follows:

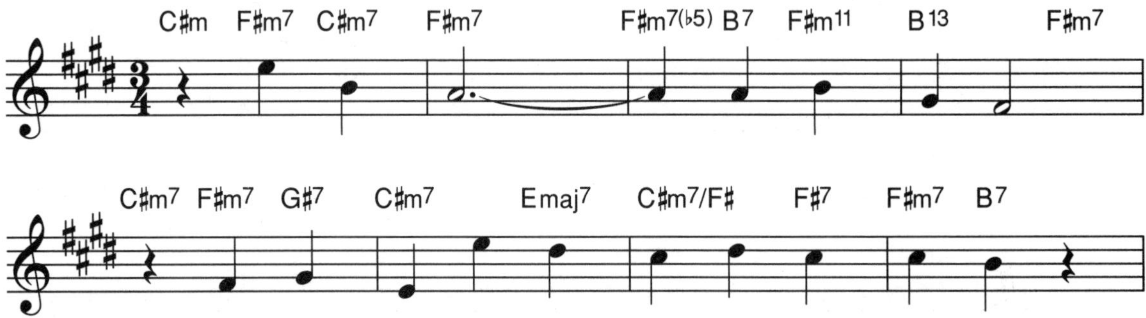

Just viewing this framework may not provide enough information to create a representative harmony. It may be necessary to acquire a deeper familiarity with the passage and its harmonic content first. Doing this will allow a player to extract notes or clusters that represent the harmony. The next exercise will explore this process.

Exercise 22-4: Creating a Representative Harmony

1. Play through the passage repeatedly until it feels thoroughly comfortable.

2. Simply knowing the notes does not guarantee an understanding of the harmony. Play through the passage again with the goal of "seeing" the harmony that resides within the notes. Proceed slowly, and try to visualize the chord occurring on each beat. Repeat this step until the harmony is clearly perceptible.

3. Repeat step 2 without the melody notes. As only the inner voices and the bass are played, imagine ways to consolidate these notes into LH chords or note clusters that represent the harmony.
4. When ready, break free from the actual notes of the passage and play the LH chords or clusters imagined in step 3. Play through the following example that offers one way to voice the harmony:

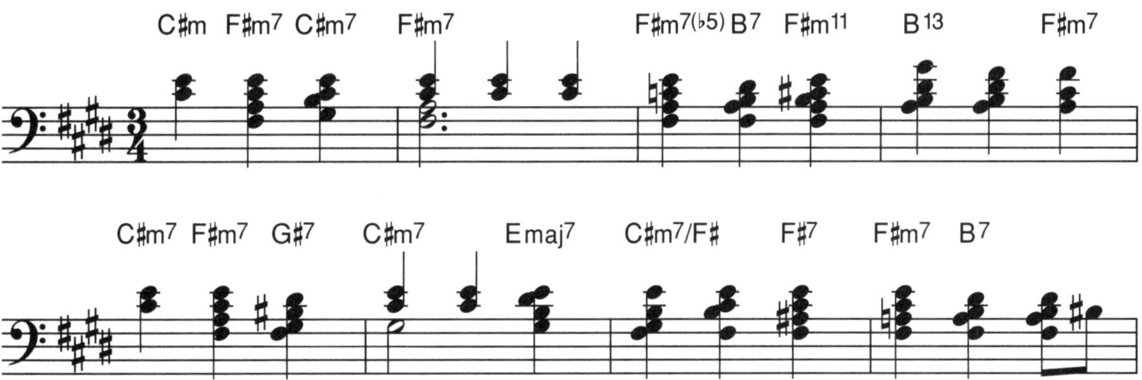

5. Return to this exercise periodically and discover new ways to express the harmony and challenge creativity.

There are innumerable ways to represent the harmony with the LH. Don't feel compelled to find one perfect progression. Experimentation will enlarge the harmonic vocabulary. Remember, the improviser has the freedom to either stay within the prescribed harmony or venture outside it. In this case, Scriabin's harmony has only been borrowed. One should not feel bound by it—exercise the freedom to explore.

Improvising Over a Representative Harmony

Having developed a LH harmony based on the Scriabin prelude, use this harmony to improvise with the RH. This exercise offers an opportunity to review the Scale Choice Questions from chapter 8:

1. What is the primary tonal focus of the passage?

    a. Does the way the passage begins and ends suggest tonal focus?

    b. Does the key signature indicate a particular tonal focus?

    c. Are there harmonic resolutions that indicate tonal focus?

    Apply these questions to the Scriabin prelude. It should be fairly clear that the tonal focus is either C♯ minor or E major. The dominant chord at the end of the passage (B7) suggests that E major is the best choice; but either way, the notes for improvisation are the same. Once the tonal focus is determined, the next question can be answered:

2. Is there a scale based on the tonal focus that can generally accommodate all chords in the passage?

    The answer is yes. The primary chords are shown below with the appropriate scales:

    Table 22-5: Appropriate Scales for the Scriabin Passage

Chord	Appropriate Scale
C♯m7	C♯ natural minor (uses notes of the E major scale)
F♯m7	F♯ Dorian (uses the notes of the E major scale)
B7	B Mixolydian (uses the notes of the E major scale)
Emaj7	E major scale

    Because all the appropriate scales utilize the notes of the E major scale, use this scale to accommodate the entire passage. Now that the best choice of scale has been determined, the last question can be addressed:

3. What alterations are required to accommodate other chords in the passage?

    The table below explains the exceptions:

    Table 22-6: Scale Alterations for the Scriabin Passage

Chord	Chord Location	Alterations
F♯m7(♭5)	Measure 3, Beat 1	Use C♮ and D♮
G♯7	Measure 5, Beat 3	Use B♯
F♯7	Measure 7, Beat 3	Use A♯

    When passing by these chords, a slight alteration may be all that is needed to navigate the passage smoothly while using the notes of the E major scale as a guide.

Exercise 22-5: Improvising Over a Representative Harmony

1. Play through the following harmony in which all the notes are consolidated into the LH. Try to "see" the harmony while playing. Repeat this passage until it can be played by memory.

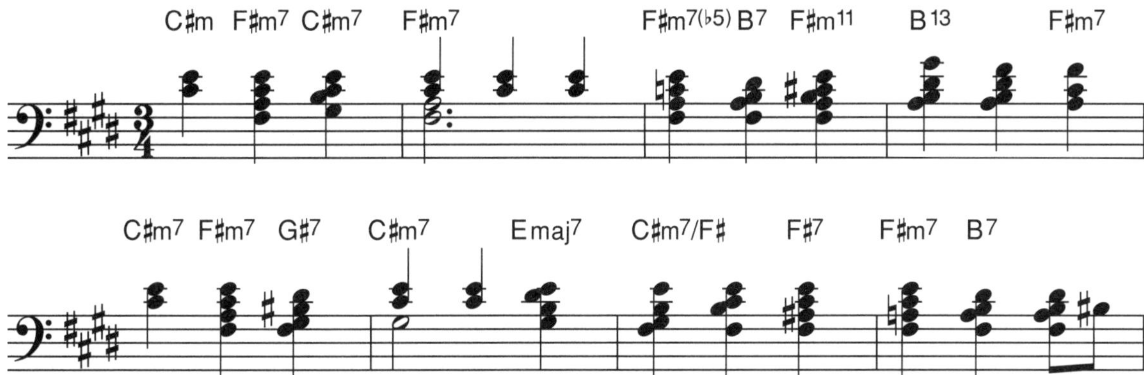

2. Once the LH harmony is memorized, play through the sample improvisation below and then experiment with the RH using the E major scale and alterations from table 22-6 when required. If this is too difficult, have a friend play the LH part.

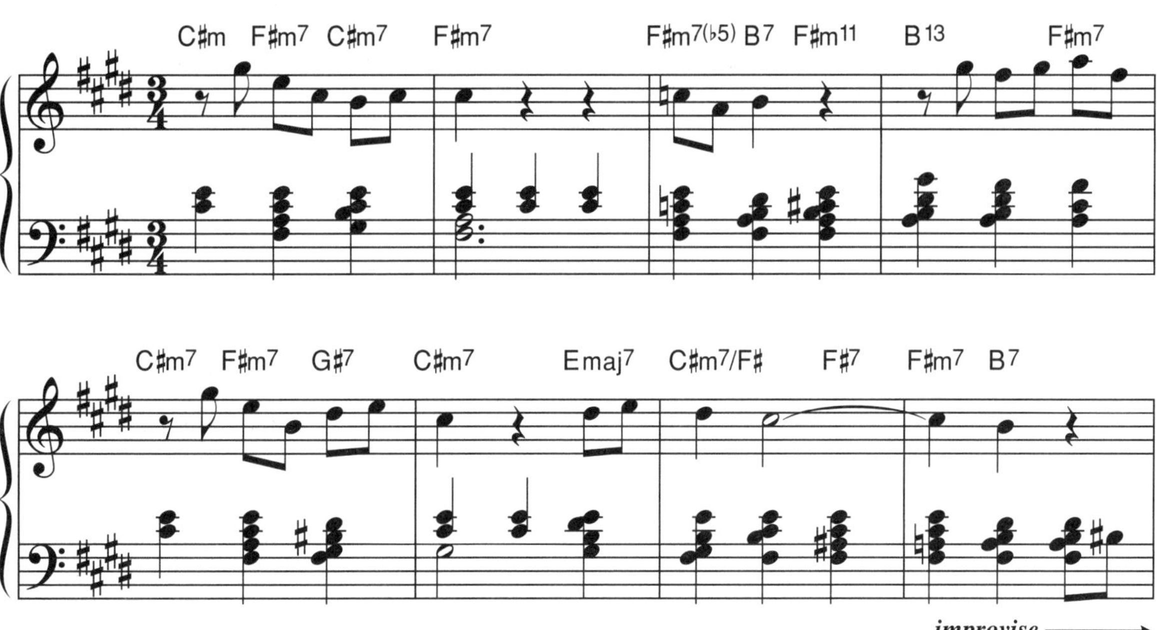

Key Points from This Chapter

- Improvisation can apply to harmony as well as melody.
- While harmony usually dictates the choice of scales, the choice of scales can sometimes dictate harmony.
- Harmony can be borrowed, revised or adapted for use with improvised melodies.

Section 4 Other Styles of Improvisation

So far, this text has focused primarily on the music of the baroque, classical and romantic periods. That is because most traditional music study is based upon the music of those eras. However, improvisation is not limited to any particular period or genre. It can be applied to any form of music, using the same tools learned in the preceding chapters.

This final section will venture into a completely different stylistic genre—jazz (chapters 23–25), and then embark on a brief evolutionary tour of improvisation across the ages (chapter 26).

CHAPTER 23 Jazz Improvisation, Part 1: Rhythm

A book about improvisation would not be complete without some mention of the art form known as jazz. After all, improvisation is the very essence of jazz. The genre was born of the innate desire to explore the wonders of spontaneous creation. But since there is already a wealth of existing instructional material on jazz improvisation, this book will not explore the topic in great depth. The following three chapters will describe some of the basic tenets of jazz and explain how to translate the tools already learned into the jazz idiom.

Many people reading this book may think they could never play jazz—as if it were a foreign language. But they may not realize that they already speak the language. In reality, everything learned so far in this book applies directly to jazz improvisation. Every scale, melodic tool (adjacent neighbors, skipping, jumping, meandering, silence, repetition, borrowing, etc.), pattern, transition method and scalar mode can be effectively used in the creation of jazz. To become a jazz player, all one needs to know are the nuances that make jazz different from traditional music. The three primary points of differentiation are rhythmic interpretation, harmony and forms.

Rhythmic Interpretation

"It don't mean a thing if it ain't got that…exacting rhythmic precision."

While this phrase might pertain loosely to a fugue by J. S. Bach, it wouldn't necessarily apply to a tune by Dave Brubeck. When Duke Ellington and Irving Mills penned that great lyric back in the 1930s, the "thing" to which they were referring was "swing." For jazz to be jazz, it has to swing.

But what makes something swing? First, take a look at this question from an academic perspective. Play the following jazz tune as written without trying to swing:

This is exactly how a tune might appear in a typical fake book (a compendium of classic tunes commonly used by jazz players). But when played in straight eighth notes, does the tune swing? The answer is definitively no.

Then, why is it written that way? The eighth notes represent jazz shorthand. When jazz players gather together to "jam," they typically play without any note-for-note written arrangement; instead, they play with something called a lead sheet that contains a basic melody and a set of chords (e.g., *Whiplash*). Perhaps because the precise notation is too cumbersome to write down, or fearing that it might extract the "soul" from a phrase, jazz composers have elected to write straight eighth notes as shorthand with an implicit command to "make it swing."

What does swing look like on paper? Unless told otherwise, jazz players interpret each pair of consecutive eighth notes with a triplet feel as follows: ♫ is played as ♩ ♪ (triplet, 3)

Play through the following revised version of *Whiplash* written with traditional notation:

An immediate change in character can be felt when the concept of swing is applied. But simply playing this rhythm precisely as written above does not guarantee that it will swing. That's because the secret component of swing is not accuracy, but rather the humanness of the performance.

Lessons from Dance

Imagine seeing a couple doing the foxtrot on the dance floor. An observer may notice that the man's steps are exactly on the beat and never wavering, but he somehow looks a bit stiff and uncomfortable. His rhythmic perfection doesn't make him a smooth dancer.

Next to him is another man whose movements are reminiscent of Fred Astaire. This dancer is relaxed and comfortable. His style conveys a sense of confidence and genuine enjoyment. While studying his movements more closely, it is surprising to find that his steps are not rhythmically perfect. Of course, most are right on the beat. But some are just a touch early, while others are ever-so-slightly late. On the whole, he is a very rhythmic and precise dancer. Yet, the subtle nudging and stretching of time in the placement of his steps (the humanness) gives him that intangible air of "cool."

The same concept applies to jazz improvisation. Jazz players rely on their strong sense of rhythm. One might listen to great jazz players and conclude that they play with exceptional precision. But when listening more closely, one will hear the same subtle nudging and stretching of time in the placement of notes that gives the music character and makes it swing.

Listening

From this point on, words fall short in attempting to describe what constitutes swing. One cannot see music swing on paper. To understand it fully, a person must listen carefully to great players and imitate their style and feel. This process will take some time and effort, but it is well worth the investment. When a player is really swinging with a tune, the feeling is magical.

Exercise 23-1: Learning by Imitation

1. Find a recording of a favorite jazz artist, and select a tune that really swings. Then, do the following:

    a. Listen carefully and identify the rhythmic elements that make the music swing.

    b. Select a particular passage and try to imitate the rhythmic elements on the piano. (If possible, play the same notes that the artist played on the recording.)

    c. Make a simple recording of the imitation. On playback, decide whether or not it swings. If it doesn't, do more listening and imitating and then record again.

    d. Repeat this process with several passages from the artist recording until a good sense of swing is acquired.

2. Apply the skills from step 1 to *Whiplash*. For now, disregard the harmony and concentrate on the melody. See if it swings better now than it did before. If not, repeat step 1.

3. Now apply the swing feel to the following jazz tune:

Ode to Glenn

Thurmond

Improvising in the Jazz Style

Once a sense of swing has been acquired, the transition from traditional to jazz improvisation is quite easy. Simply take the same improvising tools learned thus far and apply them to the jazz style. This section will walk through the process step by step.

Remember the way the LH Alberti bass was used to help build an improvisation toolbox in earlier chapters? The Alberti pattern provided a simple, repeated accompaniment that allowed the player to focus on RH improvisations. In jazz, the equivalent of the Alberti bass are classic boogie-woogie patterns as shown below:

Boogie-Woogie Pattern 1

Boogie-Woogie Pattern 2

Play through these familiar patterns several times until they feel comfortable. Begin slowly and focus on making them swing (this may require relaxation rather than deep concentration). Once they swing, commit the patterns to memory. This will provide the foundation for the following explorations into jazz improvisation.

Exercise 23-2: Improvising in the Jazz Style

1. Once the boogie-woogie patterns are memorized, begin improvising with just one note (as done in the *Foundations* section). Remember that the goal is not rhythmic accuracy, but rather to make it swing. Begin playing either of the two boogie-woogie patterns in the LH; then, add the RH part below. Play through the example several times and then experiment with short phrases.

2. Try some repetitive phrases that use multiple notes. Don't make the melodies too complicated at this point. Keep them very simple and focus on making them swing. Play through each of the following examples several times and then experiment:

Example 1

Example 2

Example 4 is a tricky one. It uses the same repeated patterns as the previous examples, but adds some harmonizing notes for added color. Take it very slowly the first time. Then, gradually speed up each subsequent time it is played.

Example 4

Using Scales and Other Tools

Although the chords shown in the boogie-woogie harmony are all major chords, jazz tradition allows them to be converted into dominant 7th chords. With this in mind, the appropriate scale mode for soloing is the Mixolydian mode. From the earlier study of modes, recall that the Mixolydian scale is a major scale with a lowered 7th. In the keys of C, F and G, the Mixolydian scales are written as follows:

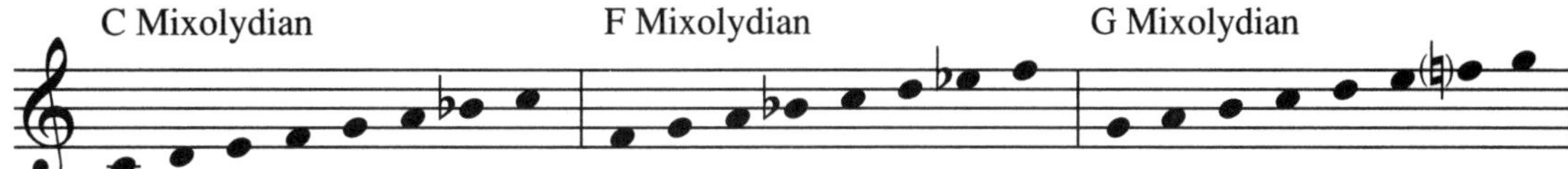

The Mixolydian scale also provides an effective scalar basis for improvising over the boogie-woogie patterns.

Exercise 23-3: Improvising with the Mixolydian Mode

1. While playing a boogie-woogie pattern in the LH, play through the following exercise based upon the Mixolydian scale (don't forget to swing the eighth notes):

Play through this step several times until the Mixolydian scales feel comfortable in this style. Don't stop until it swings.

2. After playing step 1 several times, the straight scalar line may sound tiresome. That's probably because the other available improvising tools haven't been used. The application of skipping, jumping, adjacent neighbors and repetition can add tremendous color to improvisation.

   With a boogie-woogie pattern in the LH, play the following RH example very slowly the first time to make sure it swings. Then, gradually increase speed as it is repeated.

3. Use all of the improvising tools (skipping, jumping, adjacent neighbors, repetition, etc.) to create colorful melodies over the boogie-woogie patterns.

Key Points from This Chapter

- "It don't mean a thing if it ain't got that...swing!"
- In the jazz style, consecutive eighth notes are interpreted with a triplet feel: ♫ = ♩♪ (triplet)
- Exacting rhythmic precision does not necessarily create swing.
- The best way to acquire a sense of swing is to listen to great players and imitate their style and feel.

CHAPTER 24 Jazz Improvisation, Part 2: Harmony

The second general point of differentiation between jazz and traditional improvisation is harmony. Jazz players have always used an alternative set of guidelines for creating harmony. Their goal has been to create chords with a different type of color and depth than offered by traditional chords. This section will explore the basic harmonic guidelines that have formed the foundation for much of jazz in the twentieth century.

Tone Types for Creating Voicings

Jazz keyboard players devote much of their LH playing to a chord form called the four-note voicing. In a jazz trio, the pianist intentionally and respectfully leaves the responsibility of bass notes to the bassist. The drummer provides the primary rhythmic color (a role also shared by the other players). The role of the pianist is to add harmonic color with the LH chords (called voicings) and melodic improvisation (soloing) with the RH.

There are two types of tones used in the creation of four-note voicings—identifying tones and color tones. Both are required to give a chord identity and character. The following sections will explore the use of these tones for major 7th, minor 7th, and dominant 7th chords.

Major 7th Voicings

Consider the following chord:

Traditional music commonly utilizes this exact form (and its inversions) in the creation of harmony. The jazz player in a trio setting will usually express this chord as a four-note voicing using the following steps:

1. **Remove the root:** Assume that the bass player will play the bass note (in the B♭maj7 chord, remove B♭).
2. **Select the two identifying tones of the chord:** Identifying tones are always the 3rd and the 7th intervals from the root tone. They will be major or minor depending on the type of chord desired. For major 7th chords, the following intervals are used:
   a. The major 3rd (D) identifies the chord as major rather than minor.
   b. The major 7th (A) identifies the chord as a major 7th rather than a dominant 7th.

3. **Select the two color tones:** The color tones for major 7th chords are the 9th and 6th. For the B♭maj7 chord, the following intervals are used:
   a. The major 9th (C) is the all-purpose color tone. It is played with all voicings.
   b. The major 6th (G) adds vibrancy. (The perfect 5th also can be used at one's discretion.)

These steps result in the following colorful voicing. Play the B♭ bass note with the LH and the four-note B♭maj7 voicing with the RH:

Just as traditional chords have inversions, so do four-note voicings. The root form and three inversions are shown below. Play each one with the RH while playing the bass note with the LH.

With the B♭maj7 voicing, the two most common forms (A and B) are shown below.* The B form is shown in both available octaves.

Table 24-1: Common Voicings for the B♭ Major 7th Chord

A Form	B♭maj7	B Form	B♭maj7
6th	G	9th	C
3rd	D	7th	A
9th	C	6th	G
7th	A	3rd	D

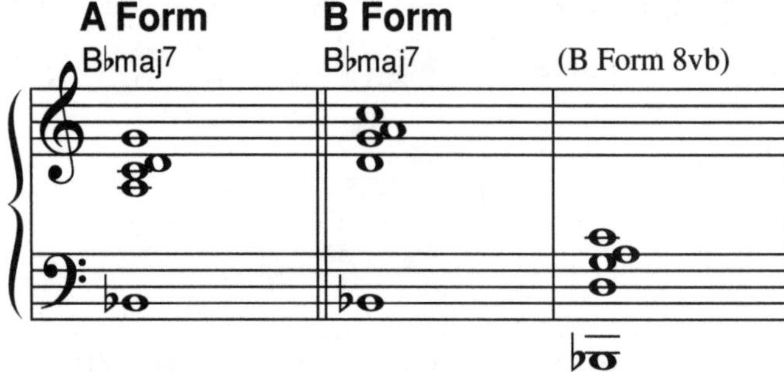

The other two inversions can also be used. However, the close intervals (adjacent notes) are more dissonant, making those forms less pleasant to the ear.

* These form names were developed by John Mehegan in *Jazz Improvisation 4: Contemporary Piano Styles* (New York: Amsco Publications, 1965).

Voicing Range

There is an optimal range for four-note voicings. When played too low, some voicings sound gruff and unpleasant. When played too high, they sound too shrill and also limit the number of notes available for solo playing with the RH. For the best tonal character, choose the four-note forms that fall within the following range:

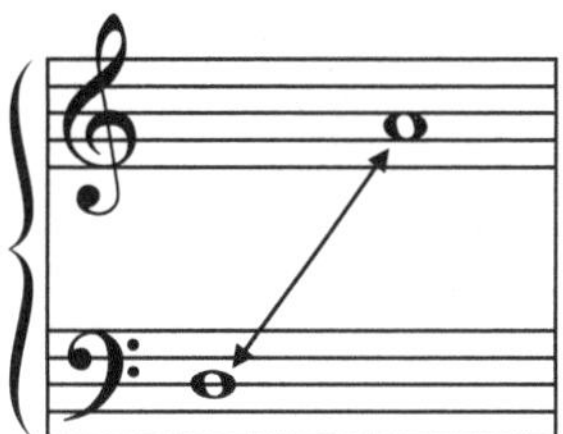

In the key of B♭, the A form voicing would normally be played, since it falls directly in the middle of the suggested voicing range. The B form is acceptable, but tends to sound slightly gruff in the lower octave and too bright in the upper octave.

For comparison, consider the Dmaj7 chord. In the example below, the B form is the preferred choice, since it falls in the center of the suggested voicing range. The A form tends to be too bright in the upper octave and too gruff when played an octave lower.

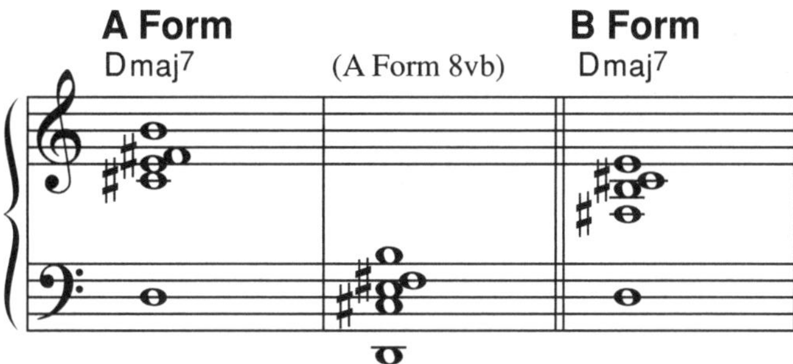

The following table will be useful in finding the four-note major 7th voicings in any key. The notes shown in bold represent the preferred voicing form. In some cases, either form is acceptable.

Table 24-2: Major 7th Voicings

	A FORM				B FORM			
Chords	7th	9th	3rd	6th	3rd	6th	7th	9th
Cmaj7	B	D	E	A	**E**	**A**	**B**	**D**
C♯/D♭maj7	B♯	D♯	E♯	A♯	**E♯**	**A♯**	**B♯**	**D♯**
Dmaj7	C♯	E	F♯	B	**F♯**	**B**	**C♯**	**E**
E♭maj7	D	F	G	C	**G**	**C**	**D**	**F**
Emaj7	D♯	F♯	G♯	C♯	**G♯**	**C♯**	**D♯**	**F♯**
Fmaj7	**E**	**G**	**A**	**D**	**A**	**D**	**E**	**G**
F♯/G♭maj7	**E♯**	**G♯**	**A♯**	**D♯**	A♯	D♯	E♯	G♯
Gmaj7	**F♯**	**A**	**B**	**E**	B	E	F♯	A
A♭maj7	**G**	**B♭**	**C**	**F**	C	F	G	B♭
Amaj7	**G♯**	**B**	**C♯**	**F♯**	C♯	F♯	G♯	B
B♭maj7	**A**	**C**	**D**	**G**	D	G	A	C
Bmaj7	**A♯**	**C♯**	**D♯**	**G♯**	D♯	G♯	A♯	C♯

Additional Color

When the RH is not soloing, it can be used to add color to major 7th voicings. Typically, two or three RH notes are played in the octave above the LH voicing. These notes are selected at the player's discretion to suit the moment. The most common RH color tones are the 3rd, 5th, 7th and 9th. Below are a few examples for the B♭maj7 voicing:

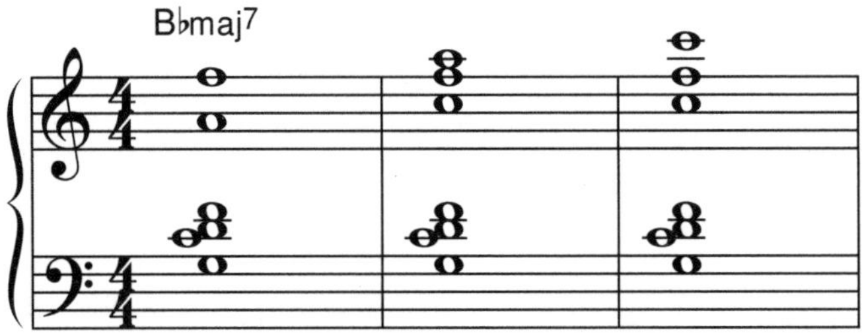

Exercise 24-1: Creating Major 7th Voicings

Use the steps below to create four-note major 7th voicings for the following chords:

Cmaj7 Dmaj7 Fmaj7 Gmaj7

1. For each chord, eliminate the bass note.
2. Locate the appropriate 3rd and 7th (identifying tones).
3. Add the 6th and 9th (color tones).
4. Play both A and B forms of the voicings for all four chords.

A player who is serious about learning jazz will want to learn and memorize these four-note voicings in all 12 keys.

Five-Note Quartal Voicing for Major 7th Chords

There is an alternative way to utilize the RH for additional color when it is not soloing. With the B♭maj7 chord, the notes can be spread out in perfect 4th intervals to form the very pleasant five-note voicing below:

The shortcut method for creating this beautiful major 7th voicing is to start with the note a half-step below the root (in this case, A). Then, add successive ascending perfect 4th intervals until a complete five-note quartal voicing is formed. The following table shows the notes for the voicings of each major 7th chord.

Table 24-3: Five-Note Quartal Voicing for Major 7th Chords

Chord	Five-Note Quartal Voicing				
Cmaj7	B	E	A	D	G
C♯/D♭maj7	B♯	E♯	A♯	D♯	G♯
Dmaj7	C♯	F♯	B	E	A
E♭maj7	D	G	C	F	B♭
Emaj7	D♯	G♯	C♯	F♯	B
Fmaj7	E	A	D	G	C
F♯/G♭maj7	E♯	A♯	D♯	G♯	C♯
Gmaj7	F♯	B	E	A	D
A♭maj7	G	C	F	B♭	E♭
Amaj7	G♯	C♯	F♯	B	E
B♭maj7	A	D	G	C	F
Bmaj7	A♯	D♯	G♯	C♯	F♯

Exercise 24-2: Creating the Five-Note Quartal Voicing for Major 7th Chords

Using the same four chords from exercise 24-1, create five-note quartal voicings by following the steps below:

Cmaj7 **Dmaj7** **Fmaj7** **Gmaj7**

1. Locate the note one half step below the root.
2. Add successive perfect 4th intervals to complete the five-note voicing using both hands.
3. Over time, try to learn and memorize these five-note quartal voicings in all 12 keys.

Minor 7th Voicings

The same guidelines used for creating major 7th voicings apply to minor 7th voicings. Follow the steps below to create a four-note voicing for the Dm7 chord:

1. **Remove the root:** Assume that the bass player will play the bass note (in this case, remove D).
2. **Select the two identifying tones of the chord:** Identifying tones are always the 3rd and 7th intervals from the root tone. For all minor 7th voicings, the 3rd and 7th are minor. For a Dm7 chord, the following intervals are used:
   a. The minor 3rd (F) identifies the chord as minor rather than major.
   b. The minor 7th (C) identifies the chord as a minor 7th rather than a major 7th.

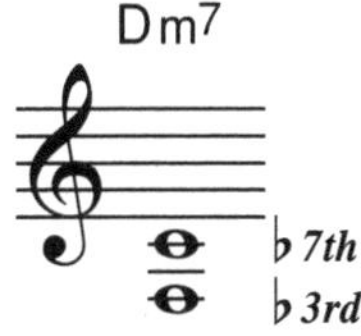

3. **Select the two color tones:** The color tones for minor 7th voicings are the 9th and 5th intervals from the root tone. For the Dm7 chord, the following intervals are used:
    a. The major 9th (E) is the all-purpose color tone. It is played with all voicings.
    b. The perfect 5th (A) is part of the basic Dm7 chord but is still considered a color tone rather than an identifying tone (since it doesn't provide critical harmonic information that identifies the chord). The 6th is not used as a color tone for minor 7th voicings because it alters the basic character of the minor chord.

Having selected these notes, the two most common voicing forms for the Dm7 chord are as follows:

Table 24-4: Common Voicings for the D Minor 7th Chord

A Form	Dm7	B Form	Dm7
5th	A	9th	E
min 3rd	F	min 7th	C
9th	E	5th	A
min 7th	C	min 3rd	F

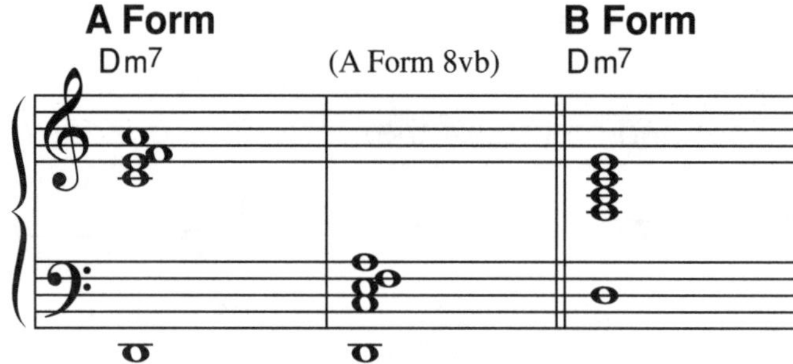

Once again, the optimum voicing range determines which form is best to use. With the Dm7 chord, both the A and B forms will work. But the B form is optimal, since it falls right in the middle of the suggested voicing range. The A form in the upper octave tends to be too bright and limits the keyboard area for RH soloing while the lower octave sounds too gruff.

For comparison, consider the B♭m7 chord. In this key, the A form is preferred. The B form is too high or too low in either octave as shown below:

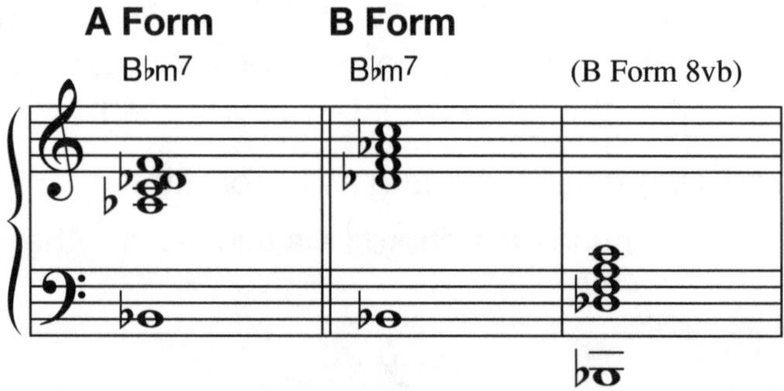

The following table can be useful in finding the four-note minor 7th voicings in all 12 keys. The notes shown in bold represent the preferred voicing form. In some cases, either form is acceptable.

Table 24-5: Minor 7th Voicings

	A FORM				B FORM			
Chord	**min 7th**	**9th**	**min 3rd**	**5th**	**min 3rd**	**5th**	**min 7th**	**9th**
Cm7	**B♭**	**D**	**E♭**	**G**	**E♭**	**G**	**B♭**	**D**
C♯/D♭m7	B	D♯	E	G♯	**E**	**G♯**	**B**	**D♯**
Dm7	C	E	F	A	**F**	**A**	**C**	**E**
E♭m7	D♭	F	G♭	B♭	**G♭**	**B♭**	**D♭**	**F**
Em7	D	F♯	G	B	**G**	**B**	**D**	**F♯**
Fm7	E♭	G	A♭	C	**A♭**	**C**	**E♭**	**G**
F♯/G♭m7	**E**	**G♯**	**A**	**C♯**	A	C♯	E	G♯
Gm7	**F**	**A**	**B♭**	**D**	B♭	D	F	A
A♭m7	**G♭**	**B♭**	**C♭**	**E♭**	C♭	E♭	G♭	B♭
Am7	**G**	**B**	**C**	**E**	C	E	G	B
B♭m7	**A♭**	**C**	**D♭**	**F**	D♭	F	A♭	C
Bm7	**A**	**C♯**	**D**	**F♯**	D	F♯	A	C♯

Additional Color

When the RH is not soloing, it can add color to minor 7th voicings. In the following Dm7 voicing examples, the RH uses the 3rd, 5th, 7th, and 9th. The last example includes the 4th to create dramatic tension.

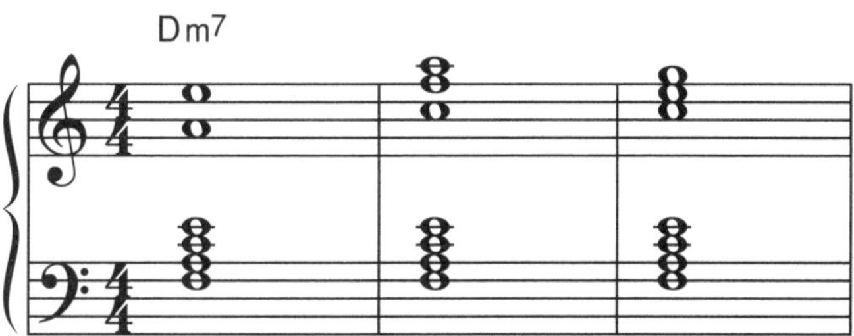

Exercise 24-3: Creating Minor 7th Voicings

Use the steps below to create four-note minor 7th voicings for the following chords:

Cm7 **Fm7** **Gm7** **Am7**

1. For each chord, eliminate the bass note.
2. Locate the two identifying tones (the minor 3rd and minor 7th).
3. Add the two color tones (the major 9th and perfect 5th).
4. Play both A and B forms of the voicings for all four chords.

Again, to evolve into a serious jazz player, it is important to learn and memorize these four-note minor 7th voicings in all 12 keys.

Five-Note Quartal Voicing for Minor 7th Chords

Five-note quartal voicings are slightly different for minor 7th chords. The shortcut for creating them is as follows:

1. Locate the note a perfect 5th above the root (in D minor, this note is A).

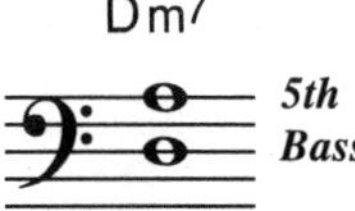

2. Add three successive ascending perfect 4th intervals (in D minor, the notes are D, G and C). This provides four-note quartal harmony.

3. This step is where the minor 7th voicing differs from the major 7th five-note quartal voicing. The fifth note is a major 3rd above the last note in the voicing (in this case, E).

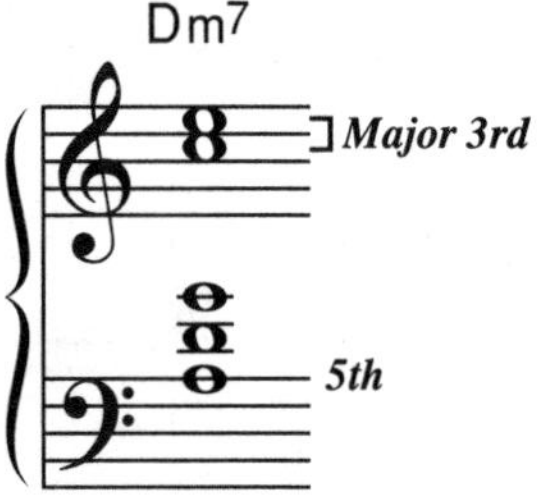

The result is a colorful five-note quartal voicing that can be used whenever the RH is not soloing. This formula will work with all 12 minor 7th chords. The table below indicates the notes for each chord:

Table 24-6: Five-Note Quartal Voicing for Minor 7th Chords

Chord	Five-Note Quartal Voicing				
Cm7	G	C	F	B♭	D
C♯/D♭m7	G♯	C♯	F♯	B	D♯
Dm7	A	D	G	C	E
E♭m7	B♭	E♭	A♭	D♭	F
Em7	B	E	A	D	F♯
Fm7	C	F	B♭	E♭	G
F♯/G♭m7	C♯	F♯	B	E	G♯
Gm7	D	G	C	F	A
A♭m7	E♭	A♭	D♭	G♭	B♭
Am7	E	A	D	G	B
B♭m7	F	B♭	E♭	A♭	C
Bm7	F♯	B	E	A	C♯

Exercise 24-4: Creating the Five-Note Quartal Voicing for Minor 7th Chords

Using the steps below, locate the five-note quartal voicing for each of the following chords:

Cm7 **Fm7** **Gm7** **Am7**

1. Locate the note a perfect 5th above the root.
2. Add three successive perfect 4th intervals (the RH will be needed).
3. Add the major 3rd above the last tone to create the fifth note in the voicing.

Over time, try to learn and memorize the five-note quartal voicings in all 12 keys.

Dominant 7th Voicings

The same guidelines used for major 7th and minor 7th voicings can be used for creating dominant 7th voicings. Follow the steps below to create a four-note voicing for the C7 chord:

1. **Remove the root:** Assume that the bass player will play the bass note (in this case, remove C).
2. **Select the two identifying tones of the chord:** Identifying tones are always the 3rd and the 7th intervals from the root tone. For the C7 chord, the following intervals are used:
   a. The major 3rd (E) identifies the chord as major rather than minor.
   b. The minor 7th (B♭) identifies the chord as a dominant 7th rather than a major 7th.

3. **Select the two color tones:** The color tones for dominant 7th chords are the 9th and 6th. For the C7 chord, the notes are D and A.

The two dominant 7th voicing forms are as follows:

Table 24-7: Common Voicings for the C7 Chord

A Form	C7	B Form	C7
6th	A	9th	D
3rd	E	min 7th	B♭
9th	D	6th	A
min 7th	B♭	3rd	E

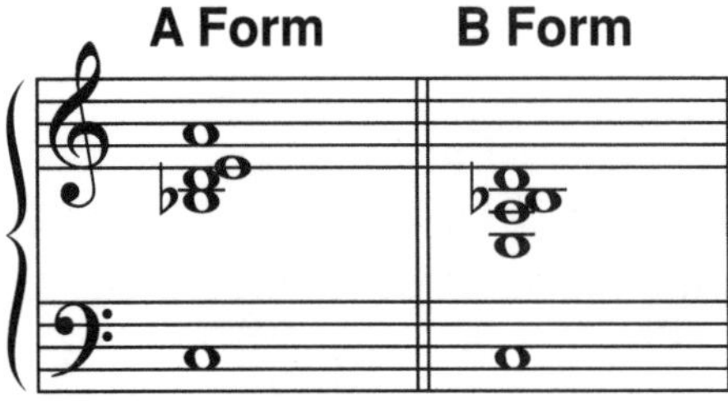

In each key, select the form that falls within the optimal range. In the case of the C7 voicing above, either form falls within the acceptable range. The table below shows the notes for all dominant 7th voicings in both forms. The preferred form of each chord is shown in bold.

Table 24-8: Dominant 7th Voicings

	A FORM				B FORM			
Chord	min 7th	9th	3rd	6th	3rd	6th	min 7th	9th
C7	**B♭**	**D**	**E**	**A**	**E**	**A**	**B♭**	**D**
C♯/D♭7	B	D♯	E♯	A♯	**E♯**	**A♯**	**B**	**D♯**
D7	C	E	F♯	B	**F♯**	**B**	**C**	**E**
E♭7	D♭	F	G	C	**G**	**C**	**D♭**	**F**
E7	D	F♯	G♯	C♯	**G♯**	**C♯**	**D**	**F♯**
F7	E♭	G	A	D	**A**	**D**	**E♭**	**G**
F♯/G♭7	**E**	**G♯**	**A♯**	**D♯**	A♯	D♯	E	G♯
G7	**F**	**A**	**B**	**E**	B	E	F	A
A♭7	**G♭**	**B♭**	**C**	**F**	C	F	G♭	B♭
A7	**G**	**B**	**C♯**	**F♯**	C♯	F♯	G	B
B♭7	**A♭**	**C**	**D**	**G**	D	G	A♭	C
B7	**A**	**C♯**	**D♯**	**G♯**	D♯	G♯	A	C♯

Additional Color

When the RH is not soloing, it can add color to dominant 7th voicings. In the following C7 voicing examples, the RH uses the root tone, 3rd, 5th and 9th:

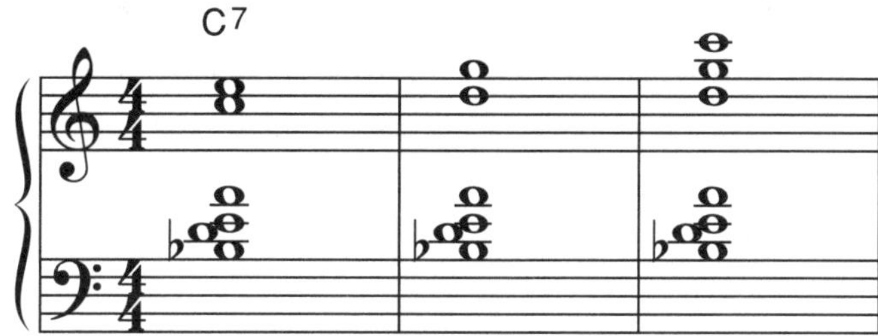

Exercise 24-5: Creating Dominant 7th Voicings

Use the steps below to create four-note dominant 7th voicings for the following chords:

D7 **F7** **G7** **A♭7**

1. For each chord, eliminate the bass note.
2. Locate the two identifying tones (the major 3rd and minor 7th).
3. Add the two color tones (the major 9th and 6th).
4. Play both A and B forms of the voicings for all four chords.

Over time, learn and memorize these four-note dominant 7th voicings in all 12 keys.

Summary of Voicing Forms

The player who has worked through the voicing exercises for all three types of 7th chords (major, minor and dominant) should now be quite proficient in creating harmony in the jazz style. The following table will summarize the tones that make up the three types of jazz voicings:

Table 24-9: Summary of Voicing Forms

Chord Type	Identifying Tones	Color Tones	A Form	B Form
Major 7th	Major 3rd, Major 7th	9th and 6th	7th–9th–3rd–6th	3rd–6th–7th–9th
Minor 7th	Minor 3rd, Minor 7th	9th and 5th	♭7th–9th–♭3rd–5th	♭3rd–5th–♭7th–9th
Dominant 7th	Major 3rd, Minor 7th	9th and 6th	♭7th–9th–3rd–6th	3rd–6th–♭7th–9th

Exercise 24-6: Switching Between Voicing Forms

The most familiar chord progression in jazz is the ii–V–I progression consisting of the super tonic (minor), dominant (major) and tonic (major) chords in any key.* This progression offers a convenient way to practice all three voicing forms in sequence.

1. Play through and repeat the following progression in the key of C until it feels completely comfortable. A sample LH bass line is provided (but remember that the pianist always leaves the bass notes to the bass player in a trio setting).

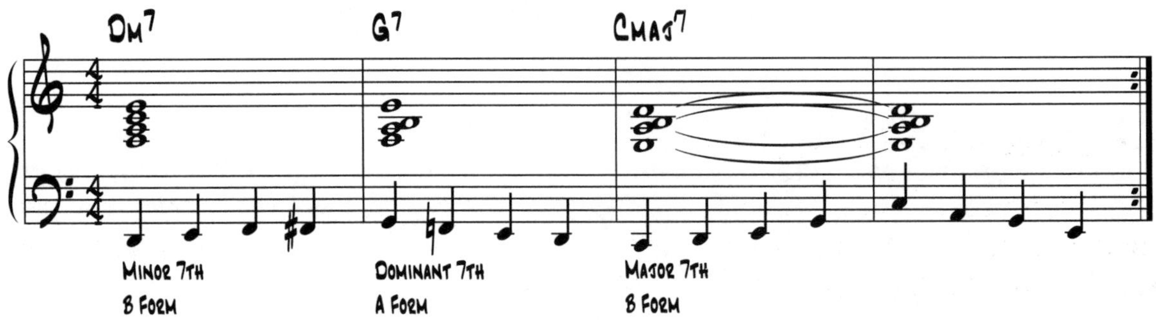

2. Play through the following two versions of the ii–V–I progression in the key of F until both versions feel comfortable. Note the change in voicing forms (from A to B or B to A) that keeps these voicings within the optimal range and ensures a smooth flow from chord to chord.

Version 1

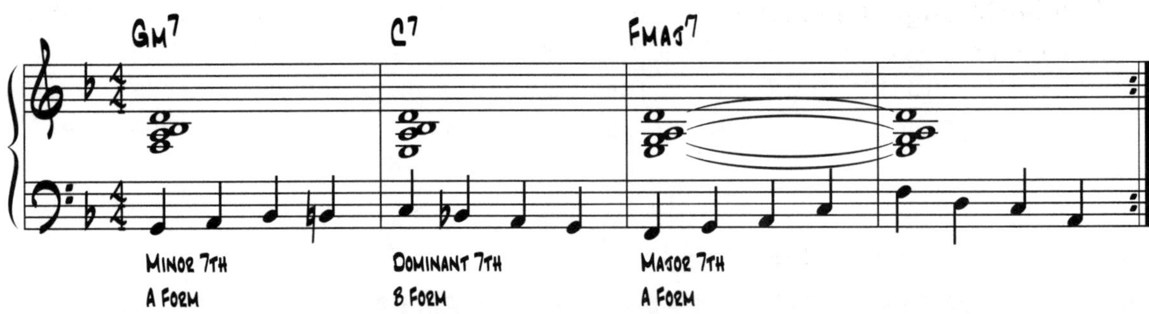

Version 2

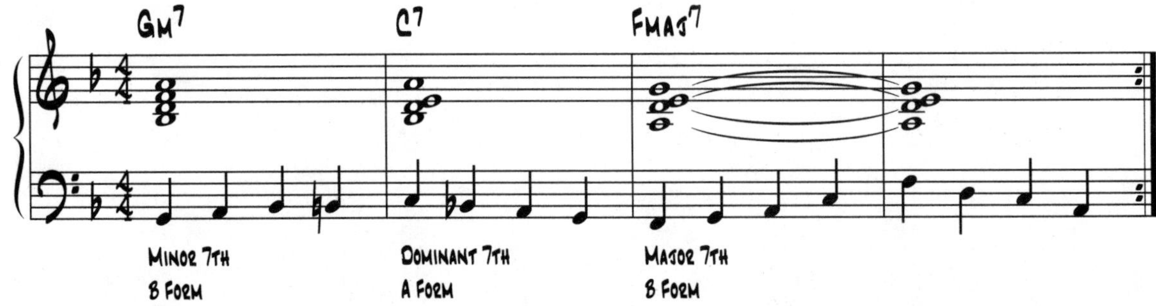

* The ii–V–I progression will be discussed in greater detail in chapter 25.

3. Try to transpose the ii–V–I progression into every key. If this seems too ambitious, try transposing the progression into the following keys first:

Table 24-10: ii–V–I Progressions

Key	ii–V–I Progression
D	Em7–A7–Dmaj7
G	Am7–D7–Gmaj7
E♭	Fm7–B♭7–E♭maj7
B♭	Cm7–F7–B♭maj7

Rhythmic Placement of Voicings

There is no set formula for the rhythmic placement of voicings. Placement is largely a matter of "feel" and experience. As always, one of the best ways to acquire this feel is to listen to recordings of great jazz pianists and emulate their playing.

Playing voicings (also referred to as "comping") contributes greatly to the sense of swing in an ensemble. As described earlier, the subtle nuances of placement—sometimes ever-so-slightly early or late—can greatly affect whether or not one's playing has a swinging character. This skill is best learned through listening and experimentation. The following exercise will introduce the most common rhythmic placement for jazz voicings.

Exercise 24-7: Voicing Placement

1. Play through the following comping rhythm, which is an example of common voicing placement, and then transpose it into various keys:

2. Try the same voicing placement from step 1 over a more active bass line. This may seem difficult at first, but it is worth the effort. Start slowly and gradually increase speed. Be sure to swing the eighth notes in the bass line.

3. Play through the alternative voicing placement below and then transpose it into various keys:

Again, there are no specific rules regarding voicing placement. The general guidelines are to:

- keep it simple (i.e., don't overplay).
- contribute to the rhythmic "groove" of a piece in partnership with the drummer and bassist.

Because voicing placement is essentially a blank canvas for the player, it offers a tremendous opportunity for creativity.

Key Points from This Chapter

- Jazz players use different guidelines for creating chords than those used by traditional musicians.
- Four-note voicings are made up of two identifying tones (always the 3rd and 7th) and two color tones (that depend upon the type of chord).
- Five-note quartal voicings are made up primarily of perfect 4th intervals and offer a colorful alternative to four-note voicings.

CHAPTER 25 Jazz Improvisation, Part 3: Forms

Jazz tends to be played in ensembles more often than in solo situations. This is because the interaction among different players is a catalyst for creative energy and communication. The most common form of jazz ensemble for the pianist is the trio, which is composed of piano, bass and drums.

As shown in chapter 22, this format has been popular for quite some time. In the eighteenth century, the *basso continuo* revolved around a figured bass (played by the *viola de gamba*) with harmony provided by the keyboardist's selection of available chords (with the LH) and an improvised melody (with the RH). Percussion was added when appropriate. This arrangement of players and functions is quite similar to that of the jazz trio. If one were to change the chord voicings and make it swing, the result could be jazz.

This chapter will explore some of the "form" elements that one will frequently encounter in jazz playing:

- the pianist's role in a jazz trio
- left hand voicings
- scalar approaches for the ii–V–I progression
- the blues

The Pianist's Role in a Jazz Trio

In a typical trio, the role of the pianist is to make harmonic, melodic and rhythmic contributions to the ensemble. The LH plays voicings (comping) based on the chord progression. The RH provides improvised melodic material (solos) and adds color to the LH voicings. Both hands work together to add rhythmic interest and creative energy.

The first adjustment for the traditional pianist in adapting to trio playing is leaving the bass notes to the bass player. Many years of performing solo does not prepare most pianists for this mindset. Therefore, heed the first rule of jazz ensemble playing—let the bassist play the bass line.

Left Hand Voicings

The second adjustment is learning to play voicings in the LH. Chapter 24 explored all three types of basic jazz voicings using the ii–V–I progression, but they were played with the RH while the LH played the bass line. The following exercise will require the player to imagine the bass line while playing voicings with the LH.

Exercise 25-1: Playing Voicings in the Left Hand

1. Play the following ii–V–I voicings with the LH until they feel comfortable in each progression:

ii–V–I in E Major

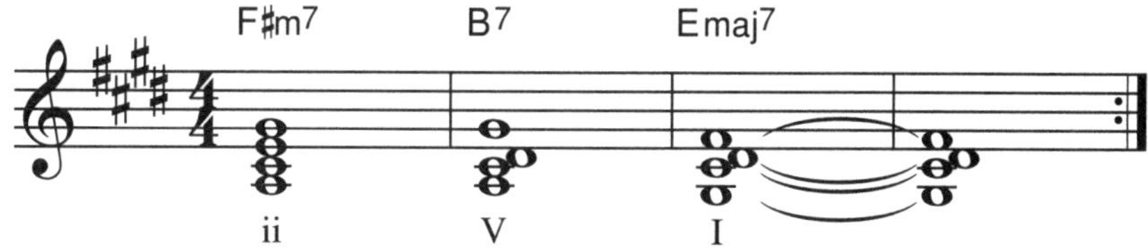

ii–V–I in G♭ Major

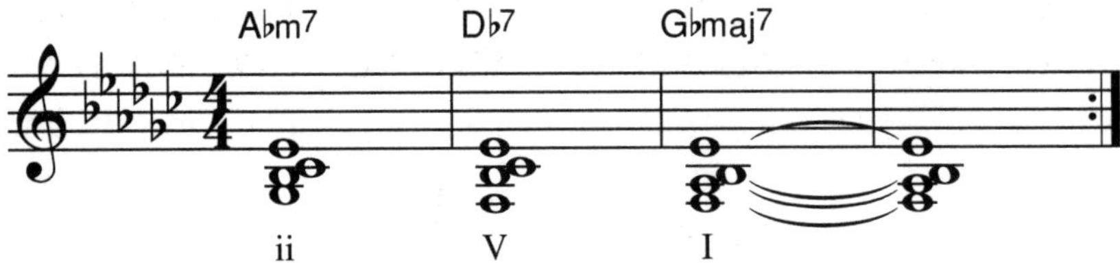

ii–V–I in B Major

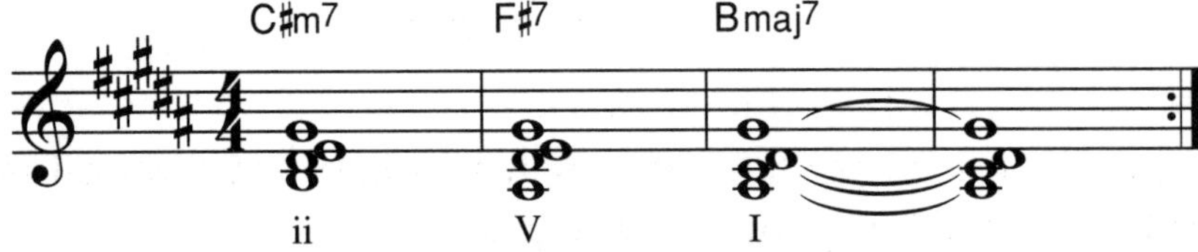

2. Transpose step 1 into the remaining nine keys.

Scalar Approaches for the ii–V–I Progression

The third adjustment for the traditional pianist is learning to solo in the jazz style with the RH while playing voicings with the LH. The following application of transitional thinking to the ii–V–I progression will make this adjustment easier.

As stated, the ii–V–I progression consists of the following chords in the key of C major:

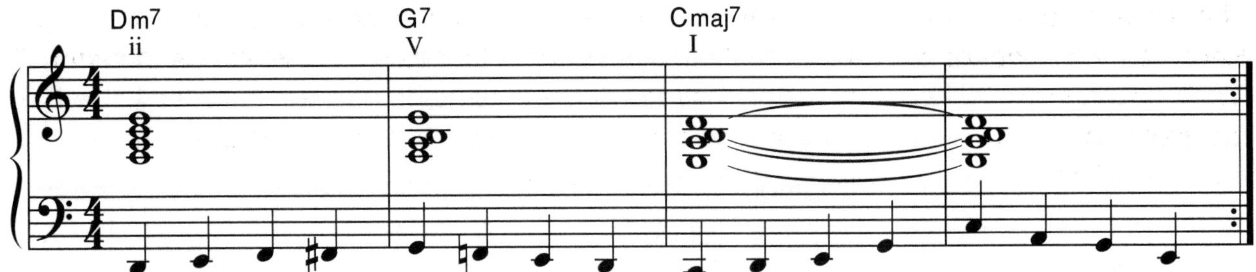

Consider the first chord in the progression, a Dm7 chord. In chapter 17, the scale suggested for minor 7th chords was the Dorian scale (see pages 107–108). For the Dm7 chord, one would play D Dorian, which is the D major scale with a lowered 3rd and 7th. The notes are the same as the C major scale starting on D. Play through the Dorian scale below:

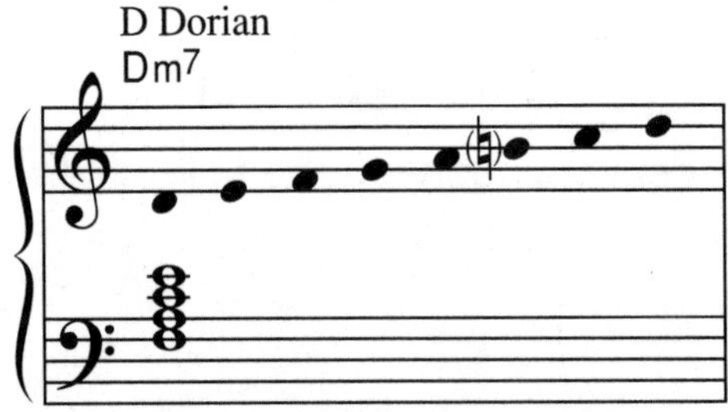

Chapter 17 also suggested the Mixolydian scale for dominant 7th chords (see page 109). For the G7 chord, one would play G Mixolydian, which is the G major scale with a lowered 7th. The notes are the same as the C major scale starting on G. Play through the example below:

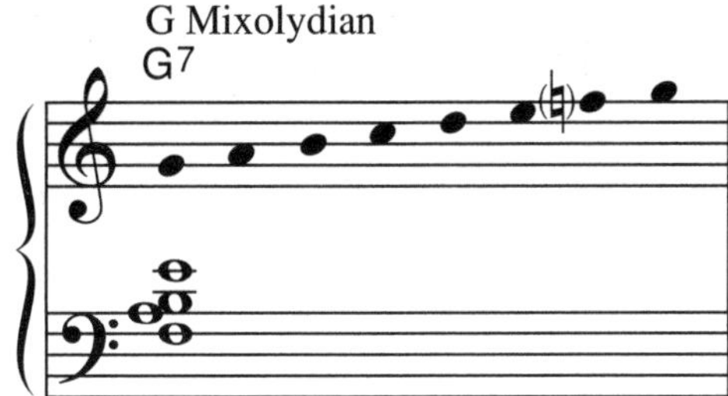

For the root chord, which is a major 7th chord, the best scale for improvisation is the major scale. For the Cmaj7 chord, one would play the C major scale.

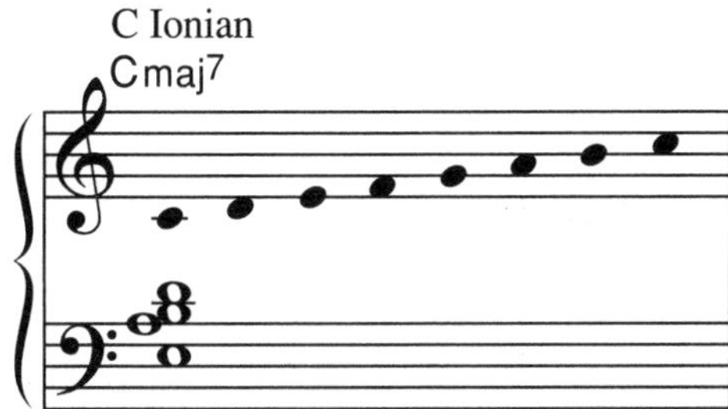

A pattern is clearly emerging—all three modes utilize the notes of the C major scale. Therefore, all three chords of the ii–V–I progression can be navigated with just one scale. Recalling the concept of transitional thinking, this could be called a "seamless transition," since no incremental changes are necessary as one moves from chord to chord in the progression. Because the ii–V–I progression occurs so often in jazz (and other genres), this mental shortcut can be of great value to improvisers in any style.

Exercise 25-2: Playing One Scale through the ii–V–I Progression

1. Play through the following example using the notes of the C major scale over the ii–V–I progression. First, play the example in straight eighth notes and then play the eighth notes in the swing style.

2. Using the notes from step 1, employ skipping, jumping, and upper/lower neighbors to improvise over the ii–V–I progression. Play the following example and then experiment. Be sure to make the eighth notes swing.

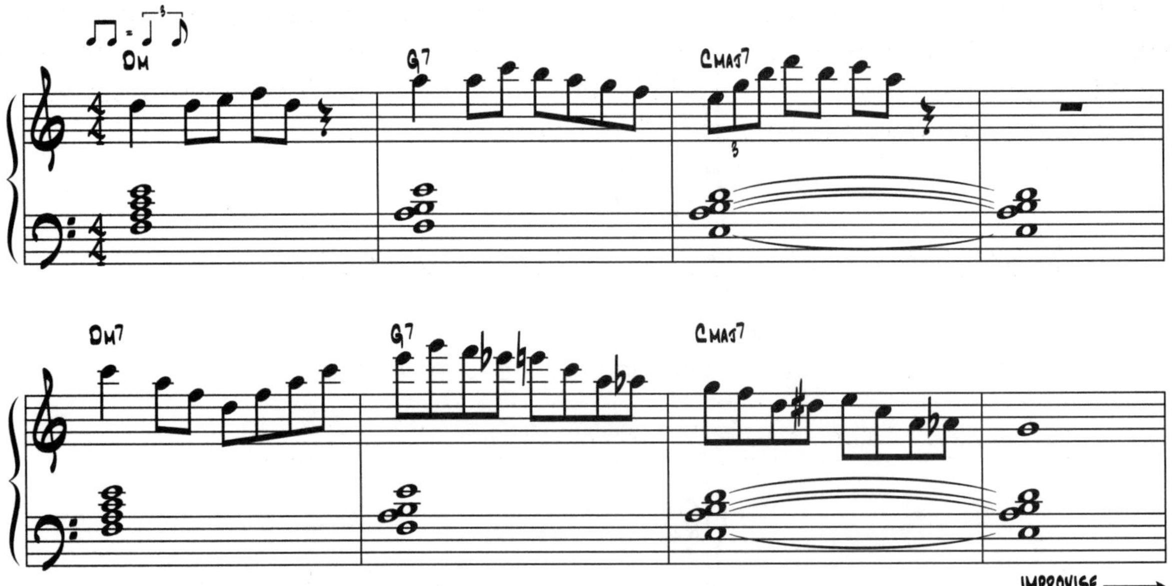

3. Add repetition and rhythmic patterns while improvising over the ii–V–I progression. Play the following example (based on three-note descending and ascending patterns) and then experiment:

4. Over time, transpose steps 1–3 into all 12 keys.

The Blues

One of the most familiar of all jazz forms is the 12-bar blues ("12-bar" referring to the length of the progression). It is an interesting fact that jazz players of any proficiency who have never met and have no printed music available can usually play well together in ensemble (and sound quite good), because they all know the blues. This is one musical form that all musicians should understand and commit to memory, whether serious about jazz or not. The generic form of the 12-bar blues is as follows:

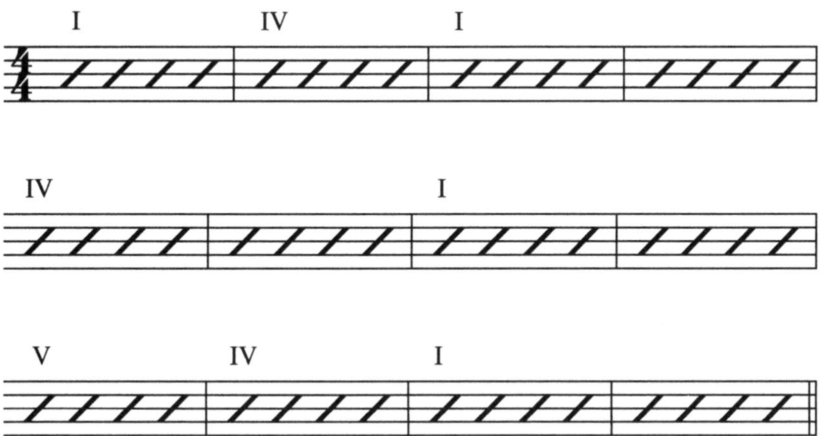

In the key of F major, the 12-bar blues looks like the following:

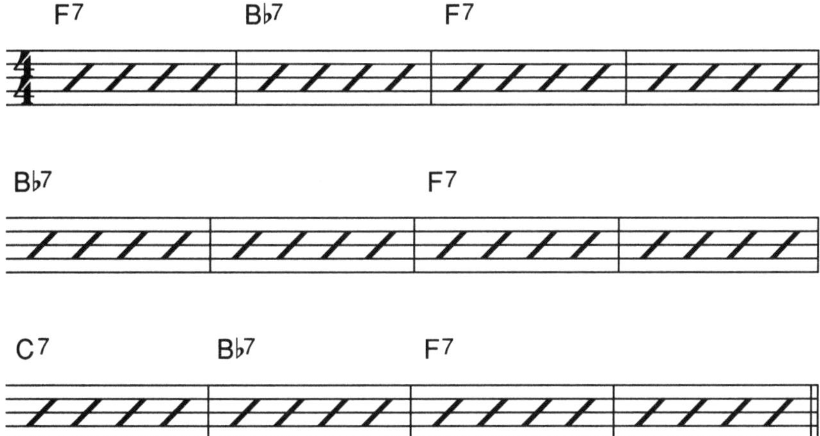

If this progression looks familiar, that's because a similar form was used for practicing the boogie-woogie patterns in chapter 23. While there are many different harmonic alterations of the 12-bar blues, this text will focus only on the most basic form shown above.

The blues progression can be played in any key, although the most frequent are B♭, C and F. These three keys work best for other jazz instrumentalists (notably the trumpet, alto sax, and tenor sax).

Exercise 25-3: Simplified Two-Note Voicings

When experimenting with the 12-bar blues *without* a bass player or drummer, it is common to play voicings in successive quarter notes to establish a steady rhythm. However, playing four-note voicings continually in this way can become tiresome to the ear. So, jazz pianists will often play only the two identifying tones (the 3rd and 7th) with the left hand.

1. The following two-note voicings are arranged in close proximity for a smooth harmonic flow that avoids jumping in wide intervals from chord to chord. Also, note that the twelfth bar has been changed to the dominant. This provides a turnaround that returns to the beginning of the progression. Memorize the following example in the key of F:

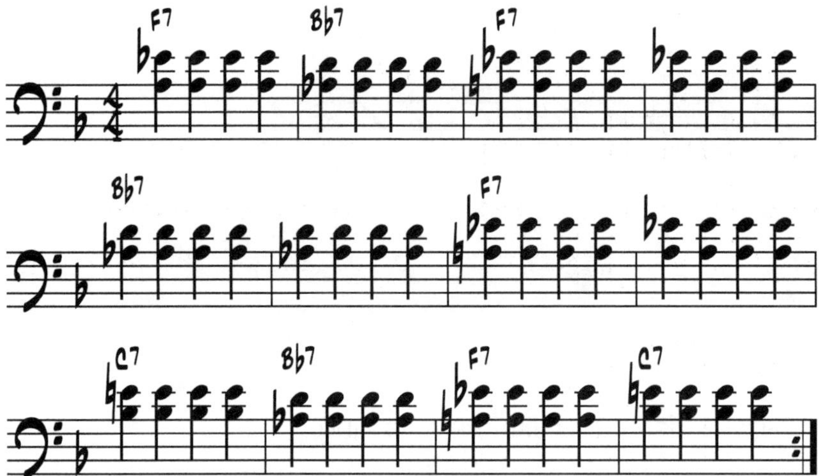

2. Once this progression feels completely comfortable, transpose it into the keys of B♭ and C (and eventually all 12 keys).

The Blues Scale

The blues is such a well-known jazz form that it has its own scale called, not surprisingly, the blues scale. In the key of F, the blues scale looks like the following:

The player who is acquainted with more exotic scales will notice that the blues scale is a minor pentatonic scale with the addition of a tritone (F♯ in the key of C) located three whole steps above the root tone. It is this tritone that gives the blues scale its unique character. In blues solos, it provides intentional dissonance (described in chapter 21), which gives the blues its edgy quality.

Exercise 25-4: Experimenting with the Blues Scale

1. While playing the two-note LH voicings from exercise 25-3, play the following example that utilizes the blues scale in quarter notes:

2. Play through the following example that utilizes the blues scale in eighth notes. Make sure to interpret the eighth notes in the swing rhythm.

3. Play through this longer example that strays slightly from the standard blues scale and uses many of the tools learned earlier (upper/lower neighbors, skipping and jumping). Then, experiment with the blues scale using all improvising tools.

4. Transpose the 12-bar blues progression into as many keys as possible.

Modes and the Blues

The blues scale is only one of many useful tools in blues improvisation. The scale modes discussed in chapters 17–19 are equally valuable for blues playing. As was done with the boogie-woogie patterns in chapter 23, use Mixolydian scales throughout the progression. With only three chords used in the 12-bar blues, the following scales apply:

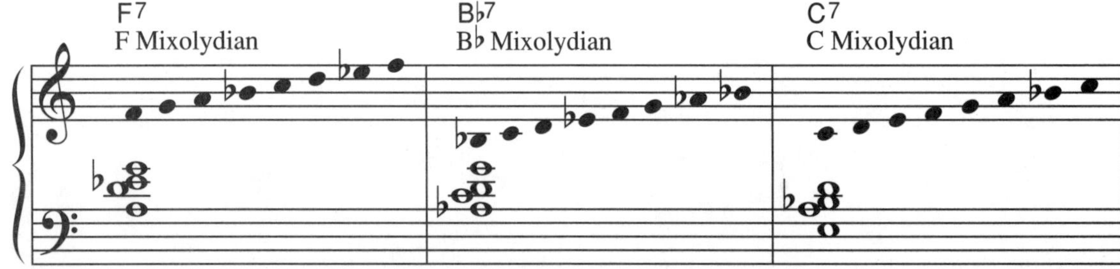

Exercise 25-5: Using the Mixolydian Mode with the Blues

1. Play through the following example that utilizes the Mixolydian scales over the 12-bar blues progression:

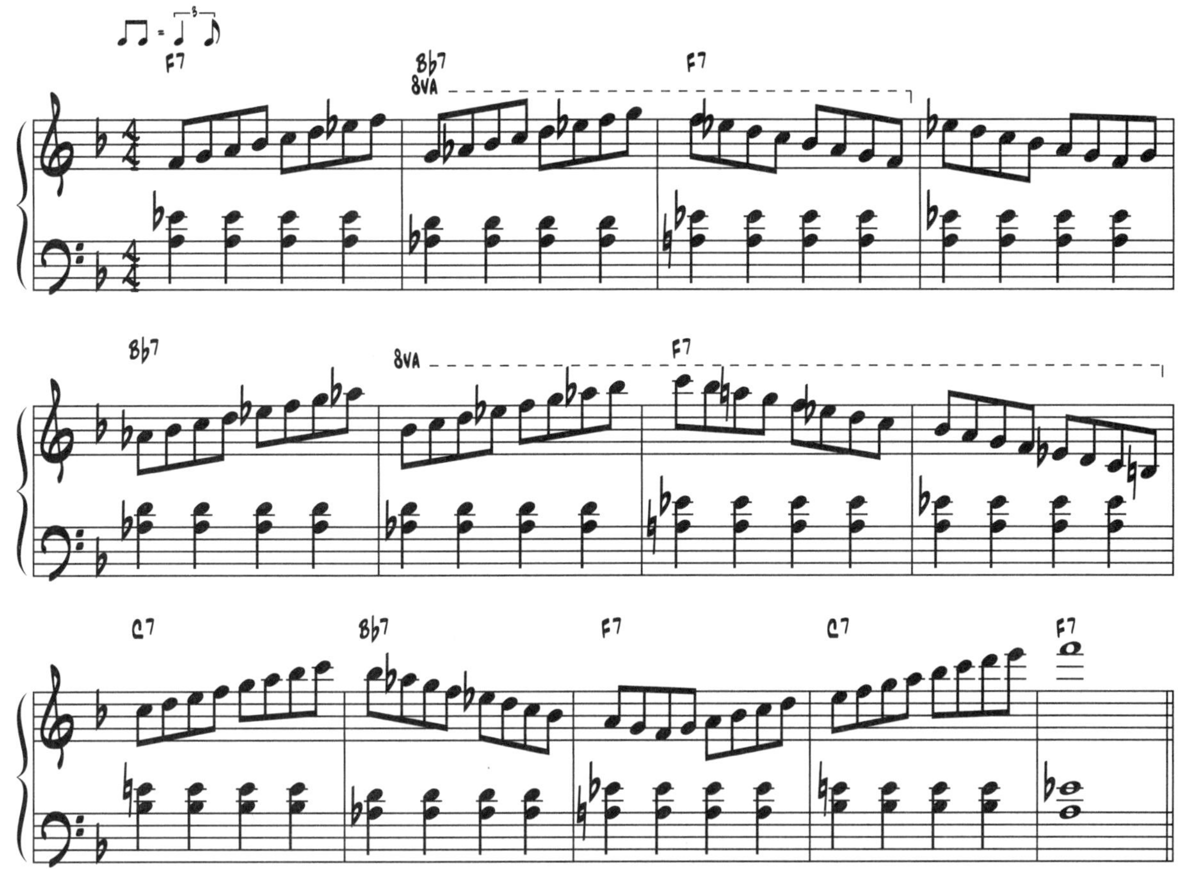

2. While playing two-note voicings in the LH, play through the following solo example that uses a repeating motif based upon the three Mixolydian scales:

3. Use all available tools to improvise with the Mixolydian scales.
4. Transpose the above steps into the keys of B♭ and C (and eventually all keys).

Learning from the Masters

One of the best techniques for learning to improvise in the jazz style is to transcribe and practice the solos of the masters. Transcription forces a student to internalize the notes played and identify patterns that can become part of one's own improvisatory palette. Below is a sample transcription of a blues solo similar to one that might be played by a jazz master.

Exercise 25-6: Practicing a Transcribed Solo

1. While playing two-note jazz voicings with the LH, play through the following blues solo that navigates the 12-bar blues progression three times. Play very slowly the first time through this passage.

2. Review the transcription and identify the various rhythmic and melodic patterns that appear throughout the solo. Select the most interesting two-measure phrases and practice them until memorized.
3. Select one section of step 1 and practice it daily for a week until memorized. Then, move to another section the following week. The goal should be to memorize the entire transcription over time.

For those who are serious about learning jazz, it is important to continue the process of transcribing and memorizing the solos of master improvisers until their styles are "imprinted" into one's consciousness. Over time, these various styles will coalesce in the mind and a personal style of improvisation will emerge. Until this occurs, the best advice for any budding jazz player is to borrow from the masters.

Improvising on a Popular Progression

Another important skill of the jazz player is the ability to improvise on the harmony of a popular tune—just as Liszt and Mozart did with the great opera melodies of the day. Below is an original melody over the chord changes of a popular jazz tune:

This is a great practice tune for aspiring jazz musicians because it is composed of several ii–V–I progressions linked by transitional chords. At first, the thought of improvising through this entire progression might seem intimidating. But the process is easier when the tune is broken into smaller groups of related chords that share common scales.

Begin by examining measures 1–5. These measures can all be navigated with scales equivalent or similar to the A♭ major scale.

Table 25-1: Choosing a Scale for Measures 1–5

Measures	Chords	Scale Types	Scale Equivalent
1	Fm7	F Natural Minor	A♭ Major
2	B♭m7	B♭ Dorian	A♭ Major
3	E♭7	E♭ Mixolydian	A♭ Major
4	A♭maj7	A♭ Major	A♭ Major
5	D♭maj7	D♭ Major	A♭ Major scale with G♭

Play the following example of measures 1–5 that uses the notes of the A♭ major scale through the entire passage:

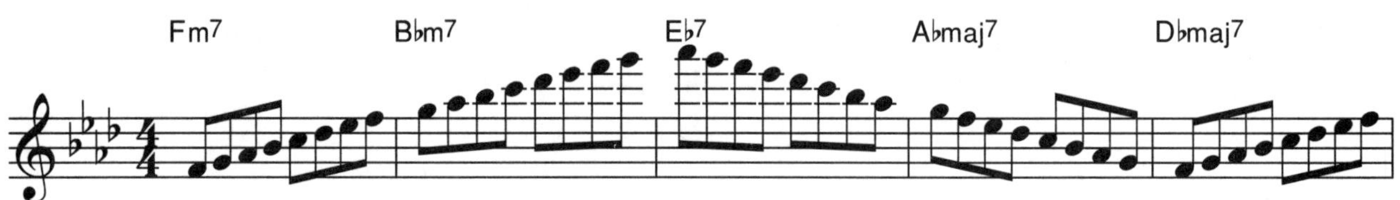

The above example illustrates a principle emphasized earlier in this text. Whenever possible, avoid reacting to a changing harmony chord by chord (literal transition). Instead, try to think in longer harmonic phrases. As one matures in the ability to see groups of related chords that share common scales, improvisation will become much easier in any style.

The table below applies this principle to the harmonic phrases of the musical example on the previous page. Note that some chords (measures 24, 30, 31 and 32) are unrelated to others and must be treated as individual transition chords with their own corresponding scales.

Table 25-2

Measures	Related Chords	Scale Types
1–5	Fm7–B♭m7–E♭7–A♭maj7–D♭maj7	A♭ Major
6–8	G7–Cmaj7	C Major
9–13	Cm7–Fm7–B♭7–E♭maj7–A♭maj7	E♭ Major
14–20	D7–Gmaj7–Am7–D7–Gmaj7	G Major
21–23	F♯m7–B7–Emaj7	E Major
24	C7(♯5)	C Whole Tone
25–29	Fm7–B♭m7–E♭7–A♭maj7–D♭maj7	A♭ Major
30	D♭m7	D♭ Minor
31	Cm7	C Minor
32	B°7	B Diminished
33–36	B♭m7–E♭7–A♭maj7	A♭ Major

Exercise 25-7: Navigating the Entire Tune

1. Play through the following exercise that further demonstrates how related chords can use the same scalar material. The common scale is shown beneath the related measures.* Note how much easier it is to navigate the passage when one learns to identify groups of related chords.

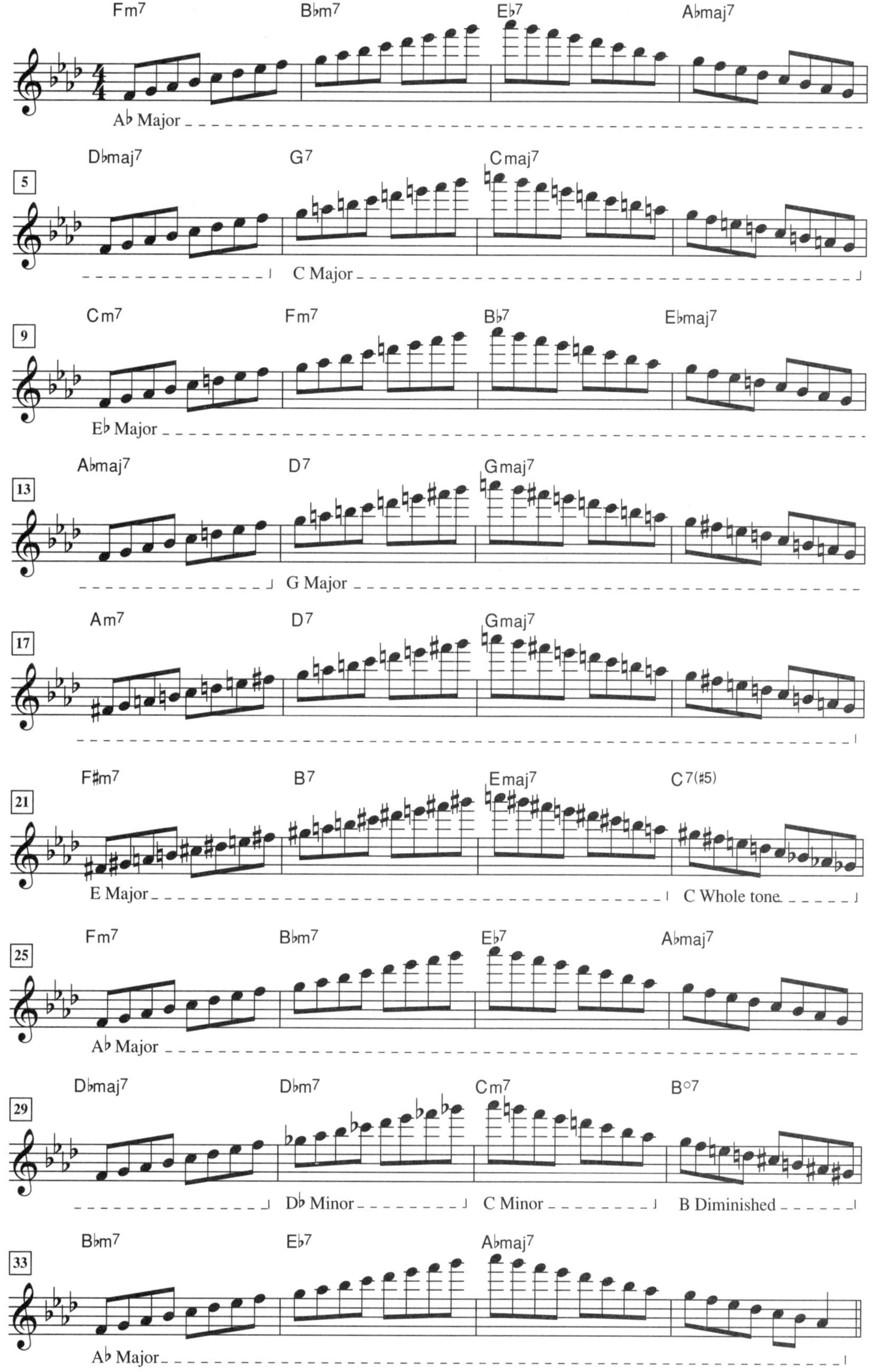

* The whole-tone scale shown for measure 24 is a useful scale for certain augmented chords. It is built upon successive whole-tone intervals. The C whole-tone scale works well with the C7(♯5) chord; the diminished scale shown for measure 32 will be discussed in detail later in this chapter.

2. Now, use a motif from J. S. Bach's Partita No. 2, BWV 826, as the basis for a contemporary improvisation:

J. S. Bach Motif

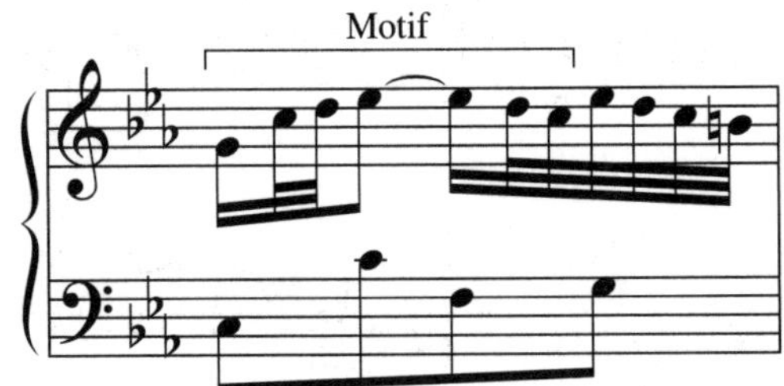

Sample Improvisation

FM7 B♭M7 E♭7 A♭MAJ7 D♭MAJ7

MOTIF

6 G7 CMAJ7 CM7 FM7

11 B♭7 E♭MAJ7 A♭MAJ7 D7 GMAJ7

16 AM7 D7 GMAJ7

21 F♯M7 B7 EMAJ7 C7(♯5) FM7 B♭M7

27 E♭7 A♭MAJ7 D♭MAJ7 D♭M7 CM7

32 Bø7 B♭M7 E♭7 A♭MAJ7

IMPROVISE →

3. Play through the following transcribed solo and internalize the various melodic and rhythmic elements for use in future jazz improvisation.

4. Use all available tools to experiment further with this progression.

The Diminished Scale

One particularly valuable tool for the jazz improviser is the diminished scale (also called the octatonic scale). It is built upon alternating half-tone and whole-tone intervals. This unique construction allows it to convey a sense of moving in and out of the key. As a result, it can provide an air of sophistication to the improvisation of jazz players at any level. There are two forms of the diminished scale—the initial half-tone diminished scale and the initial whole-tone diminished scale.

As the name implies, the initial half-tone diminished scale (hereafter called IHT for **I**nitial **H**alf **T**one) begins with a half-tone interval.

C-IHT Scale

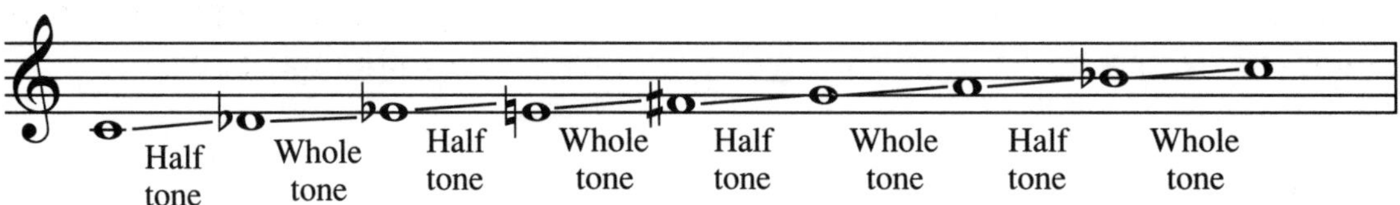

D♭-IHT Scale

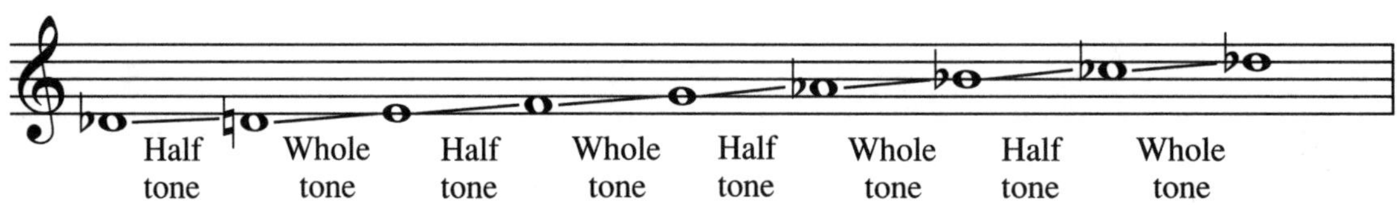

Creativity and common sense should be used to determine the best fingerings for these scales in each key. Often, the optimal method uses only the thumb, index and middle fingers. Play through the following sample fingerings:

C-IHT Scale

D♭-IHT Scale

The IHT scale works best when played over any dominant 7th voicing, as the following example will illustrate. Notice how the scale alternates between dissonance and consonance.

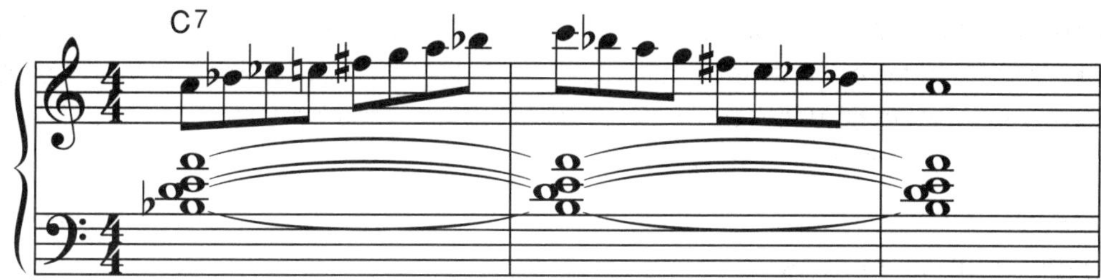

The initial whole-tone diminished scale (IWT for **I**nitial **W**hole **T**one) begins with a whole-tone interval. All the notes of the diminished chord reside within this scale.

C-IWT Scale

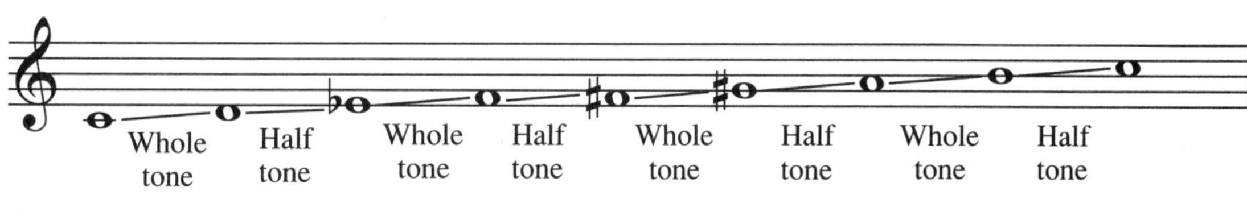

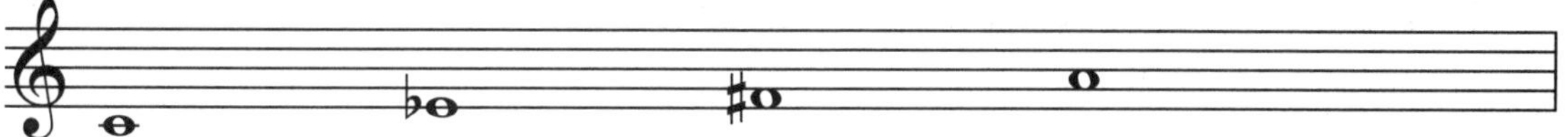
Notes of the C Diminished chord

Again, fingering is left to the discretion of the player. The following example suggests one way to navigate the scale:

C-IWT Scale

The IWT scale is best used for playing over any diminished chord or voicing as shown below:

A unique attribute of the diminished scale is that there are only three distinct scale patterns:

Scale Pattern 1 (C-IHT)

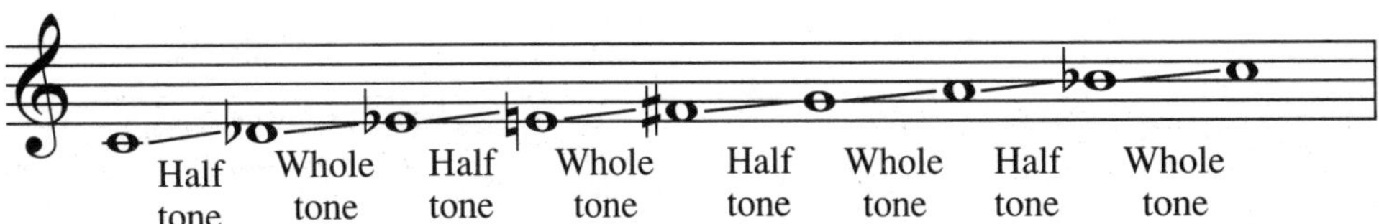

Scale Pattern 2 (D♭-IHT)

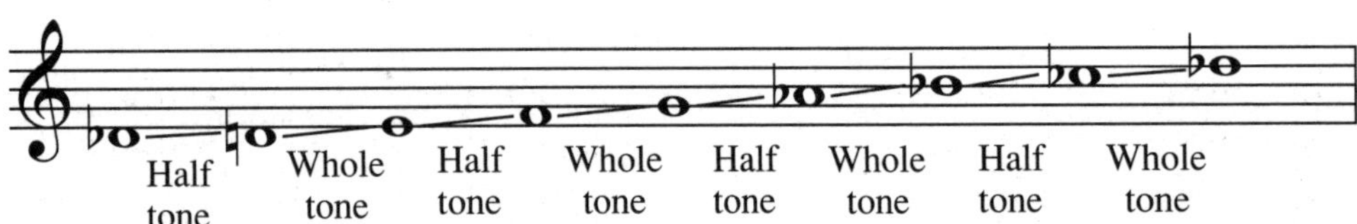

Scale Pattern 3 (C-IWT)

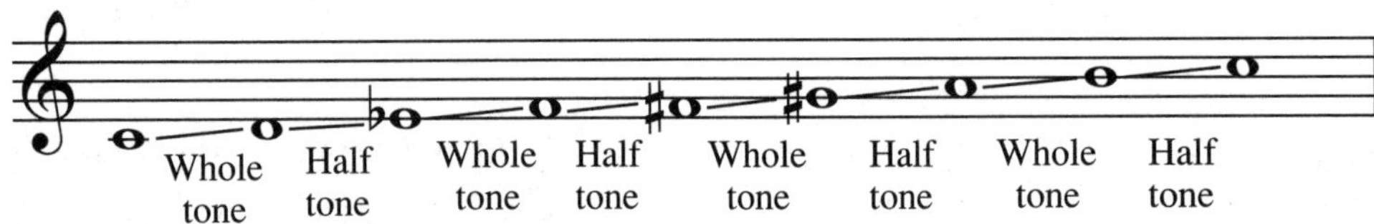

All other diminished scales are derived from the patterns used for these three scales. For example, the C-IHT scale shares the same notes with the following diminished scales: D♭-IWT, E♭-IHT, E-IWT, F♯-IHT, G-IWT, A-IHT and B♭-IWT. This is one of the fortunate benefits of learning diminished scales—to learn one is to learn eight.

The following exercises will explore all 24 diminished scales using the patterns of the three root scales above.

Exercise 25-8: Practicing the Diminished Scales

1. **C-IHT Scale:** Play through the following eight diminished scales that utilize the same notes of the IHT scale starting on C. Practice this step daily until these scales become second nature.

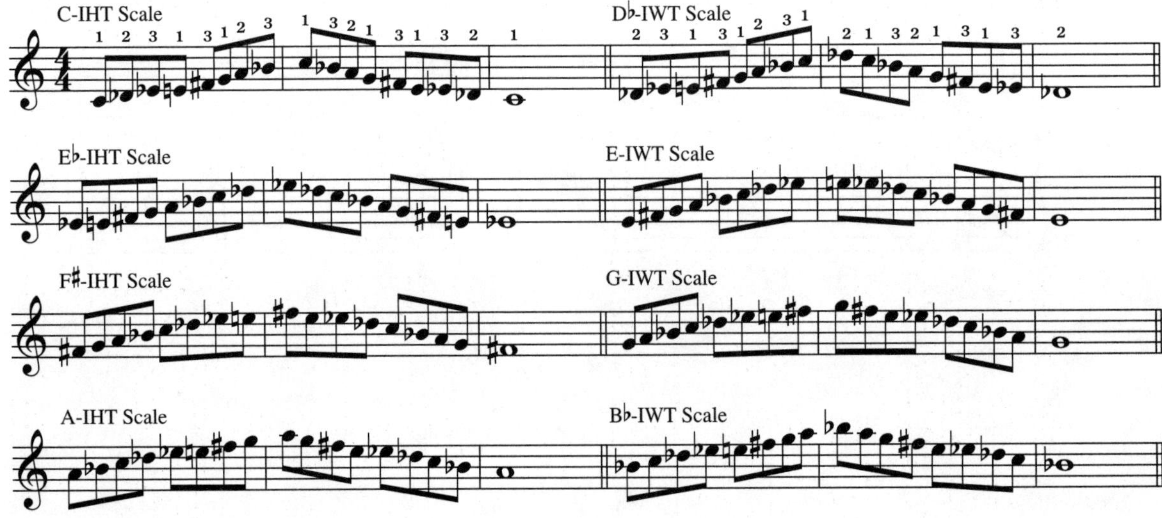

2. **D♭-IHT Scale:** Play through the following eight diminished scales that utilize the same notes of the IHT scale starting on D♭. Once step 1 is mastered, practice step 2 until the scales become second nature.

3. **C-IWT Scale:** Play through the following eight diminished scales that utilize the same notes as of the IWT scale starting on C. Once the previous two steps are completely comfortable, practice step 3 until the scales feel natural.

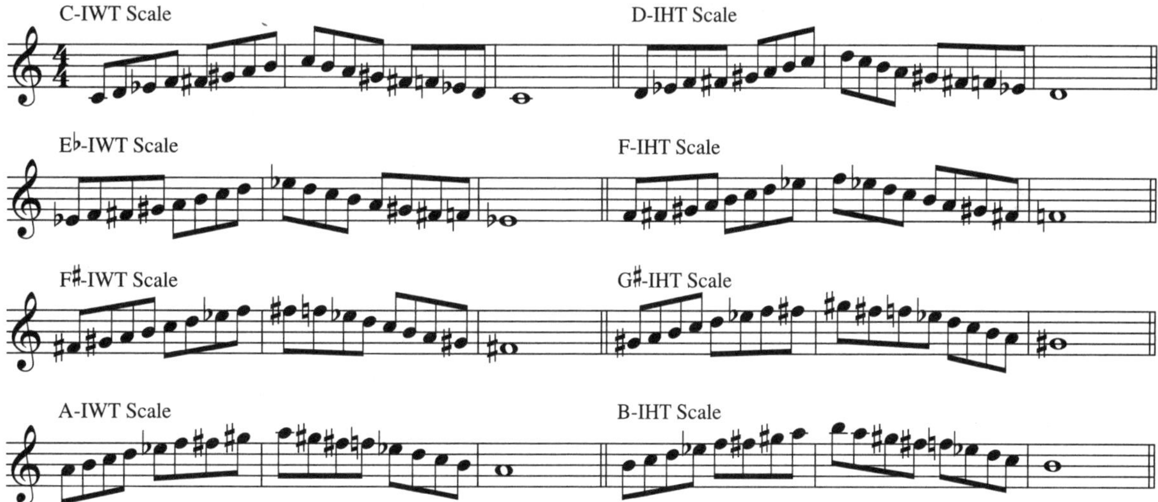

Exercise 25-9: Internalizing the Diminished Scales

The following exercise will help to drive the various diminished scales into memory.

1. **Patterns and Voicings:** Convert each of the three preceding exercises into the following contiguous scale pattern. While playing each scale with the RH, play the appropriate LH voicing (use the dominant 7th voicing for all IHT scales and a diminished chord for all IWT scales).

2. **Descending Diminished Scales:** Turn the previous step upside down by starting with the top note for each scale. Again, play the appropriate voicings in the LH.

A solid grasp of diminished scales will become a valuable asset for any improviser. Take the time to learn them well.

Jazz Summary

As mentioned earlier, this instruction in jazz is not meant to be exhaustive, but only a basic introduction that can provide a springboard to further study. One who has worked through the material diligently, however, should have enough experience to do well in a typical jam session. If these chapters have whetted the appetite for deeper jazz study, consult the many volumes of existing material that explore jazz in greater detail.

Key Points from This Chapter

- The ii–V–I progression is one of the most common in jazz.
- A single scale can usually be played through any ii–V–I progression.
- Incremental transition can simplify improvisation in any style, including jazz.
- Transcription is a valuable learning tool for the jazz improviser.
- The blues and diminished scales are important tools that can add immediate sophistication to the playing of a novice jazz improviser.

CHAPTER 26 Improvisation through the Ages

This final chapter offers a brief overview of improvisational styles used during various periods of musical history to provide historical perspective. While the general principles of improvisation have remained constant over the centuries, styles of improvisation have often changed with the times as composers probed new melodic, harmonic and rhythmic territory.

Given the breadth of the topic, this overview makes no attempt to be comprehensive. It merely offers a snapshot of selected periods that may prompt further study. Working through the examples and exercises will let the player experience the unique character of each era. Enjoy this brief tour of musical history.

The Medieval Period (500–1450)

All medieval musicians were expected to improvise. The musical notation used during the medieval period was so vague that instrument choice, melodic pitch, tempo and rhythm could all vary dramatically from one performance to another. This ambiguity presented a great challenge for the musician, but also great freedom. Play through the following Ambrosian chant entitled *Eructavit*:

Eructavit represents the most common musical form of the medieval period—song. Most pieces were sung *a cappella*. Singers typically adhered to the prescribed notes of a piece, but were free to improvise with the length of each note. Therefore, it was likely that *Eructavit* (or any similar chant) had a different character each time it was sung.

Exercise 26-1: Improvising in the Medieval Style

Sing through *Eructavit* assigning note durations and phrasing as desired. Try to create a few different versions of the chant using various note durations.

Adding Harmony to *Eructavit*

One can add interest to the above exercise by playing *Eructavit* in the context of modern harmony. Play through the following LH progression that has been popular over the past few hundred years:

By varying the note durations, one can create different versions of the chant that complement this harmony. Play through each of the following examples:

Example 1

Example 2

Example 3

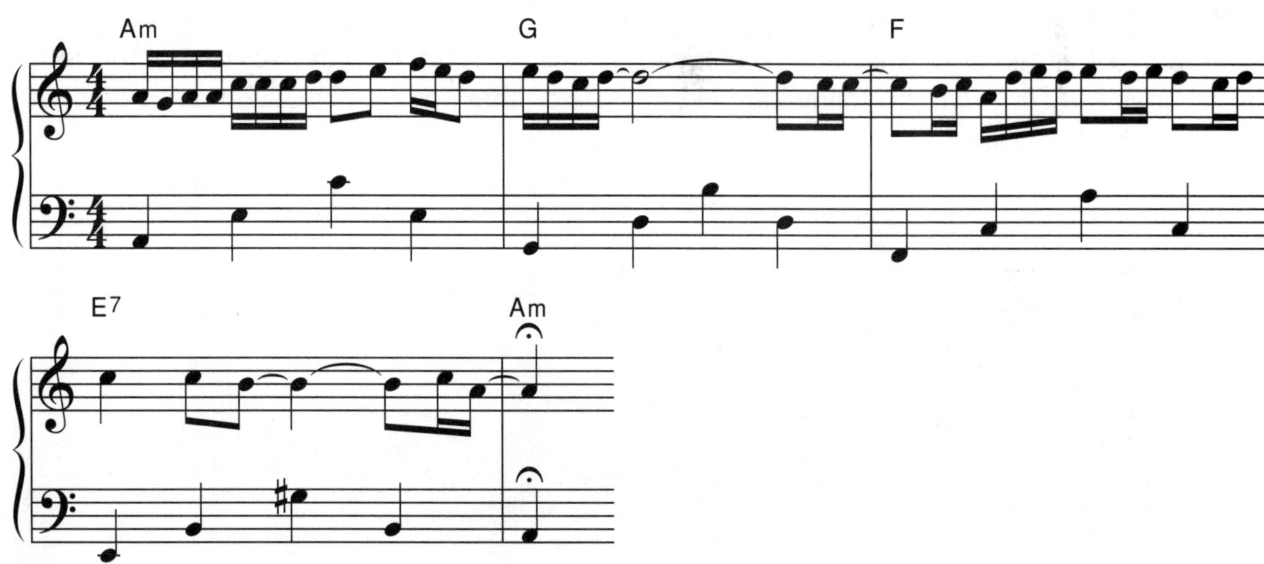

Exercise 26-2: Improvising in the Medieval Style

1. Use the notes of *Eructavit* to create an improvisation over the modern harmony as shown in the previous examples.

   Eructavit Melody

   Harmony 1

2. Try matching the notes of *Eructavit* with the following alternative harmonies:

   Harmony 2

   Harmony 3

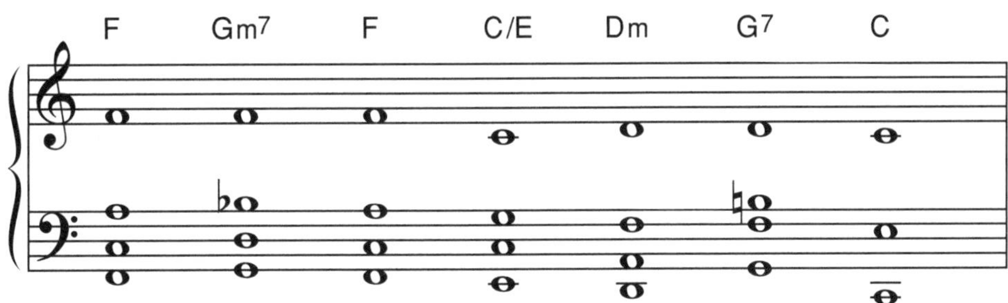

   Harmony 4

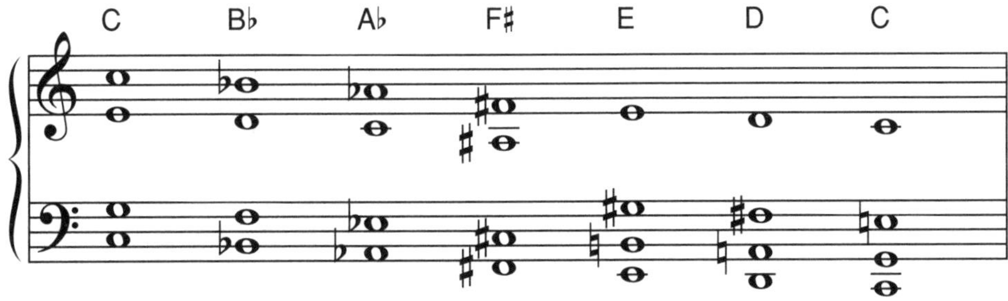

3. Create a new harmony and improvise over it using the notes of *Eructavit*.

The Renaissance Period (1450–1600)

The piano is a fairly young member of the keyboard family. Before the experiments of Bartolomeo Cristofori led to the invention of the pianoforte in the early 1700s, there was a wealth of keyboard music written during the Renaissance period for clavichord, harpsichord and virginals. Much of this music was expected to include improvisation.

To improvise in the Renaissance style, one must be aware of certain important characteristics of the period:

1. Modes were the foundation of improvisation. Musicians had not yet agreed on the major/minor system known today.
2. Parallel movement from major to minor was common, even within a single measure. Composers would often ascend with a major scale and descend with the parallel minor.

3. Frequently changing meters and the use of roll chords were common.

With fewer rules, the Renaissance improviser enjoyed great freedom to navigate harmony. To explore this period, the next two examples feature the work of two important Renaissance composers—Antonio de Cabezón (ca.1500–1566) and Claudio Merulo (1533–1604).

Cabezón's *Del Primer Tono*

Play through the following excerpt from Antonio de Cabezón's *Del Primer Tono*:

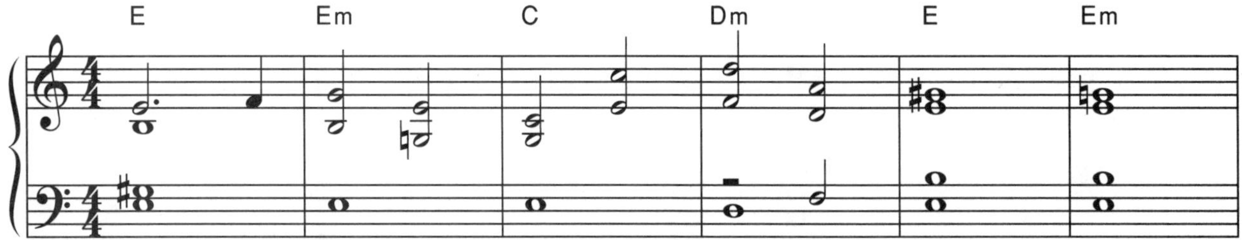

With the addition of improvised passing tones, the passage acquires more richness:

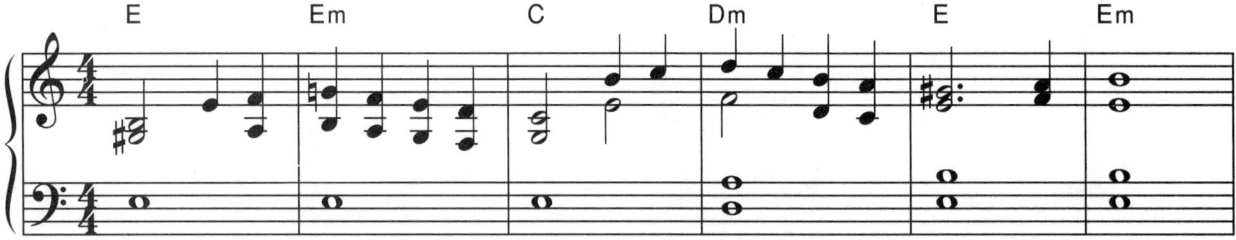

Play through the following example that suggests one way that a Cabezón improvisation might have sounded:

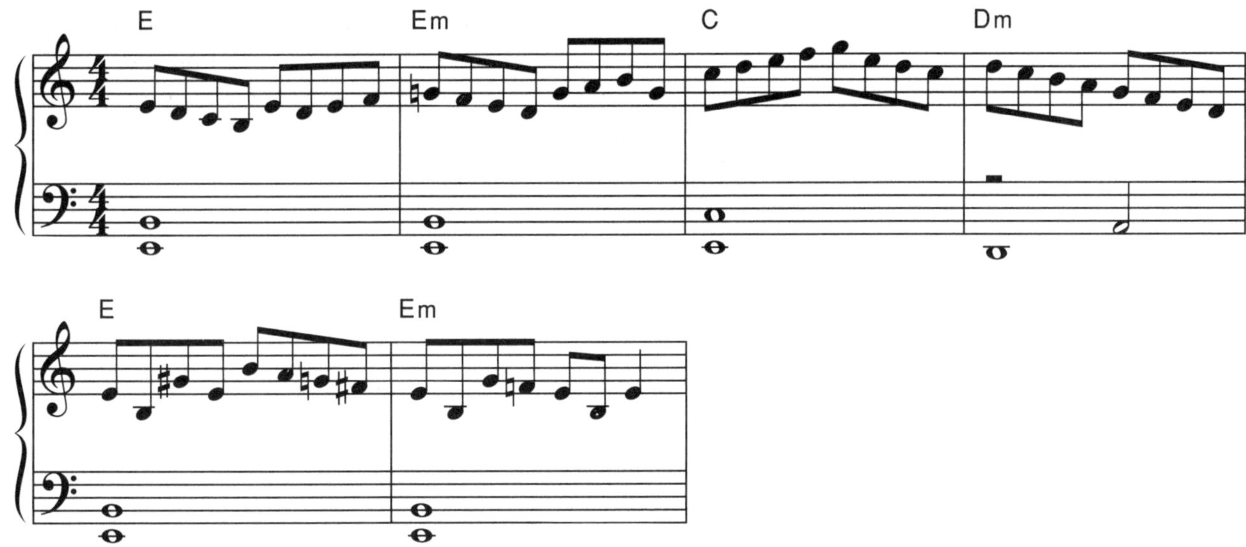

Merulo's *la Zambeccara*

Play through the following excerpt from Claudio Merulo's *la Zambeccara*:

Improvised passing tones and other modifications can enhance the passage as shown below:

The next example doubles the time signature to $\frac{8}{4}$, allowing greater improvisatory freedom:

Exercise 26-3: Improvising in the Renaissance Style

Having acquired an ear for Renaissance harmony through the preceding examples, use the harmony of Cabezón or Merulo to improvise in the Renaissance style.

The Baroque Period (1600–1750)

The word "baroque" refers to the type of artistic expression that appeared in the seventeenth and early eighteenth centuries. Generally, the baroque style involved the use of complex forms, extravagant ornamentation, and the simultaneous use of contrasting elements to create drama, movement or tension.

Two of the most celebrated composers of the baroque period were Johann Sebastian Bach (1685–1750) and George Frideric Handel (1685–1759). Bach and Handel were also known to be among the most prolific improvisers of their day. The following section examines how these two great composers approached the same type of musical work—a prelude in D minor.

J. S. Bach's Prelude in D Minor, BWV 875

Play through the first nine measures of J. S. Bach's Prelude in D Minor, BWV 875, from the *Well-Tempered Clavier, Volume 2*.

The harmonic progression can be summarized as follows:

Note Bach's use of the descending natural minor scale and broken (arpeggiated) chords in measures 1 and 2, and the LH repetition of these patterns in measures 5 and 6.

Measures 1 and 2

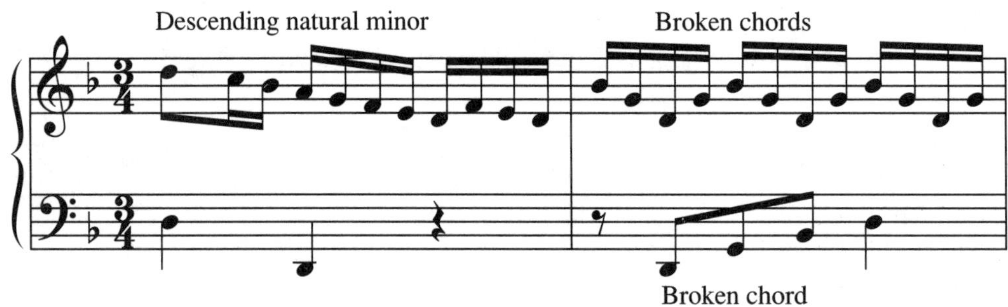

Measures 5 and 6

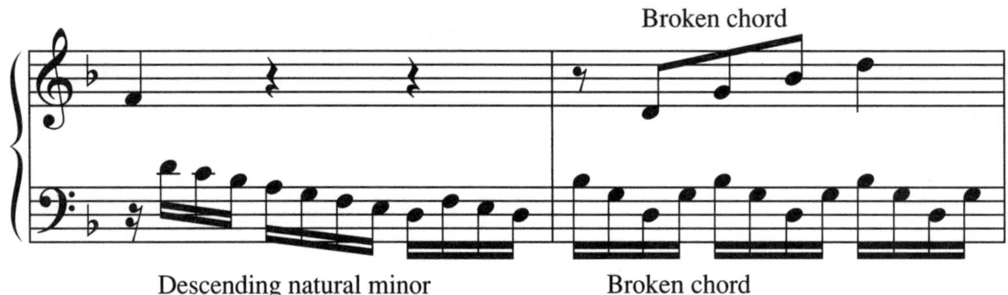

Earlier chapters discussed the importance of repeated patterns in improvisation. Bach used this technique continually throughout this prelude (in fact, throughout much of his compositional work). The following exercise will analyze the patterns he employed in this piece.

Exercise 26-4: Internalizing Bach's Patterns

1. To internalize some of Bach's patterns, play the following RH example below that starts a minor 3rd higher than the original version. Note the two elements of this pattern—the descending D natural minor scale and the arpeggiated G minor chord.

2. Play through the following phrase that applies the two elements of the previous pattern starting a perfect 5th higher than the original version:

3. Try to create a different version of the descending scale/broken chord pattern for each remaining note of the D natural minor scale (i.e., try starting on E, G, B♭, and C). The G minor broken chords can be played in any inversion that seems appropriate at the end of the descending scale.

4. Create new versions of the LH pattern using different inversions for the broken chords. Play through the examples below and then explore:

LH Pattern 1

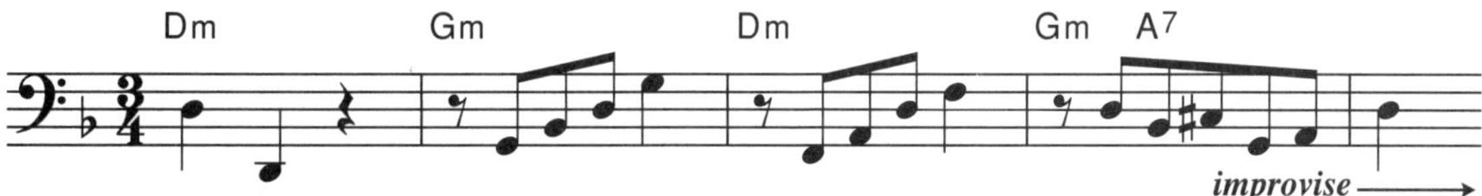

LH Pattern 2

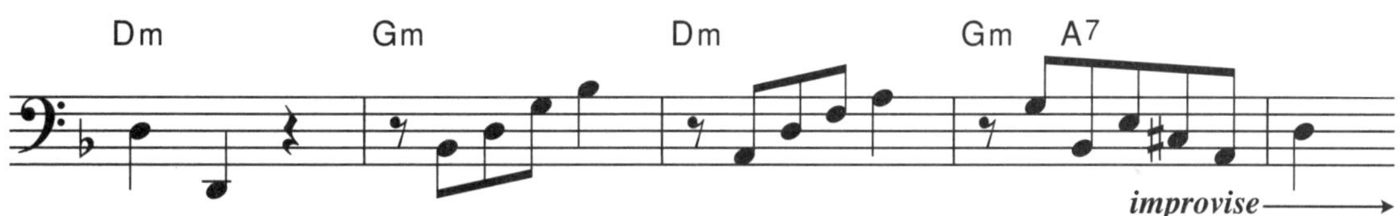

5. Use the patterns developed in steps 1–4 to create a new improvisation based upon Bach's original harmony:

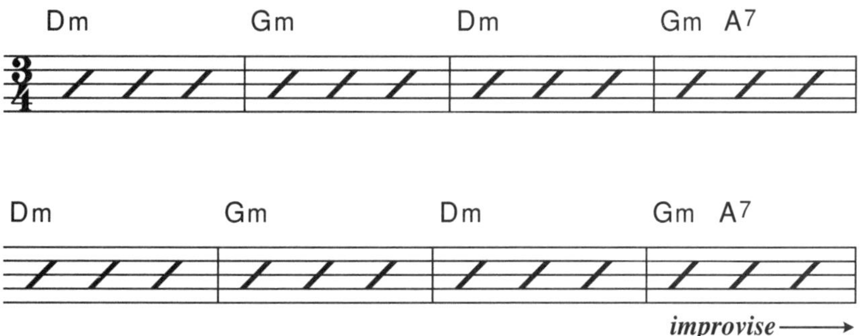

Handel's Suite in D Minor, HWV 428,

Play through the following passage from George Frideric Handel's Suite in D Minor, HWV 428:

The harmonic framework for this passage is summarized below. Note Handel's use of recurring patterns adapted to the changing harmony.

The following exercise will encourage the creation of new patterns in the style of Handel.

Exercise 26-5: Improvising in the Style of Handel

1. Play the following Handel-like phrase based on the D melodic minor scale (ascending):

2. Play through the following examples that rearrange the scale as Handel might have done:

Example 1

Example 2

Example 3

3. Repeat the above examples until they are nearly memorized. Then, select random segments from each example to create composite phrases in the style of Handel.

Exercise 26-6: Internalizing Handel's Patterns

Another valuable way to internalize patterns is to move them up by chord tones (rather than scale tones).

1. Play through the original passage several times until the pattern elements are clearly identified (scale segments and arpeggiated chords).

2. Using the elements of this passage, finish the example below that starts on the next tone of the D minor chord (F, a minor 3rd above D). The arpeggiated chords also move up by one inversion.

3. Finish the example below that moves the pattern up another chord tone (A, a perfect 5th above D). The arpeggiated chords move up two inversions from the original pattern.

4. Once the patterns are fully internalized, use all previous tools to improvise in the style of Handel.

Exercise 26-7: Improvising in the Baroque Style

Folies d'Espagne by Corelli (examined in chapter 8 and 15) provides another good foundation for improvisation in the baroque style.

1. For review, play through the Corelli passage below:

2. Play through the following sample improvisation:

3. Using the LH harmony of the Corelli passage, experiment with the RH using patterns of the baroque period.

The Classical Period (1750–Early 19th Century)

Much of this book has used music of the classical period (e.g., Mozart and early Beethoven) as a foundation for improvisation. Therefore, some of the important stylistic shifts that occurred as composers migrated from the baroque period to the classical period should be already apparent. These shifts include the following:

- An emphasis on simplicity over complexity.
- Movement away from the layered polyphony of the baroque period.
- The preference for a more formal, ordered structure.
- Movement toward a forceful melody over a subordinate harmony.

The compositions of Mozart and Beethoven certainly reflect these paradigm changes. This section will focus on another eminent figure of the classical period, Franz Schubert (1797–1828).

Schubert's Sonata in B♭ Major, D. 960

Play through the following excerpt from Franz Schubert's Sonata in B♭ Major, D. 960:

Notice the absence of layered polyphony and the use of a strong melody over a subordinate harmony—both traits of the classical period.

In the passage, the repeated eighth-note harmony shifts back and forth from the RH to the LH. The following revised passage consolidates this harmony into the LH. Take a moment to play through it.

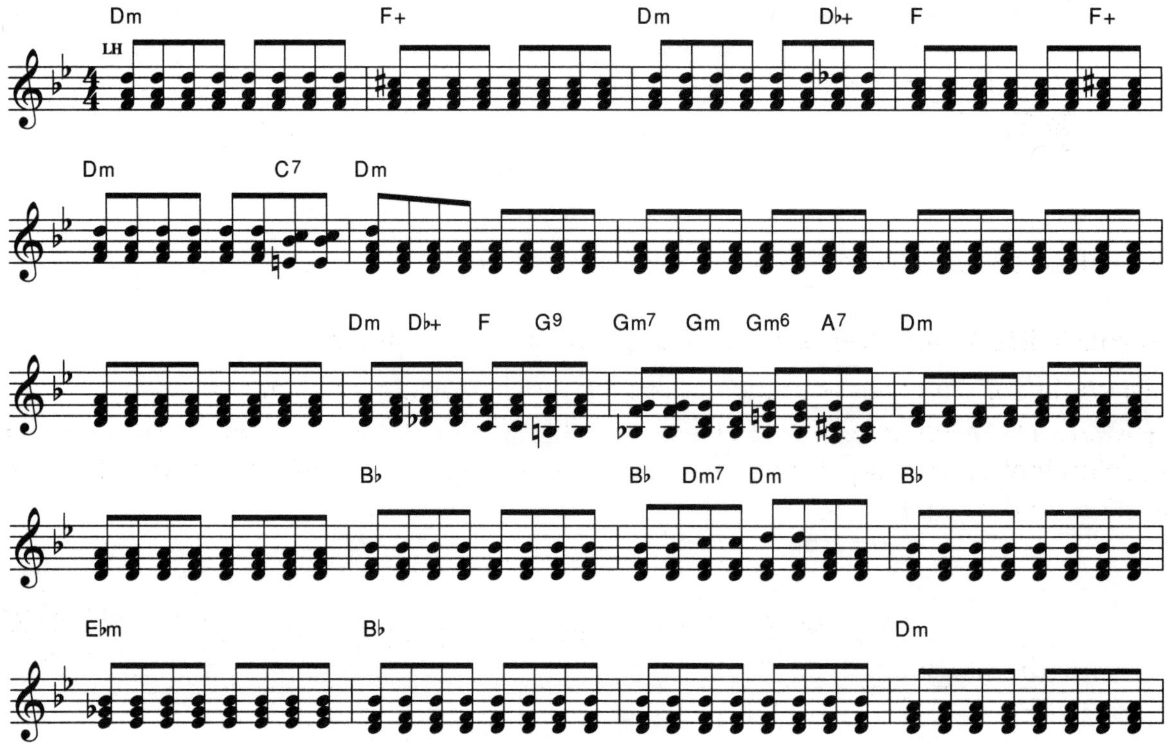

The next exercise will use this harmony as a basis for improvisation.

Exercise 26-8: Improvising on Schubert's Harmony

1. Play through the preceding LH harmony passage until a "representative" harmony (i.e., a close approximation) can be played using only the chord symbols as a guide.
2. While playing the representative LH harmony developed in step 1, play through the following RH sample improvisation that utilizes many of the tools explored earlier:

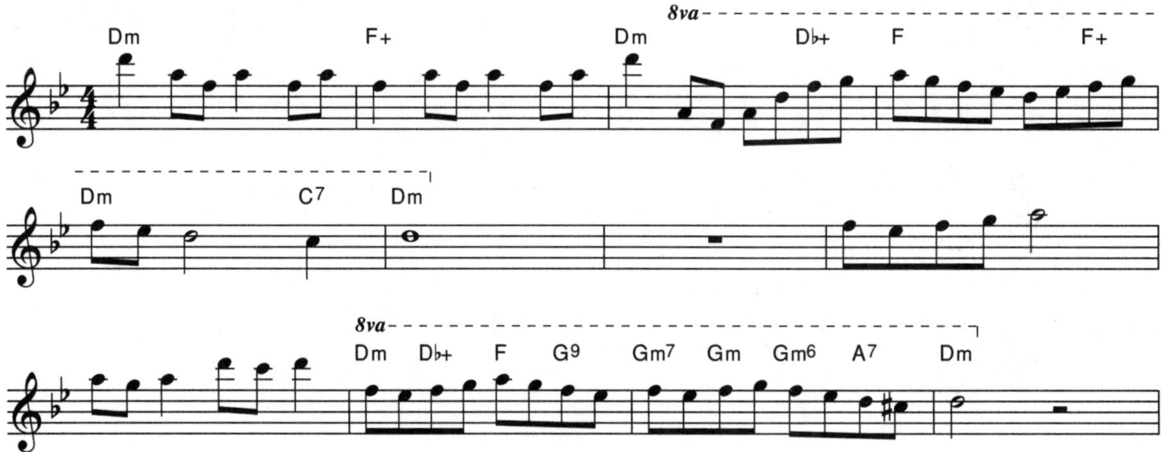

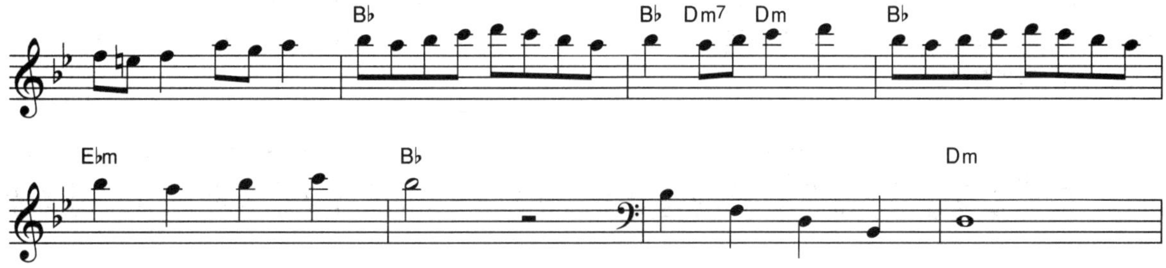

3. Use all tools to improvise over Schubert's harmony in the classical style.

Cramer's Etude in A Minor from *Studies for the Pianoforte*

A lesser-known composer of the classical period was Johann Baptist Cramer (1771–1858). Beethoven was especially fond of Cramer's etudes and used them as the basis for his teaching methods. Play through the following excerpt of Cramer's Etude in A Minor from *Studies for the Pianoforte*:

Cramer's RH patterns provide an opportunity for further exploration of the classical style.

Exercise 26-9: Analyzing Cramer's Etude in A Minor

1. Play through the Cramer passage until the structure and style of his patterns are clearly identified.
2. To internalize these patterns, move them up to the next chord tone (start on A). Play the segment below (with the LH notes from the original passage) and try to finish the passage using Cramer's harmony:

3. Move the patterns up another chord tone (start on C) and try to finish the passage using Cramer's harmony:

4. Use all available tools to improvise on Cramer's harmony.

The Romantic Period (19th Century)

The piano grew in popularity quite dramatically during the romantic period. Whereas the classical period was guided by clarity and order, the romantic period was characterized by emotion, adventure and imagination. The emergence of the piano virtuoso (the likes of Frédéric Chopin and Franz Liszt) created large audiences for piano music. Because composers of this period were more likely to create music to please themselves (rather than to satisfy the wishes of wealthy patrons), their music displayed greater passion and power than had been seen in previous periods.

Chopin's Impromptu in A♭ Major, Op. 29

Rather than further exploring Chopin's Prelude in C Minor, Op. 28, No. 20, examine one of his other styles of composition, the impromptu. Play through the following excerpt from his Impromptu in A♭ Major, Op. 29:

By definition, an impromptu is a musical composition designed to create the illusion of improvisation. Notice that the style in the above passage is far more flowing and adventurous than the prelude studied earlier. While it is a written composition, it does suggest the freedom of an improvised piece.

Attempts to improvise through the rapidly changing harmony of this impromptu might be quite difficult. A far simpler approach is to borrow the LH concept from Chopin and apply it to a more accessible harmony.

Exercise 26-10: Improvising in the Style of Chopin

Using the simplified harmony below, this exercise will experiment with scalar and chord-based patterns to form a basis for improvising in the style of Chopin.

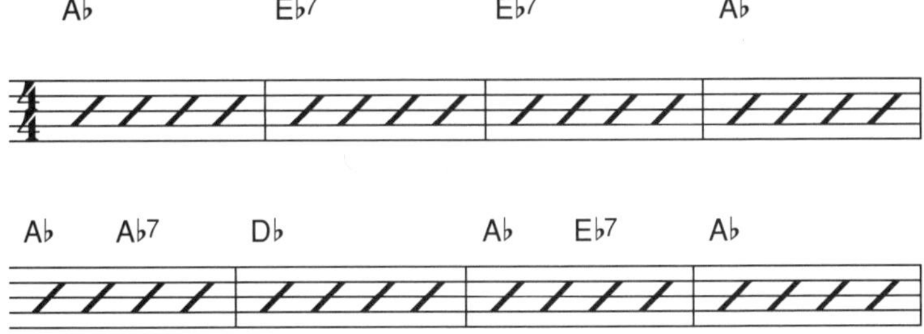

1. **LH Styling:** Memorize the following passage based on the above harmony that employs the LH style of Chopin's Impromptu in A♭ Major:

2. **RH Scale Pattern:** Play through the following RH scale pattern. Once the passage can be played comfortably, add the LH bass from step 1.

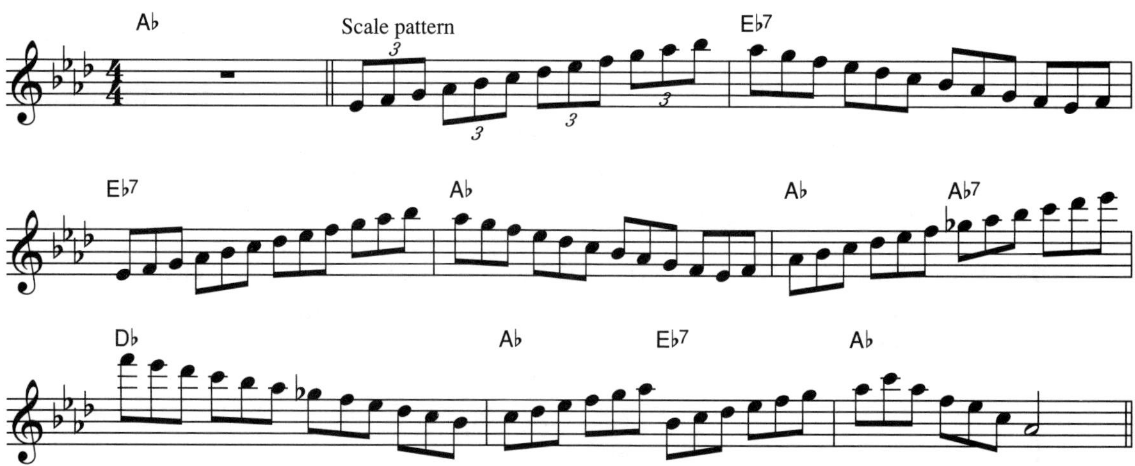

3. **Chord-Tone Pattern:** Play through the following RH passage that uses chord tones to form a simple improvisation. Once the passage can be played comfortably, add the LH from step 1.

4. **Combining Scales and Chord Tones:** Play through the following RH passage that combines the scale pattern from step 2 and the chordal pattern from step 3. When comfortable, add the LH bass pattern from step 1.

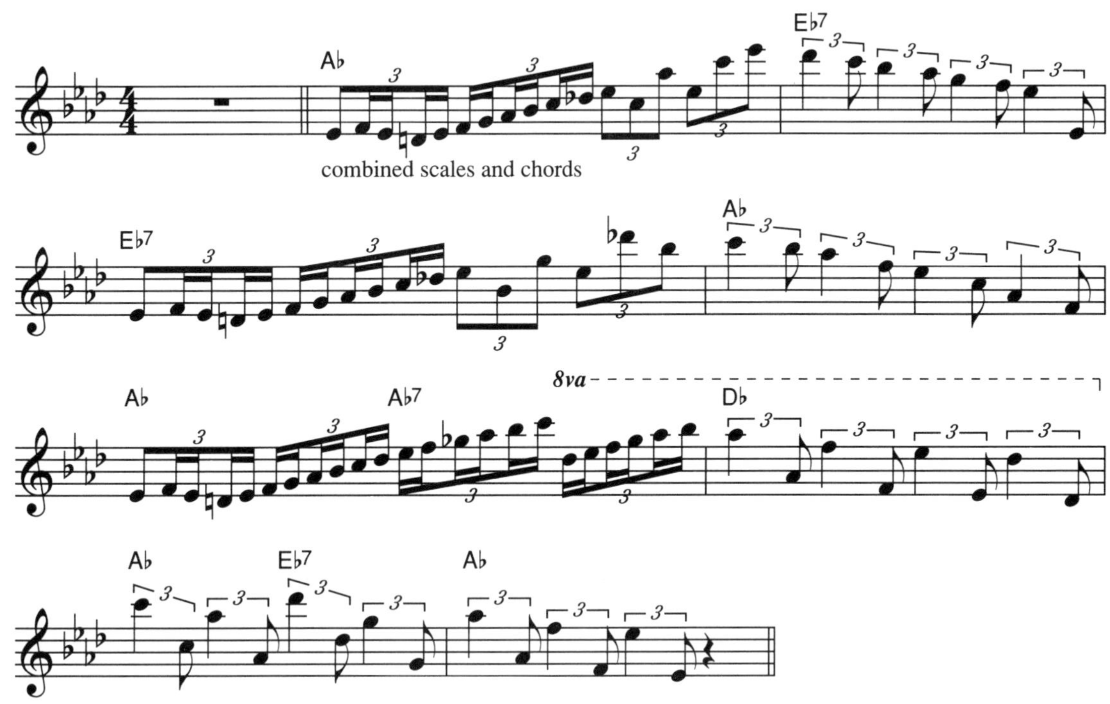

5. Use all available tools to improvise over the LH bass pattern from step 1.

Chapter Summary

This brief history of improvisation from the medieval to the romantic periods was designed to provide a broader context for exploration. Just as the improvisers of the past ventured into uncharted territory from one period to the next, the improvisers of today have the freedom to discover new and exhilarating ways of expression. Remember that there are no wrong notes within improvisation, only some that are better than others. Keep striving to find the better notes.

From the Authors

If you can talk, you can improvise.

That statement was made at the very beginning of this book.

We hope you believe it now.

If these pages have helped to open your eyes and ears to an exhilarating new world of musical opportunity through improvisation, we are most gratified. Our hope is that this book will be of value not only within the context of your own personal expression, but also in the teaching studio and the classroom. Improvisation can be of immense value to students, expanding their listening skills, their harmonic and melodic vocabulary and their understanding of the creative process. May these ideas help you to inspire a new generation of improvisers.

As a closing thought, we urge you to view improvisation more as an exploration than a discipline. The techniques you have learned can certainly be perfected through time and diligence. But never let them obscure the quintessential elements of the craft—the adventure, the curiosity, the spontaneity, the freedom—that can all flourish irrepressibly when the "script" is yours to write.

So, create and explore!

May it excite your mind and spirit.

Above all, may it bring you joy.

Brian Chung & Dennis Thurmond

For Further Reading

Below are a few sources for the classical pianist that lend a perspective on the rich history of improvisation for the keyboard:

Bach, C. P. E. *Essay on the True Art of Playing Keyboard Instruments*. 1753–1756. Translated and edited by William J. Mitchell. New York: Norton, 1948.

Czerny, Carl. *A Systematic Introduction to Improvisation on the Pianoforte, Op. 200*. 1829. Translated and edited by Alice L. Mitchell. New York: Longman, 1983.

Ferand, Ernst T. *Improvisation in Nine Centuries of Western Music: An Anthology with a Historical Introduction*. 1887. Köln, Germany: Arno Volk Verlag, 1961.

Neumann, Frederick. *Ornamentation and Improvisation in Mozart*. Princeton: Princeton University Press, 1989.

Nettle, Bruno and Melinda Russel, ed. *In the Course of Performance: Studies in the World of Musical Improvisation*. Chicago: University of Chicago Press, 1998.

Tomas de Santa Maria. *Libro Llamado Arte De Taner Fantasia*. 1570. Reprint, Geneva, Switzerland: Minkoff Reprint, 1973.

Index

Alfred